BEATING HEARTS

CRITICAL PERSPECTIVES ON ANIMALS:
THEORY, CULTURE, SCIENCE, AND LAW

CRITICAL PERSPECTIVES ON ANIMALS: THEORY, CULTURE, SCIENCE, AND LAW

Series Editors: Gary L. Francione and Gary Steiner

The emerging interdisciplinary field of animal studies seeks to shed light on the nature of animal experience and the moral status of animals in ways that overcome the limitations of traditional approaches. Recent work on animals has been characterized by an increasing recognition of the importance of crossing disciplinary boundaries and exploring the affinities as well as the differences among the approaches of fields such as philosophy, law, sociology, political theory, ethology, and literary studies to questions pertaining to animals. This recognition has brought with it an openness to rethinking the very terms of critical inquiry and the traditional assumptions about human being and its relationship to the animal world. The books published in this series seek to contribute to contemporary reflections on the basic terms and methods of critical inquiry by focusing on fundamental questions arising out of the relationships and confrontations between humans and nonhuman animals, and ultimately to enrich our appreciation of the nature and ethical significance of nonhuman animals by providing a forum for the interdisciplinary exploration of questions and problems that have traditionally been confined within narrowly circumscribed disciplinary boundaries.

BEATING HEARTS

ABORTION AND ANIMAL RIGHTS

Sherry F. Colb and Michael C. Dorf

Columbia University Press
New York

Columbia University Press
Publishers Since 1893
New York   Chichester, West Sussex
cup.columbia.edu
Copyright © 2016 Columbia University Press

Library of Congress Cataloging-in-Publication Data
Colb, Sherry F., 1966– author.
   Beating hearts : abortion and animal rights / Sherry F. Colb and
Michael C. Dorf.
              pages cm. — (Critical perspectives on animals : theory,
culture, science, and law)
     Includes bibliographical references and index.
     ISBN 978-0-231-17514-2 (cloth : alk. paper) —
     ISBN 978-0-231-54095-7 (ebook)
     1. Law—Moral and ethical aspects.   2. Animal welfare—Law
and legislation.   3. Animal rights movement.   4. Abortion—Law
and legislation.   5. Pro-choice movement.   I. Dorf, Michael C.,
author.   II. Title.

K247.6.C65   2016
179'.3—dc23   2015026814

Columbia University Press books are printed on permanent
and durable acid-free paper.
This book is printed on paper with recycled content.
Printed in the United States of America

c 10 9 8 7 6 5 4 3 2 1

Cover design: Mary Ann Smith

References to websites (URLs) were accurate at the time of
writing. Neither the authors nor Columbia University Press is
responsible for URLs that may have expired or changed since
the manuscript was prepared.

CONTENTS

ACKNOWLEDGMENTS

A great many people played important roles in our thinking about the issues addressed in this book. Gary Francione's influence on our views about nonhuman animals and on our lives has been enormous. As Sherry's colleague at Rutgers School of Law–Newark for thirteen years, he was a shining example of how we could live according to our values. We regret that it took us as long as it did to follow his example, but that was our failing, not his. In addition, he and Gary Steiner were extremely generous in urging us to submit our book for publication in their wonderful series. We are honored to be included.

Each of us has been thinking and writing about reproductive rights questions for a long time, at least since law school in the late 1980s. Our respective mentors—especially Nomi Stolzenberg and Laurence Tribe—helped us develop our views on these questions and offered us scholarly opportunities for which we will always be grateful. More recently, a teaching and scholarly collaboration between Michael and Sidney Tarrow gave us a grounding in the dynamics of social movements, discussed in part 2.

We transitioned from vegetarian to vegan in 2006, and we soon discovered an incredibly supportive community. Much of what we know and think about animal rights comes from extended conversations with our friends in and around the movement, including (in addition to those already mentioned) Jonathan Balcombe, Carol Barnett, Ted Barnett, Harold Brown, Taimie Bryant, Neil Buchanan, T. Colin Campbell, Jim Corcoran, Anne Dinshah, George Eisman, JoAnn Farb, Joe Farb, Lewis Freedman, Amber Gilewski, Stephen Glass, Ariel Gold, Amie Hamlin, Lara Heimann, Mark Heimann, Julie Hilden, Robert Hockett, Keith Langer-Liblick, Stephanie Langer-Liblick, James LaVeck, Bob Linden, Eric Lindstrom, Jen Majka, Jeffrey Moussaief Masson, Milton Mills, Victoria Moran, Ducson Nguyen, Alan Scheller-Wolf, Terri Scheller-Wolf, Mary Schuelke, Harold Schultz, Linnaea Scott, Paul Scott, Rae Sikora, Jasmin Singer, Jenny Stein, Mariann Sullivan, Evan Tasch, and Priscilla Timberlake.

We are also very grateful to Cornell Law School for supporting our work and for providing vegan options at just about every event at which food is served. For most of our time at Cornell thus far, Stewart Schwab was the dean, and we very much appreciate his leadership in this and so many other respects. Eduardo Peñalver, our new dean, has also been enormously supportive. Speaking of Cornell, we would also like to thank the students and the guest speakers in Sherry's animal rights seminars, whose challenges and insights are reflected in these pages. Special thanks to our tireless and thorough research assistants, Jesse London, Justin Mungai Ndichu, Geoffrey Parker, and Matthew Tymann, to Ernestine Da Silva and Gina Jackson for their help in formatting the manuscript, and to Estalita Slivosky for preparing the index.

Eduardo Peñalver, Sidney Tarrow, Manès Weisskircher, Alan Scheller-Wolf, and two reviewers for Columbia University Press read all or substantial parts of the manuscript and gave us extremely helpful feedback. We are also grateful to participants in workshops and conferences at Cornell University, Princeton University, Rutgers School of Law–Newark, UCLA School of Law, and the annual Vegetarian Summerfest at University of Pittsburgh at Johnstown.

Finally, we extend special thanks also to our wonderful vegan daughters, Amelia Colbdorf and Meena Colbdorf, for making our values their values; we do not take that for granted.

BEATING HEARTS

Introduction

TWO MOVEMENTS, ONE SET OF ISSUES

How can someone who condemns practices like animal farming, hunting, and experimentation favor a right to abortion? Abortion, after all, is the deliberate taking of a human life, or at least of a potential human life. Yet many people in the animal rights movement *do* support legal abortion. Do animal rights activists really care more about the well-being of nonhuman animals than they do about tiny humans?

Conversely, how can people who would ban the destruction of even a one-celled human zygote—an entity as simple as an amoeba and possessing no more consciousness than a fingernail or a strand of hair—eat and use the flesh, skin, and secretions of feeling creatures like cows, pigs, and chickens, whose lives were filled with unspeakable suffering, ended only by horrific deaths? Do pro-life activists really care more about a human cell than about the suffering of fully sentient animals whose evolutionary history, brain chemistry, and emotional repertoire closely resemble our own?

It is of course possible to favor both animal rights and the rights of embryos and fetuses, and some people are in fact active in both movements.[1] Yet for the most part the animal rights movement and the pro-life movement do not overlap. Indeed, in public debate the issues of abortion and animal rights are rarely discussed together, except perhaps when someone is trying to score rhetorical points through mockery: *You favor rights for chickens but not human babies? Your position is grotesque!*[2]

Despite the rhetorical gap between most activists, abortion and animal rights raise closely intertwined questions. Both the pro-life movement and the animal rights movement challenge conventional views about the moral relevance of membership in the human species: people in the pro-life movement regard humanity as a sufficient condition for moral rights; people in the animal rights movement contend that humanity is not a necessary condition for moral rights. Although the question of whether humanity is a sufficient condition for moral rights is logically distinct from the question of whether it is a necessary condition for such rights, the two questions call into play many of the same considerations. The pro-life and animal rights movements both ask which criterion or criteria ought to ground rights.

This book considers some of the ways in which the debates over abortion and animal rights shed light on one another. In addition to focusing on interconnected ethical questions, the pro-life and animal rights movements face many of the same tactical questions. When should activists promote regulatory measures that do not fundamentally challenge the status quo, and when should they insist on abolition? Should legal reforms precede or follow attitudinal changes? Do gory images of dead animals or dead fetuses win hearts and minds to the respective causes or merely alienate the public? Is violence against abortion providers or animal exploiters objectionable at all, and—if so—is the objection merely tactical or is it principled? By juxtaposing the considerations relevant to answering both ethical and tactical questions as they arise in the contexts of the two movements, we aim to broaden the conversation about both.

Our goals are partly explanatory. We hope this book will be of interest and use to persons of good faith, whether they are pro-life or pro-choice, for or against animal rights. By tracing the consequences of views on one set of issues for views on the other set of issues, we mean to provoke thought even if we do not change minds.

Still, we would be less than forthright were we to deny that we hold views on the issues we tackle. To oversimplify, we are pro-choice on abortion and we favor animal rights. The chapters comprising part 1 of this book provide a more nuanced explanation of our views, but we can briefly summarize them here.

This book explicates the view that sentience grounds moral rights. Sentience is the ability to have subjective experiences. A being who can feel pleasure or pain is, in virtue of that ability, sentient. Indeed, we argue that the ability to have subjective experiences is precisely what makes a being a *being*, a "who" rather than an "it."

Most reasonably complex living animals, including humans, are provably sentient. So are fetuses at some point in their development. Inanimate objects and (so far as we know) plants are not sentient. Most sentient creatures can respond to external stimuli, but such responses alone do not necessarily indicate sentience. A thermostat that directs a furnace to fire up when the temperature dips below the set point responds to an external stimulus. So does a sunflower displaying heliotropism. But we have no good reason to think that a thermostat or a sunflower feels anything. We can vaguely imagine what it might feel like to be a hummingbird, a shark, or an eight-month-old human fetus, but we cannot envision what it would feel like to be a thermostat or a sunflower. It would, to the best of our knowledge, not feel like anything.

If we acknowledge, as we do, that at some point in their development fetuses are sentient, then why do we characterize ourselves as pro-choice rather than pro-life? Our answer has three essential parts.

First, people who call themselves pro-life generally do not regard sentience as a necessary condition for the rights of the unborn. They think that one-celled zygotes, no less than newborn babies, are entitled to protection against destruction. To be sure, people within the pro-life movement sometimes express a concern for fetuses due to their sentience. For example, a number of pro-life legislatures have enacted antiabortion laws premised on the view that fetuses can feel pain at twenty weeks.[3] But we think that the emphasis on fetal pain is best understood as an effort to appeal to those elements of the general public that do not hold strongly pro-life views. As reflected in the official statements of the main pro-life organizations, the unborn have rights from "the moment of conception," long before they are sentient.[4] Because we reject this view, we hesitate to call ourselves pro-life.

Second, to be pro-life is to believe that the rights of the unborn outweigh any interest a pregnant woman might have in terminating a pregnancy. In our view, prior to fetal sentience, they do not. Moreover, even after fetal sentience, a pregnant woman might be entitled, by virtue of the tremendous physical burdens that pregnancy imposes, the particular health challenges she faces, or some other circumstance, to terminate her pregnancy. Although it is possible to say that fetuses have rights but that pregnant women have superior rights, that way of speaking would not be recognizably "pro-life." Indeed, we speak in that way, and we consider ourselves pro-choice.

Third, the pro-life movement is predominantly a movement for legal reform. Even though we agree with pro-lifers that abortions of sentient fetuses are sometimes immoral, we disagree with the further conclusion that such abortions should therefore be legally forbidden. We are both lawyers by training, and perhaps for that reason we are acutely aware of the law's shortcomings and limitations.

In some circumstances, attempts to command compliance with an unpopular mandate may backfire, causing collateral damage. That is the accepted wisdom about what went wrong with the prohibition of alcohol, and it is at least an arguable account of the regime of abortion regulation that preceded the U.S. Supreme Court's 1973 decision in *Roe v. Wade*.[5] Prohibition of alcohol led to the violence associated with bootlegging, while prohibition of abortions led to the violence associated with back-alley abortions.[6]

In other circumstances, even where there is no practical obstacle to enforcing a legal rule, it may be appropriate to commit the matter to individual conscience. Thus, constitutional democracies permit freedom of speech even though many instances of its exercise will be irresponsible and even harmful. Likewise, one might think it is appropriate for the law to permit women the freedom to choose abortion, even if one deems some particular exercises of that freedom immoral by one's own lights. Accordingly, notwithstanding our concern for sentient fetuses, we cannot cast our lot with those who draw the categorical conclusion that abortion ought to be illegal in all or even in many cases.

Our views about the proper role of law in the regulation of animal use, at least given existing realities, are not all that different from our views about the proper role of law in protecting fetuses. As a general matter, we think it is wrong to use sentient animals as resources by producing, selling, and consuming animal-derived products. Thus, we are vegans. We make every reasonable effort to avoid eating or wearing animal products, and we refuse to patronize enterprises such as aquariums and zoos that use animals for entertainment. We also generally avoid using products that are tested on animals. However, under current circumstances, we do not propose that the law should forbid the use of animal products.

Even though, as a practical matter, we would leave most decisions about whether to consume animal products to individuals, we would not characterize our views about veganism as "prochoice." We are pro-choice with respect to abortion, even though we regard some abortions as immoral, because we think that ultimate authority for deciding whether to have an abortion ought to rest with each individual woman. By contrast, we would resist writing our views about animal exploitation into law for strategic rather than principled reasons. Given current practices, there is no realistic chance of securing a legal prohibition on consuming animal products, and thus we think that advocacy efforts should focus chiefly on changing hearts and minds. In a future in which vegans constitute something like a majority of the population, we might reevaluate the wisdom of seeking legal prohibition. We reject the notion that individual consumers are entitled, as a matter of right, to consume animal products.

We would be surprised if most readers found the foregoing explanation of our views fully satisfying because to this point we have merely set out a summary of them. Part 1 of this book will provide more of the details of our positions and the reasons underlying them. We do not, however, intend this book as a comprehensive treatment of the moral or tactical issues raised by either abortion or animal exploitation and slaughter. We provide the broad outlines of an approach to each set of questions, but our chief aim is to explore the connections of those questions to one another, not to answer every question that arises in each field.[7]

How shall we go about answering the moral questions that we raise in part 1 of this book? Religion dictates or informs the views that some people hold about abortion and animal rights. Abortion is wrong, these people believe, because from the moment of conception, humans possess an immortal soul made in the image of God. Likewise, for many of the same people, animals lack immortal souls and, in any event, God gave mankind dominion over the animals to use as we please. Accordingly, they conclude, abortion is wrong and animals lack rights.

We think the religious arguments are hardly clear-cut. The original biblical regulation of abortion seems to have less to do with protecting human souls than with protecting a man's property interest in his potential offspring.[8] Meanwhile, Christian beliefs about the point at which the soul enters the body—or "ensoulment"—have varied over time, although the trend since the seventeenth century has been toward the view that ensoulment occurs at conception.[9] With respect to the rights and interests of animals, even people who think that the Bible forecloses animal rights rarely think that the Bible compels them to exploit, slaughter, or eat animals. Moreover, as thinkers like Norm Phelps and Matthew Scully have argued, dominion over animals need not be construed as license to exploit and harm them but may instead be a call to service and stewardship.[10]

Ultimately, however, we put aside arguments rooted in religious authority, regardless of where they lead. In a pluralist society such as ours, citizens hold a wide variety of religious beliefs, including nonbelief. Principles of church–state separation imply that elected officials must be able to articulate arguments that persons of different religious faiths—or persons who profess no religion—can accept. This ideal, which the late philosopher John Rawls labeled "public reason," is controversial, to be sure.[11] Many people of faith contend that preventing them from appealing to religious authority deprives them of their best arguments. Nonetheless, we ourselves accept the constraints of public reason because, whether or not they are required as a matter of political philosophy, as a practical matter we hope to reach a diverse audience whose members subscribe to a wide range of religious faiths, or to no faith at all.

Because our discussion of abortion and animal rights touches on important questions of moral philosophy, we feel some obligation to locate our approach within the centuries-old debate between the two great moral philosophical traditions of the West: utilitarianism versus Kantianism and other rights-based views (collectively sometimes called "deontology"). On the one hand, we acknowledge the enormous contribution that utilitarians have made toward advancing our understanding of the moral status of animals. Jeremy Bentham, who is rightly regarded as the father of utilitarianism, famously stated about animals: "The question is not 'Can they reason?' nor 'Can they speak?' but 'Can they suffer?'"[12] Likewise, utilitarian Peter Singer's 1975 book, *Animal Liberation*, played an extremely important role in mobilizing the contemporary movement to protect the interests of animals. Bentham, Singer, and others deserve credit for demonstrating the inconsistency between the values humans espouse and the way that humans act toward our nonhuman cousins.

On the other hand, we are uncomfortable with utilitarianism for the sorts of reasons that deontologist philosophers routinely offer in criticism of utilitarianism, most centrally that it treats people—or as we would have it, all sentient beings—as mere vessels of pleasure minus pain (or in the more sophisticated accounts, as vessels of utility).[13] Thus, in principle, if a sadist derives more pleasure from inflicting pain on an innocent victim than the pain the innocent feels, utilitarianism may hold that the sadist is morally entitled to torture his victim.

We have read enough philosophy to know that utilitarians have devised arguments that try to avoid this result and similar ones. John Stuart Mill distinguished between higher and lower pleasures. Modern "prioritarians" build deontological side constraints into their social welfare functions.[14] And so forth. Were we writing a comprehensive work of moral philosophy, we would explore whether such intellectual moves succeed and, if so, whether they fundamentally transform utilitarianism into something else.

However, we have neither the expertise nor the inclination to write a comprehensive book on moral philosophy. Our interest focuses on questions about the moral status of fetuses and animals. To the extent that utilitarian philosophers have had important insights about those questions, we gratefully draw on them, even as we strongly disagree with some of the conclusions they reach.

In rejecting full-throated utilitarianism, we do not necessarily endorse all of the views of any particular philosopher working in the deontological tradition either. Deontology has its own difficulties that in important respects mirror those of utilitiarianism. Is it really wrong to tell a lie to avoid a catastrophe? If it is not, as so-called threshold deontologists would concede, is that concession really grounded in deontological principles?[15]

We make no effort to resolve these seemingly timeless questions. As philosopher David DeGrazia observed in his 1996 book, *Taking Animals Seriously: Mental Life and Moral Status*, "first-generation" writers on animal ethics like Singer placed "extraordinary emphasis, in their books and articles, on the utility-versus-rights debate," but the real divide among the public when it comes to animals (and perhaps fetuses) is not over *how* to count their interests but over *whether* to count their interests at all.[16]

More broadly, in contemporary public debate, politicians, judges, pundits, and others rarely feel the need to enlist in any one particular philosophical camp—whether it is utilitarianism, deontology, or some ostensibly alternative view, like virtue ethics. If advocates sometimes appeal to the moral intuition that it is wrong to increase suffering in the world, while at other times appealing to the seemingly contrary moral intuition that some actions are right or wrong regardless of their aggregate consequences, that is because the moral intuitions of human beings do not neatly correspond to one or another of the axioms of the leading schools of moral philosophy.

What then is our affirmative methodology with respect to moral questions? Simply stated, we try to reconcile and refine what we take to be widely shared moral intuitions about a variety of real and hypothetical cases. Philosophers sometimes attach the label "constructivism" to this approach, but that is too highfalutin for our purposes here.[17] To reiterate, we are not building a comprehensive account of morality; we are simply testing the sorts of general statements people sometimes make about abortion and animals—like "all human life is precious" or "it is wrong to deliberately cause unnecessary suffering"—against logic, reality, and common sense.

This book presents a set of arguments, but people rarely make large changes in their substantive views—much less in their behavior—based on appeals to reason alone.[18] If we want to change how people feel and act, might we do better to dramatize our position in emotionally salient ways? We are mindful of the fact that Harriet Beecher Stowe's novel *Uncle Tom's Cabin* successfully dramatized slavery's evils without inventing any new arguments against the institution.

Nonetheless, our own experience reassures us that our project can complement other kinds of work. Our own journey to veganism began with the experience of sharing our lives with our dogs and with getting to know a few individual farmed animals. But we have also found that rational arguments played an important role in how we came to think about and act with respect to abortion, animals, and many other matters. When we talk with colleagues and friends in the animal rights movement, we find that their trajectories have been remarkably similar, regardless of whether they are left-brain-dominant lawyers like us or right-brain-dominant artists.

More broadly, we reject the dichotomy between reason and emotion, between thinking and feeling. Neuroscience teaches that the emotional centers of the brain play an essential role in decision making, including moral decision making.[19] If the logical arguments we present in this book succeed in persuading our readers, it will be in part because they engage readers' emotions.

Finally, we want to clarify in advance what may seem like linguistic sloppiness about both of our topics. In discussing the pro-life position, we will sometimes use the term "embryo" or "fetus" as a shorthand for "human zygote, embryo, or fetus." We do so because a single word is less cumbersome than a four-word phrase but also to underscore that the pro-life position in contemporary American debates about abortion confers rights on microscopic nonsentient entities, so long as they are human.

Meanwhile, in talking about animal rights, we sometimes use the term "animals" as a shorthand for "nonhuman animals," even though, of course, human beings are also animals. That is a purely stylistic choice against wordiness. In its substance, this book points in the opposite direction. We challenge readers to justify the distinctions they reflexively draw between humans and other animals.

To be sure, as we explain in chapter 1, there are some contexts in which we humans may have legitimate reasons to favor the interests of some members of our own species over the interests of members of other species, much in the way that you sometimes have legitimate reasons for conferring benefits on members of your own family or friends that you do not confer on strangers. Those reasons have their limits, however. You need not pay for your neighbor's children's college education. But it does not follow that you may kill and eat them.

PART I

ETHICS

Under what circumstances, if any, is abortion morally permissible? When, if ever, are humans entitled to use or kill animals? And to what extent should a democracy allocate these matters to individual conscience rather than to collective decision making through law?

The chapters in part 1 of this book address questions such as these chiefly as matters of ethics or morality. Part 2 comprises chapters addressing parallel strategic and tactical questions that face the pro-life and animal rights movements, although, as we explain there, questions of principle cannot always be cleanly separated from pragmatic considerations.

This part consists of four chapters. Chapter 1 develops the idea that sentience grounds moral rights. We defend the sentience criterion against the competing notion that membership in the human species is the key to moral consideration.

Chapter 2 then asks whether and when it may be morally permissible to inflict harm on sentient fetuses and animals, notwithstanding the moral consideration to which they are entitled.

Chapter 3 builds on a familiar feminist argument for the abortion right by juxtaposing the impact of abortion restrictions on women with the impact of the dairy and egg industries on the female animals—cows and hens—who are exploited for their reproductive products.

Chapter 4 considers what we call the Epicurean objection to animal rights: If the interest in avoiding suffering grounds moral consideration, then ought not so-called humane exploitation of animals be permissible? We link this objection (and our response to it) to an objection to abortion rights: If currently unconscious people have a right to live (as we acknowledge they do), then why isn't the fact that presentient embryos will eventually achieve sentience sufficient to give them too a right to live?

We draw on moral philosophy to address these issues but not because we believe that philosophers have any special moral authority. Instead, these chapters ask readers to interrogate what they already think—and how they already feel—about abortion and animals.

1

Sentience or Species?

Competent adult humans are moral agents—that is, we are beings with moral duties to others. But to which others? This chapter argues that we owe moral duties to living, sentient beings—including most animals and late-term fetuses. We consider, but reject, an alternative view that says we owe moral duties to only humans (including fetuses and zygotes). Although we may extend special benefits toward our fellow humans, it does not follow that we may ethically harm and exploit animals. Absent some very strong justification or excuse, we have a duty at least to avoid intentionally inflicting suffering or death on any sentient being, whether human or nonhuman.

As we indicated in the introduction, our strategy for inferring the content of moral duties builds on what we take to be widely shared moral intuitions. Thus, instead of beginning by postulating the general source or nature of moral duty, we begin with concrete examples.

PARTIAL-BIRTH ABORTION

In the 2007 case of *Gonzales v. Carhart*, the Supreme Court of the United States rejected a constitutional challenge to the federal

Partial-Birth Abortion Ban Act.[1] "Partial-birth abortion" is not a scientific term. It is a category created by abortion opponents to refer to a type of abortion more formally known as intact dilation and evacuation (intact D&E) or dilation and extraction (D&X) that, before the ban's enactment, had sometimes been used late in pregnancy. Abortion opponents coined the term "partial-birth abortion" to refer to the fact that during a D&X, the fetus is partially delivered before being killed.

The *Carhart* case involved a number of technical questions, both legal and factual. Did the federal law provide doctors with clearer notice of the prohibition's scope than a Nebraska partial-birth abortion ban that the Court had invalidated partly on vagueness grounds in an earlier case? How frequently did doctors perform a D&X? For what reasons? How early or late in pregnancy did a D&X typically occur? Were there circumstances in which a D&X could be considered medically necessary? Which side had the burden of proof on that question? What exactly was the government's goal in banning partial-birth abortion, given that it permitted abortions by other means at the same stage of pregnancy? Much can be, and has been, said about these and other questions, but we mention the case here for a different reason. The majority opinion contains a graphic description of the "partial-birth" procedure, and we think that the description offers an important insight into the moral force of the pro-life position. Here is an excerpt of the opinion, quoting a nurse who testified before a Senate committee about her impression of a D&X performed on a twenty-six-week fetus:

> [The doctor] went in with forceps and grabbed the baby's legs and pulled them down into the birth canal. Then he delivered the baby's body and the arms—everything but the head. The doctor kept the head right inside the uterus. . . .
>
> The baby's little fingers were clasping and unclasping, and his little feet were kicking. Then the doctor stuck the scissors in the back of his head, and the baby's arms jerked out, like a startle reaction, like a flinch, like a baby does when he thinks he is going to fall.

The doctor opened up the scissors, stuck a high-powered suction tube into the opening, and sucked the baby's brains out. Now the baby went completely limp. . . .

He cut the umbilical cord and delivered the placenta. He threw the baby in a pan, along with the placenta and the instruments he had just used.[2]

Only a psychopath can read that description without viscerally reacting with sympathy for the fetus. The clasping and unclasping hands, the kicking feet, and the startled flinch all bespeak something terrible happening *to someone*. Indeed, that is undoubtedly the point of the narrative. By calling the fetus a "baby" and by juxtaposing the fetus's apparent fear and pain with the doctor's casual disrespect for the fetus's ruined body, the nurse makes the point that the fetus was *someone* who was unjustly treated as merely *something*.

What, exactly, makes the fetus someone rather than something? The language quoted here unmistakably points to sentience—to the fact that the fetus is capable of experiencing sensation and experiences terribly painful sensations during an abortion. The fetus does not just react to stimuli in the way that sunflowers bending to the sun's rays do. He *flinches*. He is *startled*. We are meant to infer that he *suffers*. By calling attention to what the fetus does, the nurse implies that the fetus has mental and emotional states of the sort that a sunflower cannot have. And the nurse assumes that we, the audience, will attach moral significance to the fetus's suffering and death. When all is said and done, we may still end up pro-choice on abortion, but we cannot in good faith deny that harm to a twenty-six-week-or-later fetus has moral weight.

MALE CHICKS

If fetal sentience underwrites the moral revulsion most of us feel in response to the nurse's narrative of partial-birth abortion, should we not also feel moral revulsion in response to similar impositions on nonhuman sentient animals? Do we? Let us now consider a routine practice in the egg industry.

Through selective breeding, farmers have created two very different sorts of domesticated chickens. So-called broiler birds have been bred to grow large quickly so they can convert as little feed as possible into an enormous amount of meat very rapidly. By contrast, flesh on so-called layer hens is, from an economic standpoint, mostly wasted. These birds are thus relatively small, with feed inputs directed toward the frequent production of eggs. Constant egg laying takes its toll on the hens. They suffer calcium depletion, egg peritonitis, and other maladies. Although the wild cousins of domesticated chickens can live to be ten years old, even hens who avoid succumbing to illness will typically be killed at about two years of age, when their egg production diminishes. Accordingly, farmers must constantly replenish their supply of laying hens.

Hatcheries, meanwhile, cannot determine the sex of chicks until they hatch from their shells. At that point, hatchery employees separate the females from the males. The females are kept for laying, but the males have no economic value. They cannot produce eggs and, because they are from the layer rather than the broiler line, their bodies will not produce meat nearly as efficiently as a broiler's body will. With no market for male layer chicks, they are killed almost immediately after hatching—regardless of whether the female layer chicks will be sent to cages in "factory" farms or to so-called free-range farms.[3]

How do farmers kill male chicks of the layer breed? Common industry methods include suffocating them by sealing them in garbage bags, gassing them, and macerating them—that is, grinding chicks to death by feeding them along a conveyor belt into a gigantic high-speed meat grinder. The American Veterinary Medical Association (AVMA), which publishes guidelines for the euthanasia of animals, classifies those last two methods as "humane," although that classification is questionable.[4] It is difficult to imagine anyone thinking that maceration would count as a humane method of euthanasia for an ailing family pet or—for those who think voluntary euthanasia acceptable for humans—for themselves or another terminally ill human. But even if one were to accept the AVMA claims, the truth is that many male chicks are killed by methods that the guidelines acknowledge cause serious distress, such as suffocation. And that is to say nothing of the deprivation of life itself suffered by these millions of healthy rooster chicks (a subject to which we will return in chapter 4).

We now want to ask what we hope will seem like a shockingly easy moral question: Is the painful death of a newly hatched male "layer" chick a morally regrettable act? We are not yet asking whether it is an immoral act. Just as you might think that the suffering of fetuses during abortion is morally regrettable, yet you ultimately believe that women should have a right to abortion, so you might think that gassing, suffocating, or grinding up chicks is morally regrettable but nonetheless morally permissible.

Perhaps you think that eating eggs is necessary for human health, that human health is more important than harm to chickens, that in a modern market economy there is no realistic way to produce substantial numbers of chicken eggs without killing newly hatched male chicks, and that therefore what happens to the male chicks is, all things considered, justified. We consider the question of justified harm to animals (and to human fetuses) in the next chapter. Here we ask a more basic question: Even if necessity justifies killing newly hatched male chicks, is it still morally regrettable? If it is justified, is it a justified *harm*? Or is suffocating a newly hatched chick to death an act devoid of apparent moral significance, akin to cutting your fingernails or smashing a rock into pieces?

We suspect that most people will say that suffocating the baby chick is harmful. If we now ask *who is harmed by the suffocating of the chick?*, the answer will also be clear: Why, the chick himself, of course. And the reason will be just the same as in the abortion case: because the chick is someone, not something.

THE SENTIENCE CRITERION

Put more generally, late-term fetuses and newly hatched chicks are beings with interests of their own—including interests in avoiding suffering and death. That is what distinguishes them from inanimate objects and life forms like plants that (so far as we know) lack sentience. A vandal who destroys a building commits a harmful act, but it is not a harm *to the building*. Instead, the vandal harms the individuals who live in, work in, or otherwise use the building. He harms the owner of the building, whose insurance probably will not cover all of his losses. And he harms the shareholders in the insurance company, for that matter. Further, if the building was aesthetically pleasing to the eye, the vandal harms the people who now can no longer derive pleasure from admiring its architecture. But the vandal does not harm *the building* because he cannot harm the building. The building is not the sort of entity that can experience harm because the building cannot experience anything.

To be sure, we often speak about inanimate objects or artificial entities as though they had interests. For example, we might say that making a larger-than-expected quarterly profit was "good for Google," even though Google is a corporation that does not itself have experiences. Or you might say that reducing your carbon footprint is good for the environment, even though the environment is not a being with interests. We can best understand such statements as a kind of shorthand. When we say that some event is good for Google, we mean that it is good for shareholders and other people, such as Google employees, who benefit from Google's profitability. Likewise, when we say that some action is good or bad for the environment, most of us have in mind the many creatures, including humans, who benefit from robust ecosystems, rather than the environment itself.[5]

There is nothing wrong with talking about artificial entities and inanimate objects as though they had interests. But it is easy to lose sight of the fact that the entity in question is really only a shorthand for the interests of beings that have interests. For example, someone might think that the Holocaust worked a harm to the Jewish people beyond the harm that it did to each of the six million Jews the Nazis exterminated, to the survivors of the ghettos and camps, and to their relatives whose lives were thereby damaged. Indeed, we think something very much like this ourselves (which is hardly surprising, given that we are both Jewish and that one of us is the child of Holocaust survivors). But when you unpack the idea of harm to the Jewish people as such, it too turns out to be a complex kind of shorthand.

We can and do acknowledge that part of what it means to be a person is to identify as a member of a group that has properties greater than the sum of its individual members. Nonetheless, that does not mean that the group has its own interests beyond all of the interests that people (and perhaps other animals) have with respect to the group. When people speak about harm to a group, they need not, and generally do not, assume otherwise. For example, when we talk about harm to the Jewish people, we treat group membership as something that individual members of the group (and some others who are not members of the group) highly value. In addition to the harm that the Holocaust caused to its direct victims, it robbed future individuals (including Jews and non-Jews alike) of an important piece of Jewish culture. But all of those harms are harms to people, not harms to any insensate entity.

Below we discuss the question of whether an act can be wrongful even if it does no harm to any being with interests. For now, we focus on our claim that sentient beings—like late-term fetuses and newly hatched chicks—have interests. We think it apparent that, by contrast with inanimate objects and the like, animals and late-term fetuses have interests precisely in virtue of the fact that they are sentient.

The view that sentient animals have interests is uncontroversial. People who are not animal rights activists of any sort claim to hold this view as well. Consider the existence and popularity of legal restrictions on cruelty to animals. These restrictions reflect the widespread sentiment that animals have interests in avoiding harm to them. To be sure, animal welfare laws are grossly under-inclusive and arguably worse than useless.[6] For example, the federal Animal Welfare Act[7] purports to require the humane treatment of animals used in research and as pets, but it excludes all "farm animals . . . used or intended for use as food or fiber," as well as all birds, rats, and mice.[8] Nonetheless, the idea behind protecting animal welfare would be incoherent if there were not agreement that animals are beings whose welfare can be considered. And animal welfare laws do more than just say that animals have interests. They restrict human freedom on the ground that it is sometimes objectionable to harm animals. In other words, our laws reflect the view that animals deserve at least some moral consideration.

People will undoubtedly disagree about what consequences follow from giving moral consideration to animals and late-term fetuses, but we think the discussion to this point—coupled with what we take to be widely shared moral intuitions—establishes at least the following: People should not harm sentient beings without an adequate reason. We shall call that proposition the sentience criterion for moral consideration. We might equivalently state it in this way: Sentience is a sufficient condition for moral consideration.

Note that we have so far espoused the proposition that sentience is a sufficient condition for moral consideration. We have not said that acts that cause no harm to sentient creatures *ipso facto* lack moral implications. The late philosopher and legal scholar Ronald Dworkin, in a book in which he espoused a pro-choice view on abortion, developed the position—which he associated with older Catholic doctrine even while attempting to put it on a secular footing—that abortion is a waste of the precious gift of life. Under this view, very early abortion may be immoral even when it works no harm to the interests of the unborn.[9] Dworkin himself, however, clearly placed great weight on sentience, as when he wrote "that a fetus cannot have interests of its own before it has a mental life," even as he allowed that acts could be wrongful without causing a setback to anybody's interests.[10]

In distinguishing between what he called "derivative" moral interests (those that derive from the interests of beings capable of having interests) and "detached" moral interests (those that are detached from the interests of any such beings), Dworkin believed he had found the key to unlock the abortion debate. People who oppose abortion may *say* that it is wrong to abort a zygote because of the harm *to* the zygote, but, as Dworkin would have had it, what they really think, or what they really *would* think if they worked it through, is that abortion of a zygote is wrong because it shows disrespect for human life in general, quite apart from any interests or rights a zygote might have.

We are not as confident as Dworkin was that we know the real reasons why people hold the views they hold about abortion (or anything else), and so we will take seriously what people in the pro-life movement actually say in support of their position. And many of them say exactly what Dworkin is at pains to deny that they might actually mean—namely, that abortion is wrong because of the harm it does to zygotes, embryos, and fetuses, even well before they are sentient.

Before coming to the pro-life argument as it is usually made in American public debate, we do want to credit Dworkin with an important insight: For many people, the obligation to avoid doing unjustified harm to others is only one sort of moral obligation; there are other grounds for moral obligations as well. Nonconsequentialist Kantian ethics often works in this way, as when Kant says it is wrong to lie even if no one is made the worse for the lie—indeed, even if the lie would do only good.[11]

Dworkin's own views about abortion and some related matters seem closer to what is sometimes called "virtue ethics" than to pure Kantianism. In virtue ethics, the rightness or wrongness of particular conduct depends on the character traits it exhibits in the person who has chosen to undertake that conduct. Dworkin expressed a version of virtue ethics when, in the last years of his life, he likened the leading of the right kind of life to a performance. "It is *important* that we live well," he said, "not important just to us or to anyone else, but just important."[12]

We are ambivalent about virtue ethics. On one hand, we agree with much that Dworkin and others have to say about the inherent value of a life well lived. On the other hand, we are not persuaded that virtue ethics is really an alternative to other approaches to morality, such as utilitarianism and deontology. Most of the hard moral questions that people face are not questions of *whether* we ought to do our moral duty but of *what* our moral duty is. An ethical theory that tells us that we ought to act in the way that exemplifies the character traits of a virtuous person appears to depend on some further account of what behavior is virtuous, and we have doubts that such an account can be specified by virtue ethics alone.

To be fair, Dworkin himself distinguished morality (how we treat others) from ethics (how we ought to live)[13] and so perhaps we are knocking on an open door. In any event, as we have noted, we are not building a case for or against any comprehensive view of moral obligation. We invoked Dworkin's views about the inherent value of life simply to acknowledge the possibility that we might have moral obligations that are not obligations to any being with interests (except perhaps ourselves). We do not need or want to contest (or defend) this possibility because we mean only to advance the sentience criterion as a sufficient condition for moral consideration. For purposes of much of the argument in this book, we can be agnostic on the question of whether there are moral obligations that are independent of the interests of sentient beings.[14]

To return to the main current of the argument: even though we sometimes encounter people who expressly reject the sentience criterion, the sentience criterion both appeals to widely shared intuitions and is consistent with the three leading approaches to moral philosophy we have discussed. First, for utilitarians, harming beings who are capable of experiencing harm should be avoided because doing so decreases aggregate utility—unless the harm inflicted leads to compensating increases in utility; that is, unless it is adequately justified. Second, for a deontologist who believes that there are rights and duties that cannot be reduced to any calculation of costs and benefits, no duty seems more basic than a duty to refrain from causing unjustifiable harm.[15] And third, to the extent that virtue ethics is, as in Dworkin's formulation, only about ourselves, it neither affirms nor rejects the sentience criterion, which concerns how we act toward others.

Of course, we do not claim that all or even very many adherents of these various strands of moral philosophy endorse the sentience criterion. Moral philosophers typically begin by asking what obligations we owe to humans, without even pausing to consider whether the arguments they advance for their views should also imply obligations to sentient nonhumans. Even then, however, there are exceptions. As we noted in the introduction, Jeremy Bentham, the father of modern utilitarianism, is a notable example, as is Peter Singer. Likewise, some contemporary deontologists find little difficulty extending moral consideration to nonhumans.[16] And the same is true for virtue ethics, as the work of Martha Nussbaum illustrates. Nussbaum is a leading modern proponent of virtue ethics. Although she is more skeptical than we are about the capacity of utilitarianism and deontology to fully embrace sentient animals' interests as a proper subject of moral concern, she confidently (and, subject to reservations about some of her conclusions, we would also say insightfully) develops an alternative account—which she calls the "capabilities" approach—that builds on the sentience criterion.[17]

Accordingly, we think the sentience criterion can fit comfortably within any of the leading schools of moral philosophy. That should not be surprising because the sentience criterion should be so self-evident as to be axiomatic within almost any defensible moral system. Certainly we hope that most readers will have come along at least so far as the sentience criterion, in light of the partial-birth abortion example, the male chick example, and our discussion to this point. Much hard work remains to be done regarding what does and does not count as adequate justification for harming sentient beings, but the principle that one should not inflict harm on beings capable of experiencing such harm without a very good reason, seems so obvious that we find it almost embarrassing to have to articulate and defend it.

HUMANITY AS AN ALTERNATIVE CRITERION

We nonetheless do find it necessary to articulate and defend the sentience criterion because it is routinely denied (or at least downplayed) in public debate over both abortion and the use of animals. The moral force of the description of the partial-birth abortion that we quoted earlier arises from the sentience of the fetus. Yet the pro-life view typically emphasizes something quite different: the humanity of the fetus.

The pro-life movement is diverse, but to the extent that one can find a consistent "official" position, the movement is committed to the proposition that human beings have a right to life from the "moment" of conception.[18] For example, in April 2013 Kansas became the eighth American state to enact a law declaring that life begins at fertilization, and although such laws are mostly symbolic in light of federal constitutional limits on abortion prohibitions, what they symbolize is a view that accords moral consideration to human zygotes.[19] As a National Right to Life Committee Web page explains: "A new individual human being begins at fertilization, when the sperm and ovum meet to form a single cell."[20] Pro-life doctors, politicians, and advocates frequently say that scientific evidence proves that conception—the fusion of human sperm and human egg—marks the beginning of each new human life.

In some versions of the argument, the assembly of twenty-three chromosome pairs marks the beginning of a unique human life. In any event, two elements appear to be crucial to the argument: First, that after but not before conception, there is a unique life that can develop into a baby, then child, then adult; and second, that because this unique new life belongs to the human species, it is a proper object of moral concern.

Note that sentience plays no apparent role in this view. Modern pro-lifers do not subscribe to the theory of homunculi or animalcules, according to which each sperm (or in some versions, egg) contains a tiny but fully developed human being, who simply expands to baby-size during pregnancy. They appear to recognize, among other things, that zygotes are not sentient.

To be sure, the "core" of the pro-life movement still seeks to appeal to centrist American public opinion and thus articulates arguments that have broader resonance. We think that explains why the pro-life movement has waged a vigorous campaign against "partial-birth" abortion and in favor of laws regarding fetal pain[21]—a topic to which we will return in chapters 4 and 5. By focusing on fetuses that are sufficiently developed to feel pain, the movement appeals to people who (regardless of how they would express their views) believe that sentience grounds interests, which in turn makes a sentient fetus the proper object of moral concern.

Fetal sentience, however, is not necessary to the standard pro-life case against abortion. Although there is some controversy over how long it typically takes for a fetus to develop sentience, the answer is certainly going to be measured in weeks or months. Sentience does not emerge in the first seconds, minutes, or days after conception.[22] For the pro-life movement, sentience is accordingly *not* a necessary condition for protecting the unborn.

As we explained, however, one can accept the sentience criterion without also insisting that avoiding harm to sentient beings is the *only* possible moral imperative. The sentience criterion states only that sentience is a sufficient condition for moral consideration. It is thus possible to favor animal rights on the ground that all sentient beings deserve moral consideration *and* to oppose all abortion based on moral considerations of the sort that Dworkin discussed: considerations that are independent of the interests of particular beings. And in fact, we have friends in the animal rights movement who are also pro-life on abortion. They see both commitments as flowing from a view about the regard they owe to life.

We respect the commitments of our animal rights / pro-life friends, but we also recognize that they constitute a small minority of a minority. Regardless of whether they are pro-choice or pro-life on abortion, most people do not treat animal sentience as sufficient to ground robust animal rights. Moreover, the arguments most commonly advanced by the pro-life community do not rely on sentience as either a necessary or a sufficient condition for moral consideration. They rely instead on the humanity of the zygote, embryo, or fetus, and for that reason, these arguments tend to cut against recognition of animal rights.

Why do most people who oppose abortion think that humanity, rather than sentience, establishes that zygotes, embryos, and fetuses are worthy of moral concern? For some, no doubt the answer is that sentience cannot ground moral concern for zygotes, embryos, and early fetuses because most of them are not sentient. These abortion opponents begin with the conviction that human zygotes deserve moral concern, and they then search for a criterion that justifies that conviction. Humanity suits; sentience does not.

If someone truly holds a settled conviction that human zygotes are proper objects of moral concern, nothing we can say will change that conviction. That is, after all, simply what it means to have a settled conviction. But we note that in public debate over abortion, people who take the pro-life position typically do not rest on their settled convictions. They offer ostensible reasons for *why* they hold—and why, in their view, others should also hold—the view that zygotes are entitled to moral concern.

The core of one common argument goes like this: From the moment of conception, a zygote has a full complement of his or her unique DNA, the instructions that will enable that zygote to develop into a human baby, then a child and eventually an adult. Therefore, from conception onward, a unique human individual is present.

We think that the foregoing claim trades on a crucial ambiguity in the meaning of the term "human." A zygote is a human cell, just as any cell in a human's own anatomy is a human cell. No one, however, would suggest that other human cells have rights and interests independent of the living, sentient person to whom those human cells belong. If you decide to pluck a hair out of your arm or face, you thereby terminate the life of some cells, yet no one thinks that you thereby commit a homicide. Indeed, when a surgeon cuts out a cancerous growth from your body, she removes an assortment of human cells, a tumor that in some respects behaves as an organism. Yet again, no one would suggest that you or the surgeon engages in a homicide by removing the tumor—and not only because you are defending yourself from an invading pathogenic process when you do so. The fact that a living cell or organism contains human DNA is simply insufficient to qualify the cell or organism as a "human" being for purposes of allocating rights such as the right not to be killed.

One difference between a human zygote and these other cells is that the human zygote is programmed to grow, eventually, into what we can all agree is a human being. Unlike a cancer cell, if we do nothing to stop the zygote's further development, then—assuming that conditions are right for its development—the zygote will become a human being. But this fact cannot be sufficient to establish that a zygote *already is* a human being. If it were, then each of the cells of your body would also already be a distinct human being (rather than simply a microscopic part of the human being that you are). After all, technology that has already been used to clone mammals such as sheep could soon enable doctors to remove the nucleus of a somatic (that is, an ordinary) cell, inject it into a denucleated egg cell, and program it to grow into a human being: a clone. Therefore, all individual human cells are *potentially* people—the hair cell as much as the zygote.

Furthermore, long before the development of cloning technology, eggs and sperms were potential people too. The differences among the various potential people—between zygotes, sperm cells, eggs, and ordinary body cells—are thus a matter of probabilities that they will become human beings, a matter of degree rather than of kind.[23]

Do such probabilities matter for moral purposes? Some people think so. For example, in an important 1970 pro-life essay, then law professor (now retired federal judge) John Noonan noted that "life itself is a matter of probabilities" and proceeded to offer the following illustration: "If the chance is 200,000,000 to 1 that the movement in the bushes into which you shoot is a man's, I doubt if many persons would hold you careless in shooting; but if the chances are 4 out of 5 that the movement is a human being's, few would acquit you of blame."[24] As two of the people who *would* hold the shooter careless (or worse) for shooting at what could be a bird, a rabbit, or other animal, we cannot help but notice Noonan's implicit but obvious disregard for the moral consequences of taking animal life. Nonetheless, we set that concern aside to note that even on its own terms the example is a non sequitur. The question that Noonan was ostensibly addressing was whether the probability that a known biological entity will *become* a human being in the future is relevant to the morality of killing it in the present. Noonan's example, however, concerns the morality of killing an unknown entity, given various odds that the entity is *currently* a human being.

With respect to the zygote, the pertinent probabilities revolve around what will happen in nine months because we already know what it is today. With respect to the movement in the bushes, by contrast, the shooter is attempting to calculate who is *now* behind those bushes, not what he or she will later become. The question of whether the shooter acts wrongly by firing at the movement in the bushes has no clear relevance to the question of whether it is wrong to kill a zygote (or egg or sperm), even if we know with *certainty* that the zygote (or egg or sperm) would otherwise become a person. One could know, in other words, that some action destroys a zygote and that absent such an action, the zygote would one day become a human being; yet those probabilities are simply irrelevant to the question of whether the zygote is already a human being, absent some further argument that Noonan fails to provide.

Does anyone offer a better justification for distinguishing between the different kinds of potential to become human beings that we find in zygotes, sex cells, and ordinary cells? Two leading pro-life philosophers have attempted to do so. Here is what Patrick Lee and Robert George say:

Human embryos are (just as more mature human beings are) whole human organisms, and, as such, living (albeit immature) members of the species homo sapiens; somatic cells are not. Human embryos have the epigenetic primordia for internally directed maturation as distinct, complete, self-integrating human individuals; somatic cells do not. Thus, the "potential" of somatic cells is nothing remotely like the potential of the embryo. Like sperm and ova, somatic cells, though they themselves are not distinct, self-integrating human organisms (but are rather parts of other, larger human organisms), can contribute constituents to a process that brings into being a new, distinct, self-integrating human organism—a human embryo. By contrast, an embryo—whether brought into being by sexual union or cloning—is already a human being. That human being, given nothing more than an hospitable environment, will actively develop itself from the embryonic through the fetal, infant, and adolescent stages of his or her life and into adulthood with his or her unity and identity fully intact.[25]

This effort is problematic in at least four respects. First, note that Lee and George describe the hard work that pregnant women do as the mere passive provision of "an hospitable environment." Yet feminists and others have long argued that abortion prohibitions are so burdensome precisely because pregnancy and childbirth are physically and psychologically demanding impositions.[26] To be sure, the burdensomeness of an unwanted pregnancy primarily relates to the question of whether women ought to be entitled to have abortions notwithstanding the harm that abortion does to fetuses. The moral status of the fetus is a separate question. But we nonetheless raise the objection here because in mischaracterizing what pregnancy entails, Lee and George draw a false contrast between the interventions needed to create a human being by cloning and the supposedly automatic process of natural gestation, in which, as they would have it, the active work of pregnancy has disappeared.

Second, that distinction—between ostensibly passive pregnancy and active cloning—breaks down even further if we consider yet another means by which human beings now routinely come into existence: in vitro fertilization (IVF). Just like clones, embryos created through IVF require intervention to develop into persons. Yet people who say that a human being's life begins at conception in fact (and quite logically) regard embryos conceived by IVF as human beings; for that reason many of them regard stem cell research on such embryos as immoral "human experimentation."[27] Pro-life thinkers who call a zygote a person therefore cannot persuasively invoke the fact that a zygote will grow into a person without any deliberate intervention because the criterion of no deliberate intervention would exclude embryos conceived by IVF from the class of human beings.

Third, we note that by distinguishing the potential of a zygote from the potential of a sperm, egg, or somatic cell (in a world with cloning), the pro-life argument tacitly concedes that the zygote itself—as a zygote—lacks present interests. If we have moral duties with respect to zygotes, the pro-life argument acknowledges, that is for one of two reasons: Either because, to use Dworkin's terms, respect for life as detached from the interests of any individual requires us to treat zygotes as though they were comparable to late-term fetuses, babies, children, and adults, or because the future fetus-then-baby-then-child-then-adult that this zygote could become has interests and, to use a legal phrase, the interests of those future beings "relate back" to the current zygote. We think it clear that by attempting to associate the current zygote with the future sentient being, the pro-life argument offered by Lee and George as well as others unwittingly acknowledges that sentience, not humanity, grounds interests and thus grounds moral consideration.[28]

Fourth and finally, we note that in our considerable (albeit nonexhaustive) reading of the pro-life literature, we have found virtually no attempt whatsoever to defend the moral relevance of the fact that zygotes, embryos, and presentient fetuses belong to the human species. It is simply assumed that this fact makes a moral difference. For example, Noonan began the conclusion to the essay we quoted earlier as follows: "The most fundamental question involved in the long history of thought on abortion is: How do you determine the humanity of a being?"[29] But why? Noonan considered but rejected the objection that "humanity" is merely a secular disguise for the religious notion of ensoulment because he assumed that just about everyone—including nearly all pro-choice secular philosophers—

would share the premise that human beings have a moral right to avoid being killed simply in virtue of their humanity.[30]

And Noonan was right about that. For the most part, people who are pro-choice on abortion share the assumption of the pro-life community that only people are entitled to moral consideration. They simply disagree over who counts as a person. As the late pro-choice philosopher Mary Anne Warren contended in response to Noonan, personhood grounds moral entitlements, but not all humans are moral persons. Pro-choice theorists seem to assume, then, that all moral persons on the planet must necessarily be human, even as these theorists reject the assumption that humanity is a sufficient condition for moral personhood.

Interestingly, Warren allowed that extraterrestrial beings might count as persons but apparently not that nonhuman animals here on Earth could.[31] More importantly, for purposes of this discussion, her quarrel with Noonan illustrates the general pattern of the pro-life/pro-choice debate among those who think that the moral status of the fetus is dispositive on the question whether abortion is immoral: Most participants in that debate begin with the premise that *only* humans are worthy of moral consideration and then argue over whether zygotes, embryos, and fetuses are sufficiently like paradigmatic rights-bearing humans to qualify for moral consideration. Perhaps because debates about abortion are debates about members of the human species, participants rarely think it necessary to justify rather than simply stipulate the line that divides humans and nonhumans.

Two notable exceptions are Gary L. Francione and Peter Singer. In chapter 3, we build on Francione's feminist argument for assigning the abortion decision to individual pregnant women, notwithstanding the fact that doing so results in the abortions of some sentient fetuses, which we and Francione regard as a serious harm.[32] Here we consider Singer's argument because it calls attention to the common ground among utilitarians (like Singer) and others (like ourselves) while also providing an opportunity to see beyond some of the limits of utilitarianism.

With characteristic directness, Singer writes that "whether a being is or is not a member of our species is, in itself, no more relevant to the wrongness of killing it than whether it is or is not a member of our race," adding that "those who protest against abortion but dine regularly on the bodies of chickens, pigs and calves, show only a biased concern for the lives of members of our own species."[33] Singer thus concludes that we ought "to accord the life of a fetus no greater value than the life of a nonhuman animal" with similar capacities.[34]

We agree with Singer's main point here. A fetus lacks interests before it attains sentience, and thus abortion cannot be a wrong *to* a fetus (or embryo or zygote) before the fetus (or embryo or zygote) attains sentience. We likewise agree with Singer that once one recognizes that sentience grounds interests, there is no reason other than species favoritism to deny that sentient nonhumans (like chickens, pigs, and calves) have interests that, for many purposes, are no different from those of sentient fetuses. Accordingly, we share Singer's conclusion that if abortion is wrong because of the harm it inflicts on sentient fetuses, then killing nonhuman sentient animals is similarly wrong.

We would, however, note an important reservation. In the passage we have quoted, Singer could be read to say that humans are obligated to extend the same consideration to all sentient beings with comparable capacities. We think that view—which appears to implement Singer's categorical declaration in *Animal Liberation* that "[a]ll animals are equal"[35]—fails to capture what we believe to be the permissible place for favoritism both within and between different species. It is in fact possible to recognize the sentience criterion without insisting that we may never favor members of our own species (or of some other species, for that matter).

WHICH CAPACITIES MATTER?

Thinkers who oppose extending moral consideration to animals sometimes point to various gaps between the capacities of humans and of other animals. We note that some of the supposedly unique human capacities—such as the ability to fashion tools, to use language, to show empathy, or to form a conception of oneself (as manifested by being able to use a mirror or otherwise)[36]—have proved not to be unique when biology showed their presence in nonhumans.[37] In some respects the efforts of animal rights opponents to identify criteria that distinguish humans from all other animals resemble the shifting rationales for ill-conceived policies, like the decision by President George W. Bush to invade Iraq in 2003—justified at one time or another by a concern about weapons of mass destruction (which proved to be false), ties to al-Qaeda (which also proved to be false), human rights violations (which were real but also occurred when Saddam Hussein was a U.S. client), and the promise of bringing democracy to the Arab world (which proved to be naïve).

Likewise with respect to the capacities that supposedly distinguish humans from other animals. Just as one suspects that Bush began with the determination to invade Iraq, so one suspects that the proponents of the various capacities began with the conviction that humans are categorically superior and then went looking for evidence to defend that conviction. They provisionally settled on some criterion—like language or tool-making—that humans supposedly uniquely possessed, only to shift their ground when the evidence contradicted the uniqueness assumption. But the evidence did not cause them to reexamine their rejection of the sentience criterion because their belief in human uniqueness preceded their search for evidence and was thus not actually founded upon evidence in the first place.

That is perhaps an understandable approach if one begins with the religious conviction that God gave humans dominion over the animals, although even then one could invoke religious tradition in favor of recognizing animal interests and according them moral consideration.[38] Still, at least one type of religious view—Biblical literalism—could rationally lead to a search for some crucial factual difference between humans and animals. If humans were specially created by God on the sixth day and (much later) given divine permission to eat other animals, then we would expect to find differences in kind, not just degree, between humans and other animals.

However, anyone who accepts the overwhelming scientific evidence for evolution would expect most human capacities to be found to varying degrees in at least some other animals. And indeed, just as we see obvious morphological similarities between humans and other animals, so has science increasingly discovered similarities between the mental lives of humans and other animals.[39]

Humans find the existence of impressive animal mental capacities fascinating, as evidenced by the popularity of YouTube videos of cats and dogs playing musical instruments, singing, or dialing 911.[40] However, none of these capacities is necessary for moral consideration. If one asks why the torture of a human being is wrong, surely the answer has nothing to do with the particular torture victim's ability to play the piano, to dial 911, or to write in a diary. The intentional infliction of suffering on human beings is presumptively wrong because suffering harms human beings, and it is wrong to cause harm to other beings capable of being harmed, absent adequate justification.[41] Likewise, the intentional infliction of suffering on nonhuman animals is presumptively wrong for the same reason.

We quoted Jeremy Bentham in the introduction to note the important contribution that utilitarians have made to the development of our understanding of moral obligations to animals. We quote him again here because his point grounds a moral obligation regardless of whether one accepts utilitarianism. Bentham said: "The question is not 'Can they reason?' nor Can they speak?' but 'Can they suffer?'"[42] That one should generally avoid inflicting unnecessary suffering on beings capable of suffering is so basic a moral principle that it seems to us nearly impossible to argue for it except by pointing to what we and, we think, most readers would regard as the morally disastrous consequences of establishing more stringent criteria for moral consideration. Some of the more stringent criteria—such as language use—would disqualify from moral consideration not only late-term fetuses and many animals but also human infants as well as severely disabled and some elderly humans. And yet widely shared moral intuitions tell us that, so long as such beings are sufficiently developed to have any present experiences at all, we might even regard the infliction of suffering on such individuals as *worse*, not better, in virtue of their inability to comprehend why they are suffering.

Nonetheless, some philosophers now argue that a being cannot really feel pain unless it understands that it is experiencing pain.[43] This strikes us as almost exactly backward: the most searing pains render one incapable of understanding pain or anything else; they are raw sensory experiences, and much the worse to endure as a consequence of that fact.

Of course, sometimes anticipation can make suffering worse, as torture victims attest. And some argue that the ability to anticipate the future may bear on the important question of whether the deprivation of life itself—apart from the infliction of suffering— does harm to the being deprived of life. As we explore in chapter 4, it is surprisingly difficult to explain what interest any of us— human or nonhuman—has in our continued existence. But so far as eligibility for any moral consideration at all is concerned, nothing turns on these distinctions. The only capacity relevant to the question whether it is presumptively wrong to inflict suffering on a being is the being's capacity to suffer.

To be sure, the distinct capacities of different animals, including different humans, are relevant to some moral questions regarding other aspects of our treatment of the various beings. For example, isolation of herd or other social animals (including humans) from others of the same species will typically cause distress, whereas some animals (such as adult male orangutans) rarely come together with others of their species except for mating. A complete list of the varying capacities of different animals would be useful for developing a full theory of what we owe to other animals—what Nussbaum calls a "capabilities approach" for "animal entitlements," "animal dignity," and animal "flourishing."[44]

Nussbaum's concern for flourishing raises an important question about our duties to both human and nonhuman animals. Many people think that we have moral obligations to assist just those among our fellow human beings whose limited capacities place them in need of help. Notably, the late moral and political philosopher John Rawls argued for what he called the "difference principle," according to which inequalities in the distribution of society's material goods were justifiable only insofar as those inequalities were the result of arrangements calculated to maximize the goods available to the least well off.[45] To be sure, no human society has ever implemented Rawls's difference principle; Nussbaum herself, in discussing the duties we owe to disabled persons (and others) rejects social contractarianism of the sort Rawls embraced. But Rawls remains broadly influential, and even those, like Nussbaum, who part company with Rawls on some matters do not deny that human beings have moral duties to the most disadvantaged in virtue of their disadvantage. In other words, incapacity, not just capacity, can give rise to moral entitlements.

But that brings us to the question: Does the widely shared intuition that it is at least permissible and probably laudable to provide affirmative aid to the needy among us entail the proposition that we must provide aid to needy nonhuman animals as well? And if so, does that render the notion that we owe moral consideration to animals a kind of *reductio ad absurdum* due to the prohibitive cost of providing such aid?

Let us put numbers behind those questions. The average cost of medical care for each American is over eight thousand dollars per year.[46] However, those costs are distributed unevenly. Care for the sick and the old costs much more. Although the United States does not have universal health care coverage—even after the enactment of the Patient Protection and Affordable Care Act in 2010—we do provide free medical care for the very poor (Medicaid) and the old (Medicare). Many people (including the two of us) regard such spending as not mere charity but a matter of national responsibility to the poor and the aged. Indeed, it is now common to speak of the government programs that provide health insurance as "entitlement" programs. So now we come to the question: If we believe that it is right for society to spend many thousands of dollars to improve the health of humans, do we have any justification for refusing to spend comparable sums to improve the health of wild animals? Most pointedly, can we defend this and other disparities in treatment without undermining the sentience criterion?

THE DIFFERENCE BETWEEN AFFIRMATIVE AND NEGATIVE CONTRIBUTIONS TO OTHERS' WELL-BEING

Like many other people in the animal rights movement, we came to veganism through personal experience with animals—in our case, at least initially, our dogs. As we got to know our dogs, we came to understand them as beings with independent interests and desires. Eventually, we came to see other animals that way too. Other vegans have shared similar accounts with us. They asked themselves and then they asked others: If you would not eat a dog, why do you eat pigs?[47] People who oppose animal rights have begun to develop an answer, and while we think that their answer is unsatisfactory, as we shall show, it contains an insight that helps explain why it is possible to grant animals moral consideration without concluding that we have bottomless duties to animals.

Consider a 2010 essay in the *Atlantic* magazine by rancher Nicolette Hahn Niman, reacting to the claim that pigs and dogs are morally indistinguishable. We eat what we eat, Niman says, for cultural reasons. Thus, she opines that "[i]t's no more contradictory to eat a pig but not a dog than it is to eat arugula but not purslane."[48]

Niman's claim confuses a moral question with a sociological question. We vegans acknowledge that cultural factors explain how various eating habits developed, but we are asking whether those habits can be justified. Niman's comparison of eating some but not other animals to eating some but not other vegetables is comparable to a nineteenth-century slaveholder responding to the question of why he enslaves some but not other human beings by saying that he enjoys some but not other types of paintings or, at the level of a society as a whole, that in some cultures men wear neckties while in other cultures they do not. Niman's answer and the answer given by our hypothetical slave owner amount to saying "there's no accounting for taste." That answer does not respond at all to the claim that enslaving *anyone* is wrong or that eating any sentient animal is wrong.

At various points in her brief essay, Niman flirts with the notion that there is nothing wrong with eating pigs *or* dogs. She invokes, without any apparent revulsion, the fact that various human cultures do in fact eat dogs. And she calls the revulsion that most Westerners feel toward eating dogs a mere "taboo." But Niman also calls the revulsion against eating human flesh a mere taboo, thus suggesting that Niman thinks that only cultural tastes distinguish those societies that have killed and eaten other humans from those societies that forbid such conduct as murder and cannibalism.

We doubt that Niman actually believes that. Believing that taboos against murder and cannibalism reflect nothing more than cultural tastes amounts to a radical form of moral relativism that most people reject. If Niman really is a radical moral relativist, then she should say so forthrightly: she should simply admit that she thinks that eating pigs is morally acceptable because she believes that there is no such thing as morality or immorality. But, of course, had Niman openly embraced a radical moral relativist view in that way, *Atlantic* readers would have properly dismissed her as unqualified to offer any opinions about right and wrong.

The people who ask whether it is possible to draw a moral distinction between pigs and dogs assume that it is not just taboo or icky to eat dogs but that it is *wrong* to eat dogs. The moral question we vegans pose is this: *If* it is wrong to eat dogs, why is it not also wrong to eat pigs?

Despite Niman's confused and confusing flirtation with radical moral relativism, her essay hints at a potential answer to a different question. She states that "[f]or as many as 30,000 years, dogs have literally been indispensible members of the human family. Quite naturally, many humans have qualms about eating a family member."[49] Niman correctly implies that we have special duties to family members that we lack to strangers. Hence, she concludes that in societies in which dogs are regarded as family members, it is wrong to eat dogs for the same sorts of reasons that we treat family members as special. And so long as pigs are not treated as family members, the rest of the argument goes, we need not afford the same solicitude to pigs as we do to dogs, even though pigs have the same basic capacities as dogs. After all, your neighbor's children might have the same basic capacities as your own children, but you nonetheless may—and in many circumstances must—treat your own children specially.

There is something at least partly right about Niman's view. Some of our duties do vary based on our relationships. If a custodial parent fails to feed, clothe, or shelter his or her own children, the parent acts immorally and commits the crime of neglect, whereas if that same person fails to feed, clothe, or shelter a random stranger's children, he or she commits neither a moral wrong nor a legal wrong. To be sure, a person who voluntarily provides aid to the children of strangers acts nobly, but what makes such conduct noble is precisely the fact that it goes beyond the call of duty. Moral philosophers refer to such acts that go beyond the call of duty as supererogatory.[50]

Having in mind the difference between moral duties and supererogatory acts, it becomes easy to see what is wrong with the argument that eating pigs but not dogs is morally permissible because dogs but not pigs are considered family members: Just about all of the agent-relative duties that we owe to family members but not to strangers are duties of affirmative aid rather than duties of nonharm. By contrast, nearly everyone acknowledges that we owe most duties of nonharm to strangers and to family members alike. And more broadly, we may discriminate between kin and non-kin (and those for whom we feel empathy and those for whom we do not) in distributing positive benefits owed to no one, but, in most circumstances, we must equally respect everyone's right to be free from violence by refraining from violent acts.

The point is painfully obvious in the case of humans. A parent has a duty to care for her own children and for those over whom she has otherwise assumed responsibility, but she has no similar duty to care for the children of strangers. Furthermore, a parent may favor her own children with expensive gifts even as she fails to give impoverished strangers the money to put a roof over their heads. Even people who donate considerable sums to the poor typically provide their own children with many more material benefits than they give to strangers, and they see no moral inconsistency in doing so.

In contrast, every competent person has a duty to refrain from abusing or otherwise harming any child (or adult, for that matter). Although a parent is permitted to buy her child a new iPad rather than to spend her money on the poor, she may not stab or shoot at either her children or a stranger's children. We applaud the person who performs the supererogatory act of aiding strangers in need, but we would not say that anyone who fails to aid a person in need has thereby wronged that person. Conversely, we most certainly would say that affirmatively harming others—whether or not they are part of our families—is wrong (absent a strong justification).

There is no reason to think that the structure of moral duties differs when the objects of those duties are nonhuman animals. Most "pet owners" would likely say that it is wrong to abandon the family dog on the street, even though it is not wrong to fail to adopt every stray dog in the neighborhood.[51] Adopting stray dogs would represent a noble act, but it would be supererogatory, whereas pet owners believe (and the law provides) that they have affirmative duties to their own pets.

Just as with duties toward humans, the special duties we owe and the extra kindnesses that we extend to those animals we regard as family members are matters of affirmative aid. And as with our conduct toward humans, so with our conduct toward animals; though we may legitimately show favoritism toward our own family members when it comes to providing affirmative benefits, the duty not to harm is universal. Just as you cannot beat up a stranger's child even though you need not care for a stranger's child, so you cannot beat a stranger's dog or a stray dog even though you need not care for the stranger's dog or the stray dog.

So far we have been taking Niman's example literally by asking about special benefits we extend to particular animals whom we keep as family members, but she used the example in a more general way to refer to whole categories of beings. Her suggestion was that societies that treat dogs as family members may have obligations to *all* dogs in virtue of the family membership enjoyed by some, rather than in virtue of any capacity that dogs and pigs both have. Might Niman's argument for killing and eating pigs work better at the categorical level than it does at the individual level?

We think the answer is plainly no. Consider the fact that liberal democracies provide various benefits to citizens and to some other residents but not to persons who fall outside of the relevant political community. What justifies the United States in providing Medicaid and Medicare for (respectively) poor and elderly Americans but not for the poor and elderly citizens of the impoverished nations of Africa? Surely it cannot be a matter of need because the typical African has greater need of assistance in obtaining medical care than the typical American does. Instead it is a kind of family distinction at the categorical level. Notwithstanding our ideas of human equality, we permit ourselves to provide greater aid to our countrymen and countrywomen than to foreigners. Indeed, many people think that a developed country has a moral obligation to meet the basic health care needs of its citizens. Yet notably even countries with generous social welfare states and generous foreign aid programs spend orders of magnitude more on their own citizens than on foreigners.[52]

Meanwhile, the important distinction between aiding and not harming continues to apply when we move from talking about the difference between agent-relative duties and agent-neutral duties we owe to specific beings to talking about agent-relative and agent-neutral duties we owe to classes of beings. Thus, even though most people would find nothing objectionable about the United States spending much more to meet the health needs of its own population than it does to meet the health needs of foreigners, nobody thinks that we are therefore entitled to kill and eat foreigners.[53] At the categorical level no less than at the individual level, duties and charitable choices to provide affirmative assistance may be specific to our group, but duties of nonharm are universal.

Accordingly, Niman's suggestion that the reason we do not eat dogs is that they are family members fails to justify the different and far worse treatment we accord pigs and other animals with relevantly similar capacities. Both at the individual and categorical levels, we may legitimately offer affirmative aid to family members that we deny to strangers, but family membership does not bear on the duty to refrain from causing affirmative harm. Niman's argument no more justifies eating pigs but not dogs than it justifies eating strangers but not family members.

The distinction between family members and others, however, does provide us with an answer to the question with which we ended the last section: Might anything justify our provision of health care and other benefits to some humans but not to animals? The answer is that favoritism—in the sense of treating some but not others, whether human or nonhuman, as members of our categorical family—is a permissible basis for distinguishing between those to whom we provide affirmative benefits and those to whom we do not. There is no contradiction in thinking that all sentient beings are entitled not to be killed and eaten but that we may pick and choose how we wish to distribute various forms of affirmative aid, on bases that include national connections, species, or many other dimensions along which people choose to share their wealth. Nicolette Niman may legitimately choose, in other words, to adopt a dog but not a pig, but it in no way follows that she may therefore choose to kill the pig and spare only the dog's life.

Thus, any puzzles about why we may choose to favor particular categories of animals should not obscure the larger truth. The fact that we understand ourselves as owing special, agent-relative duties of affirmative aid and hold the option of preferentially granting charity to some humans and some select nonhuman animals does not in any way excuse us from our obligations to avoid harming animals absent an adequate justification.

CODA 1: ACTS AND OMISSIONS

In this chapter, we have argued for the sentience criterion—the very modest claim that sentience is a sufficient condition for moral consideration. As our discussion of family obligations makes clear, acceptance of the sentience criterion does not preclude the possibility that we may choose to provide special affirmative aid to some humans and deny it to other beings, including members of other species. To be more precise, however, we should say that *for us* the sentience criterion is compatible with favoritism in dispensing affirmative benefits because we are not utilitarians. The notion of tolerating any favoritism does—or at least should—pose a problem for thoroughgoing utilitarians. Utilitarianism has difficulty justifying the distinction between acts and omissions, and that is the distinction we have drawn between the affirmative aid we may provide on an unequal basis to our chosen favorites and the negative injunction against causing harm to any sentient being.

To be sure, it is possible to construct a version of so-called rule-utilitarianism in which acts that affirmatively cause harm are deemed worse than omissions that result in comparable or greater harm.[54] But for present purposes it suffices to note that the act/omission distinction is central to deontological moral theories in a way that it is not central to (or necessarily even compatible with) utilitarianism. To advert to an overused example, utilitarians are more likely than deontologists to think that it is morally permissible to throw a large man in the path of a runaway trolley so that it kills that one man rather than leaving it on course to kill two or more people.[55] Likewise, utilitarians who have not made their peace with the act/omission distinction but who nonetheless think that sentient animals are worthy of moral concern may have difficulty explaining why it is nonetheless morally permissible to do more for humans and dogs than we do for other animals.

Our goal is not to delineate the precise contours of our disagreement with utilitarians like Peter Singer. Instead, we invoke Singer because the deserved widespread influence of *Animal Liberation* may have led many people to think, mistakenly, that affording animals moral consideration must be grounded in utilitarianism. That mistaken thought might then lead people to worry that favoring some beings for affirmative aid is incompatible with the sentience criterion, and thus to reject the sentience criterion as too demanding. That too would be a mistake, for the sentence criterion is quite modest—although, as we argue in the next chapter, it has important implications for how we should act.

CODA 2: FAMILY OBLIGATIONS AND ABORTION

Our discussion of the act/omission distinction and special duties to family members also has potential implications for how to think about abortion. Begin with acts and omissions. Some of the heated disagreement over the moral permissibility of abortion depends on a characterization question: Does a woman who has an abortion harm a fetus—that is, perform an aggressive act—or does she refuse to incubate that fetus with the collateral consequence that the fetus dies, an omission? As we explain in chapter 3, each characterization is at least partly correct.

Yet one might think that abortion is morally impermissible regardless of whether abortion is best characterized as an act or an omission because a pregnant woman aborts her own baby, to whom she has a special duty of affirmative aid. We think that is indeed true, at least presumptively, with respect to a sentient fetus.

To say that a woman has a presumptive moral duty to carry a sentient fetus to term because she is (or will be) its mother is to say only that she has such a duty unless there are sufficient countervailing considerations that justify abortion. For sentient human fetuses as for other sentient creatures, that is all that the sentience criterion requires: moral consideration.

In the next chapter, we begin to address the sorts of concerns that might be sufficient to justify deliberate harm—or, in the case of creatures to whom special duties of affirmative assistance are owed, sufficient to justify either harm or a failure to provide such affirmative assistance—to sentient beings. We close this chapter with two final caveats.

First, with respect to both animals and abortion, we have been talking about moral duties, not legal duties. One might well conclude that a woman has a moral duty not to abort a sentient fetus but might still think that the law ought not to forbid her from doing so. Perhaps one worries that criminalizing abortion will simply lead to "back-alley" abortions. Or one might worry about sex equality: After all, laws criminalizing abortion convert moral duties of women into legal duties without converting comparable moral duties of men into legal duties. We have been using the term "pro-life" in this chapter somewhat imprecisely—to refer to moral arguments against abortion—but most people who describe themselves as pro-life believe abortion should be illegal. We have not yet considered the further question of whether, even if abortion in general or some particular category of abortions is immoral, it ought to be legal or illegal.

The second caveat takes us back to our central concern: sentience. Might one think that among the special duties that parents have to their children is a duty not to abort even a presentient fetus, embryo, or zygote? Well, yes, one might think that, but we would regard such thinking as confused. As we indicated in discussing Dworkin's view, one can regard even very early abortion as problematic because it is a waste of human life, even though the particular abortion does not harm the interests of any being. That is why we have been at pains to argue that the sentience criterion is a sufficient basis for concluding that some particular conduct has moral implications, but we have left open the possibility that other bases for moral obligations may exist as well. However, the view that a woman has a moral duty *to* her presentient zygote, embryo, or fetus is mistaken because a presentient zygote, embryo, or fetus is not the sort of being to whom moral duties can be owed. It is still *something*, not yet *someone*.

To be sure, a presentient zygote, embryo, or fetus is a *human* something, and for that reason there may be reasons to show respect for it—in the same way that one might think it important to show respect for a dead person's body. But the humanity of a presentient embryo or fetus is not a reason to think that it has interests, or that abortion is a harm *to* the embryo or fetus, regardless of the fact that the person deciding to have the abortion would be the mother of the sentient baby that the embryo or fetus would become if she carried her pregnancy to term. Sentience, not humanity, gives rise to interests.

2

The Necessity Defense

We hope that most if not all of what we said in the last chapter struck readers as obvious. Of course sentient animals and sentient human fetuses are entitled to moral consideration, we imagine readers thinking, but the hard questions involve whether and when other interests—like survival, pleasure in eating, and reproductive autonomy—have sufficient weight to override the interests of sentient animals and fetuses. We agree entirely with this perspective. We did not begin with the question of whether sentient animals and sentient fetuses deserve moral consideration because we think it is difficult. We began with that question because, even though it should be easy, it remains surprisingly controversial.

In this chapter we address questions that seem more challenging: Under what circumstances do people have sufficient reason to exploit or kill sentient animals and to have abortions? The short version of the first half of our answer is that nearly all of the existing uses that humans make of animals, their products, and their body parts are plainly unjustified because humans can thrive without such use of animals; indeed, in most respects, the alternatives to animal products are better for human health and for the environment.

By contrast, we think that most abortions are morally unobjectionable because they occur before fetal sentience. As we explained in the previous chapter, one might regard abortion of even a zygote, an embryo, or a presentient fetus as raising moral questions because it wastes human life or because it violates God's commands or for any of a range of other reasons that do not involve harm to the interests of living beings. We shall not attempt to persuade readers that such reasons are mistaken. But neither will we consider the question of when one might plausibly offer other kinds of moral objections to the abortion of a zygote, embryo, or presentient fetus when it harms no sentient being. We are chiefly interested in the light that we might shed on abortion and animal rights issues by considering them together, and the view that abortion might be wrong when it harms no sentient being has no clear parallel in the domain of animal rights.[1]

We focus in this chapter on the reasons that might justify exploiting and killing animals or aborting a sentient fetus. With respect to both questions, we examine the moral defense of necessity.

ANIMAL PRODUCTS AND HUMAN HEALTH

Most people—whether or not they are vegans—will say that they oppose "unnecessary" cruelty to animals. Like us, they believe that Michael Vick committed a serious harm against the dogs he used in fighting—the dogs he hanged when they lost a fight, or beat to death, or buried alive—and the nonfighting dogs he routinely used as bait for training other dogs to fight.[2] But in discussing human infliction of harm on other animals, most people distinguish Michael Vick's actions from the actions of producers and consumers of animal-derived products, such as flesh, dairy, and eggs. They maintain that although the animals used in agriculture may suffer as much as (or, often, even more than) the animals used by Michael Vick in dog fighting, the enterprise of dog fighting is unnecessary and therefore inflicts unjustified harm while the enterprise of feeding the human population is necessary and therefore inflicts justified harm.

At first blush the distinction between the infliction of suffering for entertainment and for food may appear sound. No one *needs* to watch (or to benefit financially from) a dog fight, but we all need to eat. Choosing to refrain from attending dog fights therefore poses no threat to our well-being, but choosing to refrain from eating clearly would pose such a threat. The flaw in this analogy, however, is that it describes the two activities at two very different levels of generality. It describes dog fighting as either just dog fighting, which is the specific act at issue, or as frivolity or sadism, which are broad normative classifications. One could, however, more narrowly describe dog fighting as a form of cultural expression, as a manifestation of human skill, or as an important opportunity to gather with other people to socialize and connect, all of which sound like far more dignified and laudable sorts of engagements.

Meanwhile, the analogy describes the consumption of animal products as "eating" rather than, for example, as culinary entertainment that involves participating with our dollars and cents in the infliction of tremendous pain and slaughter on innocent sentient beings. To justify animal product consumption and production, or even to argue that it is a morally better enterprise than dog fighting, one must first obscure the particulars of what is involved and describe it more broadly as "eating" or "feeding people." Perhaps as importantly, one must also assume implicitly that there is no feasible alternative way of eating, even as we fully comprehend that there are ways of expressing one's culture, of manifesting one's skill, and of socializing other than operating and attending dog fights.

In reality, in modern times, the consumption of animal-based food is completely unnecessary for the overwhelming majority of the planet's human inhabitants. Contrary to popular myth, we can get all of the proteins, fats, and carbohydrates we need from an exclusively plant-based diet consisting of vegetables, fruits, nuts, beans (legumes), and grains. Even the very conservative Academy of Nutrition and Dietetics (formerly known as the American Dietetic Association) has confirmed that a vegan diet can fulfill the dietary needs of human beings at every stage of life, including infancy and pregnancy, and can even offer important health benefits.[3]

Elaborating on the health benefits offered by a plant-based diet, numerous medical doctors, scientists, and nutritionists have separately—and in the face of much industry resistance—argued

persuasively that a whole-food, plant-based diet protects its consumers from many common cancers such as breast, prostate,
and colon cancers; from cardiovascular disease; from diabetes;
and from obesity.[4] In the spring of 2013 Kaiser Permanente, the
nation's largest integrated managed-care consortium, released
the following statement based on research about healthful diets:
"[P]hysicians looking for cost-effective interventions to improve
health outcomes are becoming more involved in helping their
patients adopt healthier lifestyles. Healthy eating may be best
achieved with a plant-based diet, which we define as a regimen that
encourages whole, plant-based foods and discourages meats, dairy
products, and eggs as well as all refined and processed foods."[5]

At the same time, we have learned from a growing body of evidence that dietary cholesterol and animal protein—the constants
in virtually all animal-based foods—are not only unnecessary for
human health but also measurably detract from health in a variety
of ways, including protein toxicity for kidneys and an increase in
IGF-1, a factor in the initiation and virulence of diabetes and cancer.[6] Countries in which people consume the most animal products,
especially dairy, have higher rates of breast cancer, cardiovascular
disease, and osteoporosis. In short, far from being *necessary* to
human health, the dietary consumption of animal products is affirmatively *harmful* to human health.[7]

ANIMAL PRODUCTS AND THE ENVIRONMENT

The creation of animal products to satisfy humans' appetites for
them also has harmful effects on the environment, thereby undermining the claim that consuming them is beneficial to human flourishing and welfare, let alone necessary to these objectives. While
many people mistakenly believe that they need animal protein or
cow-milk-based calcium, almost no one maintains that our global
environment benefits from animal agriculture.[8] Indeed, the United
Nations has specifically identified animal agriculture in general—
and flesh and dairy consumption in particular—as primary culprits
in the accelerating pace of global climate change and other forms
of environmental degradation, including deforestation and water

pollution.[9] Further, several prominent scientists have authored a paper arguing that more than *half* of the greenhouse gases in our environment are a result of animal agriculture, when one takes into account the need to grow huge amounts of food (and thus to use an enormous amount of land) to feed the tens of billions of animals whose flesh and secretions will then be purchased and sold as food.[10]

To put it succinctly, animal agriculture is an environmental nightmare.[11] In light of the harmful health effects and destructive impact on the natural environment on which human (as well as other) life depends, the suffering we inflict on animals can hardly be deemed "necessary" to human well-being.

ISN'T "BETTERING THE WORLD" OPTIONAL?

Even if you are persuaded that it would be better for you and for the planet if you adopted a vegan diet and lifestyle, you might think that you are not morally obligated to do so. After all, there are many things you might do that would be better for you or the environment; yet none of us is perfect. Most of us could give more of our money to charitable causes, spend more of our time actively helping the less fortunate among us, and otherwise work to make the world a better place.

Despite surface similarities, however, there is an important difference between becoming vegan and donating our time and money to good causes. Veganism is essentially a refusal to participate in paying people to deliberately hurt and slaughter sentient beings; donating to good causes represents affirmative acts of aiding and rescuing others.

As discussed in chapter 1, our law and morality generally recognize an important distinction between negative duties and affirmative ones, between nonharm and rescue, between what we do and what we refrain from doing. We have negative duties toward every being to refrain from inflicting unnecessary harm on him or her, even as we have affirmative duties to relatively few beings (for whom much of what we do can be understood to extend well beyond what our duties truly require). For example, we do nothing extraordinary or charitable in choosing *not* to murder any of the other billions of humans on this planet. Indeed, it would be laughable for a murderer to complain that "everyone is talking about how I killed this one guy, John Doe, while no one has said anything about all of the billions of people whom I did *not* kill!" This is what made it so amusing when 2012 Republican presidential primary candidate Herman Cain responded to allegations of sexual harassment by seeming to ask why no one was talking to all of the women who did *not* accuse him of harassing them.[12]

We rightly receive little or no credit for each murder that we refrain from committing, but we receive a great deal of blame for even one murder that we do carry out.[13] By contrast, if you gave a large amount of money to a poor and uninsured child who needed a bone marrow transplant, you would receive a lot of credit for doing so, and you would not have to justify your failure to donate to everyone else who needed a transplant. Donating aid is largely optional (supererogatory) while refraining from murder is mandatory.

This distinction between nonharm, on the one hand, and rescue, on the other, helps illuminate our discussion of veganism versus other good things that you might decide to do for other people, animals, or the planet. People who work at animal sanctuaries or adopt homeless animals are carrying out acts of kindness, generosity, and rescue toward our nonhuman animal neighbors, acts for which they deserve praise. Many of these same people are also vegan, but their veganism is not an act of aid; it is simply a choice to refrain from inflicting violence on our nonhuman animal neighbors. Though some animal organizations obscure this difference by telling us that vegans "save" a large number of animals each year—by not consuming the flesh or secretions of these animals[14]—it would be more accurate to say that vegans "spare" such animals, much as a man who might feel tempted to assault or kill another man (and has the opportunity to do so) "spares" his human neighbor when he chooses to forgo that opportunity.

The distinction between "saving" and "sparing" a nonhuman (or human) animal is significant because the first represents an act of (typically optional) beneficence while the second manifests fulfillment of a basic obligation to avoid harming *anyone*. When people say "I am not vegan, but I adopted a dog and donated to an animal shelter," they are therefore confessing to a mixture of behaviors that most would regard as very strange in relation to humans—a mixture of harmful action and generous rescue. By consuming animal products, the person in question is participating in hurting and killing farmed animals. At the same time, by adopting a dog and donating to an animal shelter, the very same person is acting in an altruistic fashion toward homeless dogs or cats.[15]

In the realm of humans, an analogous person might regularly beat and ultimately murder his spouse but also spend time volunteering at a homeless shelter and donating money to feed starving children. Of such a person, it would be inaccurate to say "well, he does some bad and he does some good, so he is imperfect." Instead, with the possible exception of some strict act-utilitarians, just about everyone would say that he has behaved outrageously toward his spouse, and that his voluntary acts of kindness toward homeless people and starving children do not compensate for his violence. He is, in other words, not comparable to the person who does no violence to anyone but also fails to donate to charity: we generally do not average violent misconduct with contribution. The first, a violation of the basic duty to avoid hurting the innocent, comes first. Similarly, a person's saving several people's lives in a fire—though a praiseworthy act—will not provide a "freebie" if he then wants to turn around and kill a different person that he hates.

In short, one may choose to donate only a little (or nothing at all), even though one *could* donate more (or something), without being guilty of wrongdoing. It may be unnecessary for you to go dancing or ice-skating on Saturday night, but you may nonetheless do so without feeling like a wrongdoer for not instead volunteering your time at the local homeless shelter. Going vegan is something quite different, however, because it is an act of nonviolence rather than affirmative aid or rescue. To excuse one's own decision to purchase and eat a chicken thus calls for a "necessity" defense in a way that excusing one's decision to dance rather than donate to the needy does not, much in the way that killing a stranger would call for an excuse or justification even when a refusal to help a stranger would not. Turning back to our nonhuman neighbors, we would suggest that this nonharm/rescue distinction helps explain why most people who are polled agree with the proposition that it is wrong to cause animals unnecessary suffering.[16]

IS PLEASURE NECESSARY?

One might agree with our arguments and acknowledge that, yes, a person can be healthy—even healthier—by eating vegan rather than nonvegan foods, and, yes, the consumption of nonvegan foods is not simply a failure to save animals (i.e., a bystander's omission) but an affirmative act of violence against animals that requires a necessity defense. Nonetheless, one might say what many nonvegans have said: pleasure is a necessary part of my life, and eating bland and tasteless meals—however healthy and environmentally sound—would represent a deprivation of necessary pleasure.

We would begin by suggesting that this argument is laughably weak on its own terms. Pleasure is, of course, an important part of life, but one can experience pleasure in many different ways, and a decision to refrain from consuming animal-based products does not amount to a decision to stop experiencing pleasure. By analogy, a person who cannot find anyone with whom to have consensual sexual relations is not thereby entitled to rape someone on the theory that sexual pleasure is a necessary part of life. As a general matter, we do not regard the pursuit of any *particular* sort of pleasure as something that justifies violence as a matter of necessity.

In any event, it also happens that culinary pleasure—indeed, even ecstasy—is easily achieved without the consumption of any animal products. The sorts of pleasure that people crave in eating are as readily available from the plant kingdom as they are from the animal kingdom. As two people who became vegan in 2006, each of us remembers worrying that we would feel deprived once we stopped eating animal products, but we rapidly found out that this worry was unwarranted. When people crave pleasure foods (of the sort that might be described as "addictive"), they are craving salt, fat, and sugar—not animal products as such.[17] One can happily and easily feast on irresistibly delicious food without ingesting any animal flesh or secretions.[18] Thus, even if one were to characterize culinary pleasure as a "necessity," one still could not rely on it to excuse the violence in which we participate when we consume animal-based foods.

ANIMAL EXPERIMENTATION AND MEDICAL USE

When considering the issue of necessity, it is useful to distinguish between the consumption of animal-based foods, which is plainly unnecessary, and the use of animals in scientific experimentation, for which one could mount a more plausible case for necessity. After all, scientific experiments on animals aim to produce medical treatments that save, extend, or improve the quality of human (and nonhuman) lives. Prima facie, these purposes appear to be more compelling than palate pleasure or fashion.

Oddly, although the case for consuming (and producing) animal-based foods is weaker than the case for experimentation, much of the pro-animal protest movement has historically revolved around the latter rather than the former. Mark Twain, for example, consumed animals and animal products but spoke out passionately against animal experimentation.[19] He wrote: "I believe I am not interested to know whether vivisection [i.e., experimentation on live animals] produces results that are profitable to the human race or doesn't. To know that the results are profitable to the race would not remove my hostility to it. The pains which it inflicts upon unconsenting animals is the basis of my enmity towards it, and it is to me sufficient justification of the enmity without looking further."[20] This emphasis, by Twain and other pro-animal activists, on what numerically comprises a relatively small proportion of animal exploitation and which is easier to defend than other uses is puzzling, particularly given that ethically motivated vegetarians and vegans have existed for a very long time and could have provided a model for a more expansive critique of the infliction of suffering on "unconsenting animals."[21]

Having said that animal experimentation may be more defensible than some other sorts of violence against animals, it is nonetheless the case that the overwhelming majority of vivisection is utterly unnecessary and accordingly indefensible.[22] Laboratories subject living animals to confinement and harmful experimentation to confirm the safety (or dangerousness) of ingredients in cosmetics, detergents, and other household items for which known, safe analogues already exist. The most famous of such experiments is the Draize test, in which live rabbits are immobilized with their eyes held open so that scientists can drip chemicals into their eyes and monitor the harmful impact of those chemicals.[23] It would be absurd to suggest that we "need" more brands of oven cleaner, floor detergent, lipstick, and eye shadow, or that subjecting animals to confinement and suffering followed by "sacrifice" (i.e., being killed in the laboratory) is a justifiable moral price to pay for access to new versions of these products.[24]

It is also becoming increasingly clear that high school students, medical students, and even veterinary students can learn everything they need to know about anatomy and physiology without having to subject nonhuman animals to the captivity, harm, and premature death that precede classroom dissection. Indeed, some countries outlaw secondary school dissections, and an increasing number of medical schools and veterinary schools either use computer models to replace dissections across the board or at least protect the right of their students to opt out of dissections for ethical reasons.[25] Unlike animals subjected to vivisection, animals used in dissection are generally dead by the time students slice into their bodies. However, like the animals whose flesh and secretions may be eaten long after the animals have been slaughtered, the industry that captures and breeds the animals for such use subjects them to captivity, pain, and an early death before their lifeless forms make their way into school cooling units.[26]

The one area in which someone could, at least upon initial consideration, make a plausible necessity argument is in the context of subjecting animals to experiments to find cures for human ailments. In the United States, the law currently requires that all medicines be tested on nonhuman animals before they can be approved for human therapeutic use.[27] And many human diseases are "modeled" in animals—that is, introduced into captive animals in a laboratory so that the course of the illness may be studied for what it may teach about the course of the disease (and potential remedies) in humans. Examples include cancer and bacterial research.[28]

Although animals suffer tremendously in medical experimentation, one might say that their use is "necessary" on the grounds that without it, we would not know as much as we do about human disease and how to cure it. This claim is hardly self-evident, however. Nonhuman animals often respond quite differently to cancer, viruses, and bacteria than humans do, and the differences go in both directions.[29] One well-known example involved thalidomide, a drug that was first introduced in Europe in 1957 and was soon marketed worldwide as an effective treatment for the nausea associated with pregnancy.[30] The drug produced no birth defects in the offspring of animals in the laboratory (who were impregnated and then forcibly given the drug), so it was deemed presumptively safe for human use.[31] In pregnant humans, however, thalidomide produced major deformities in offspring, so that babies were subsequently born without arms and legs and with other serious birth defects.[32] At the same time, drugs that cause great harm to various species of animals in the laboratory can prove to be safe and effective in humans.[33]

The problem of drugs and diseases that behave one way in nonhuman animals but a different way in humans highlights a more general weakness of medical research that uses live animals: it draws resources, time, and creativity away from alternative ways of evaluating the utility and safety of medications and from other ways of treating and preventing disease. Consider the fact that we currently spend hundreds of millions of dollars in the United States alone to do research on animals to find treatments and cures for breast cancer.[34] Meanwhile, with all this research in progress, the American Cancer Society estimates that nearly three hundred thousand American women will be newly diagnosed with breast cancer in 2014 alone.[35]

In other countries—as diverse as Papua New Guinea, Japan, and China—the breast cancer incidence rate is between five and fifty times lower than that within the United States.[36] Although Japan is an advanced country, and parts of China are as well, Papua New Guinea is not. Thus, the lower incidence of breast cancer cannot be due to better medicines in these other countries, developed through more intensive regimes of animal testing. What, then, counts for the differences? In part, we have strong reason to think that women in mostly poorer countries have benefited from their relatively lower intake of animal-based foods. Such women are, as a result, at much lower risk of developing and dying of breast cancer. They therefore also avoid having to undergo the surgeries and chemotherapy that have been repeatedly tested on animals.[37]

The irony is that if animal experimentation with some of these drugs is even arguably "necessary" to treat the large proportion of sick people in the population, it is due in part to the *unnecessary* consumption of animal-based foods by these very same people. And yet anyone who visits a hospital can attest to the fact that the food there is as far from a whole-foods, plant-based diet as one can find outside of fast-food restaurants (which some hospitals actually have in their lobbies).[38] We have been appalled to find out what friends and family are typically given to eat as patients in a hospital, as when postoperative heart patients are routinely fed heart-disease-inducing egg-based French toast and chickens' flesh.[39]

The exploitation of animals in medicine, then, even when arguably "necessary" to save human lives, may be comparable to an armed robber's "need" to use a gun against a police officer. Such necessity for using violence is a product of prior *unnecessary* violence—in the form of exploitation of animals for food choices. In the law, this sort of necessity is at best classified as "imperfect self-defense," which does not justify the violent actions, although it may be thought mitigating for sentencing or other purposes.[40]

In spite of all of this, we would not deny that sometimes an experiment on an animal might produce a breakthrough in the treatment of an otherwise untreatable human disease. For those limited cases, would we concede that animal experimentation is necessary and therefore justifiable? In our view, the answer here is still no, although the "no" is not as patently obvious as it is in the case of animal-based foods, articles of clothing, or redundant testing for household products. Let us therefore assume, for argument's sake, that some small proportion of animal research leads to the discovery of successful disease treatments that would not be discovered absent the animal experiments. What then?

In such cases, we think that the harm we inflict on animals is *easier* to defend than is the most common form of violence against animals, which people rarely question—their consumption as food and clothing. One can say that when we hurt and kill nonhuman animals so that we can save humans, that behavior—to paraphrase legal scholar and animal rights philosopher Gary Francione—is the one reason to hurt animals that is not patently frivolous.[41] Nonetheless, we would suggest that even when an animal experiment might result in information that could save human lives, the experiment is still not justified.

Why not? To use the lives of other sentient beings to help save our own is to do more than simply treat their lives as unequal to ours. It is to treat their lives as instruments. To understand the difference, consider the clichéd "burning building" scenario. A building is burning, and you can save one but not both of the following two people: a brilliant school teacher who educates hundreds of children every year and helps many of them achieve their dreams or an independently wealthy recluse who sits in his house watching television all day long and has no friends or family. Although you could choose to save either one of these two people without being fairly accused of wrongdoing, it would be understandable for you to think the first person is more worthy of being saved than the second and to select her for rescuing on that basis. In such a triage situation, you might find yourself drawn to the proposition that not all people are equal—some are more deserving than others, and you are inclined toward saving the more deserving if there is a choice that must be made.

Changing the scenario, however, yields a very different result. Now the brilliant school teacher is dying of a rapidly failing heart, and the person in the next bed at the hospital is the independently wealthy television-watching recluse. The recluse, it turns out, has a heart that is a perfect match for the school teacher. As in the triage case, we might believe that the school teacher is more worthy than is the recluse, but it would be monstrous (not to mention illegal) to remove the recluse's heart and use it to save the life of the teacher. Preferring one life over another, even when it really is life itself at stake in both cases, may be unobjectionable when we are engaging in rescue, but it does not entitle us to instrumentalize the life of the less worthy to serve the life of the worthier. Infecting nonhuman animals with disease and subjecting them to "treatments" to try to save human lives does precisely that: it instrumentalizes animals' lives and says that their lives may be taken from them to offer us hope for saving ourselves.

To be sure, the fact that an experiment on animals would save humans does, in our view, mitigate the culpability of the scientist who performs the experiment. The behavior of the scientist is less reprehensible than the behavior of paying for the infliction of suffering and slaughter on animals for food or clothing. The latter behavior serves only to satisfy culinary and fashion tastes that are easily satisfied by other means, even as the chosen means also threaten our own health and the global environment. But the possibility of saving human lives does not fully redeem animal experimentation, even on the assumption that such experimentation does in fact save human lives. And in reality, this assumption is not entirely warranted.

Are there any circumstances in which we would find the use of animal products necessary? In a limited sense, yes. We believe that individuals may sometimes face choices—due at least in part to the poor choices about animal use that we have made in other areas of our lives—that make the decision to consume an animal product excusable, if not justifiable, a difference between "understandable but wrong" and "truly justified" behavior. We have in mind vaccinations and medications that are the products of animal testing and that contain animal ingredients. For an individual who is sick, it is often no longer feasible to pursue a non-animal-based alternative. Medications in the United States have, under the law, *all* been tested on nonhuman animals, despite the fact that such testing appears not only unnecessary but potentially quite misleading.[42] Furthermore, pharmaceutical companies routinely use animal-based binders in medications, so it is quite difficult, if not impossible, to obtain vegan forms of a medication needed to treat illness, even though a vegan version would almost certainly be just as effective.[43] Similarly, a sick person who needs a heart valve transplant might have to choose between dying and receiving a valve from a slaughtered pig or cow, although nonanimal alternatives show promise.[44]

These examples—especially the last one—resemble the common hypothetical example that nonvegans present to vegans: what would you do if you were on a desert island and you had to choose between starvation and eating an animal? Our view is that in these situations, people do face a form of necessity—that is, without using the animal, one will either become extremely sick or die. This is far removed from the case of the person who enjoys eating fishes and thus does so on the theory that "you have to eat!"

Yet even "necessary" violence might be morally unjustified. We would not want to say that violence is justified whenever it is necessary to avoid dying. Even if you needed a heart transplant, you could not lawfully kill your neighbor to get his heart. It is accordingly your duty to refrain from inflicting violence against an innocent other who does not threaten your life, even if such violence *would* succeed in saving your life and no other alternative would. For the same reason, if you have a healthy heart and lungs, it would be unjustifiable violence for two people with an ailing heart and lungs, respectively, to set upon you for your organs, despite the fact that the violence against you, one person, would be saving the lives of two people.[45]

We accordingly reject the notion that necessity justifies violence against animals, even in the extreme case of the desert island or the need for organs or medication. Nonetheless, we believe that people will, understandably and excusably, do what they have to do to survive. For this reason we think that the Queen's Bench was wrong in the famous nineteenth-century case of *Dudley & Stephens*, where the judge sentenced the defendants to death for killing and eating one of their fellow lifeboat passengers— Richard Parker—when they all faced starvation.[46] Although killing and eating Parker was not justifiable in the sense of being the *right* thing to do, it was understandable and thus excusable. For similar reasons, we consider it excusable for people who need medications to take those medications, notwithstanding the fact that such consumption contributes to violence against animals. Unlike the other cases—eating animals and their secretions outside of desert islands and lifeboats, wearing animals' skin and hair, and even experimenting upon animals—a sick person faces an imminent harm and lacks the plentiful nonviolent options available in the other circumstances. However, as more of us become vegan and take advantage of the many alternatives to consuming the products of animal suffering and slaughter, people will be motivated to find nonviolent alternatives both to animal testing and to the current use of animal ingredients as binders in medications.

ABORTION'S NECESSITY: LIFE OF THE MOTHER

In the case of abortion, we can achieve a great deal of clarity, we think, by beginning with what most people would regard as a scenario presenting the strongest case for justification: the scenario in which continuing a pregnancy will likely end the life of the woman who carries it. In this situation, even prior to the Supreme Court's decision in *Roe v. Wade*, the laws of this country permitted abortion.[47] And currently, although *Roe* and the cases that have followed permit states (and Congress) to ban most abortions after fetal viability, the precedents still provide that a woman has a constitutionally protected right to an abortion, even postviability, if abortion is needed to save the woman's life.[48]

It may therefore seem uncontroversial to suggest that at least in the case of a pregnancy that threatens a pregnant woman's life, abortion is justifiable out of necessity. Yet even in this least controversial type of abortion, it is possible to argue against the justifiability of abortion as such.

Consider official Catholic doctrine, which holds that abortion, even for the purpose of saving the woman's life, is prohibited.[49] Yet under the so-called doctrine of double effect, the same religious authority does allow a pregnant woman to undergo a treatment aimed at remedying a life-threatening illness, even if the treatment will have the incidental effect of killing the fetus she carries.[50] Catholic doctrine therefore profoundly values the pregnant woman's life and generally allows her to do what she must to save herself. What accounts for the apparent distinction it draws between abortion and other lifesaving treatment that would kill the fetus?

Broadly understood, the core distinction inheres not only in Catholic religious doctrine but in customary international law as well:[51] there is a difference between *intentionally* causing a harmful outcome (such as a death), on one hand, and intentionally pursuing a different objective that has the *incidental* side effect of bringing about a harmful outcome, on the other. The doctrine of double effect operates on the battlefield no less than in the womb. Thus, it is an impermissible war crime to deliberately target and kill civilians, but it is permissible to target and deliberately kill enemy soldiers (or to bomb an enemy's munitions plant) even though the shooter (or bomber) knows that civilians are present and will foreseeably be killed by the shooting (or bombing).[52] Collateral civilian casualties may be morally (and legally) tolerable if they are proportionate relative to an intended legitimate military objective, whereas intended civilian casualties are intolerable, full stop.

This distinction plays a role in Catholic doctrine in the context of debates over physician-assisted suicide as well as abortion. It is impermissible to deliberately kill a patient who is suffering and wishes to die. On the other hand, it may be permissible to give the patient an amount of pain medication needed to relieve the patient's pain, even if the quantity of medication necessary for this purpose will foreseeably end the patient's life as well. One may, in other words, bring about a patient's death, if one does so only as a side effect of pursuing a distinct and legitimate objective, such as the provision of palliative care. (Of course, if one could provide nonlethal but effective palliative care, then the provision of the lethal version would be impermissible.) Necessity itself may be a necessary but insufficient condition for justifying actions that end lives.

With respect to abortion to save the life of the mother, from the Catholic perspective, one can attempt to save the mother's life in a manner that endangers and that may even predictably kill the fetus. This can happen, for example, in administering chemotherapy to a cancer patient that will prove lethal not only to cancer cells but to the developing fetus as well.[53] In such a case, the fetus is like the civilian standing near the enemy's munitions plant—a collateral casualty of an otherwise legitimate mission. On the other hand, Catholic doctrine forbids a doctor from saving the woman's life by attacking the fetus directly through an abortion. By analogy, it would be impermissible to deliberately target civilians during a war, even though the ultimate goal is to win a just war (for example, by demoralizing a virulent enemy), just as the goal in bombing a munitions plant would be to win the same just war. It is legitimate to try to save the woman's life and to win a just war, but—if one takes this approach—there are some actions that may never be taken even in the pursuit of legitimate ends, and such actions include the deliberate killing of civilians and of fetuses.

To help illuminate what may seem to most readers a rather extreme position on the question of abortion, consider two ways of thinking about abortion. One could envision abortion as an act of affirmative violence against a living being because abortion does in fact actively kill a fetus. Or one could envision abortion as a failure to help a fetus because one (also accurately) views pregnancy as an active and very taxing intimate intervention to save the fetus that would die without the intervention. As we elaborate at greater length in chapter 3, either vision is incomplete because abortion is simultaneously both an act of affirmative violence *and* a failure to provide active, intimate, and demanding lifesaving intervention.

If one focuses on the "active violence" element of abortion, then even in the case of an abortion to save the mother's life, it appears that the woman is inflicting death on an innocent as a means of saving herself. To understand this perspective, consider a hypothetical scenario. Two people, John and Joan, are both dying of thirst. There is one and only one cup of water within reach of the two of them, and the cup contains only enough water to save one of their lives, not both. As John reaches for the water, Joan shoots him to stop him from taking the cup, and she then grabs the cup and drinks the water herself. In this situation, Joan acts as she does to save her own life. Had she permitted John to reach the water, she would have died of thirst. Nonetheless, conventional morality would say that her act was, at most, excused rather than justified. She is not *entitled* to kill John just because he is trying to do the same thing that she is trying to do—gain access to lifesaving water.

Note too, in this hypothetical example, that what John is attempting to do—get himself a drink of water—will have the same ultimate consequence (death of the other person) as what Joan is doing—killing John to prevent him from saving himself and thereby depriving her of access to water. Yet John's action would have had the *collateral* effect of harming Joan while Joan's action was specifically *aimed* at killing John (albeit as a *means* of saving herself). While taking the water seems legitimate, permissible, and justifiable, deliberately killing the other person to keep him from getting it does not. Likewise, if two people were in a lifeboat equipped for only one person, throwing one's mate overboard would not be justified (and under the law is impermissible).[54] Sometimes, in other words (as in the case of using animal parts to save a human life), it may be "necessary" to kill someone in order to save oneself while at the same time wrong to do so (although potentially excusable). What distinguishes the justifiable from the unjustifiable cases is subtle, but it is an established component not only of Catholic doctrine but of secular legal doctrine as well.

So how do pregnancy and abortion map onto the division between impermissible direct harm and permissible collateral harm? As noted earlier, the answer very much depends on whether one regards pregnancy as action (and abortion as a failure to rescue) or whether one regards pregnancy as inaction (and abortion as affirmative violence). If pregnancy is, as many pro-choice people envision it, an ongoing act of intimate assistance to a fetus in need of life support, then the pregnant woman (the donor) is absolutely entitled to terminate her donation by having an abortion as soon as providing such life support to the fetus threatens her own life.

From the pro-life perspective, however, the correct response to the life-of-the-mother scenario is far less clear. If you are pro-life, you may regard the woman and her fetus as occupying a space in which they coexist, each legitimately drawing sustenance from her and his respective environments.[55] Just as the woman draws oxygen from the air when others in the world may also need that oxygen, so then does the fetus draw oxygen, nutrients, and everything he needs from the bloodstream of the woman, even when the woman may truly need what the fetus absorbs. They are like co-occupants of a lifeboat, and neither one has a greater right to be where she is or to get what he needs than the other does. The woman was there first, but so what? Older people do not categorically lay claim to a superior right to sustenance over everyone younger than they.

Accordingly, one's conception of pregnancy as active or as passive has potentially decisive implications for what ought to happen when a woman faces the choice between remaining pregnant and dying, on one hand, and having an abortion and surviving, on the other. Nonetheless, most people in the pro-life movement in this country and elsewhere readily accept the life-of-the-mother exception to their proposed ban on abortion.[56] Perhaps this acceptance betrays an understanding of pregnancy, at least in some contexts, as extracting difficult, painful, intimate, and in some cases potentially fatal aid from a woman rather than as simply and passively "letting nature take its course."[57] If the woman and her fetus were equally entitled co-occupants of a lifeboat, then preserving or saving the life of the mother would not justify the woman in throwing her fetus overboard. Notwithstanding this difference between people within the pro-life movement who, respectively, support and oppose the life-of-the-mother exception, however, it is likely that many on both sides of this question would be prepared to *excuse* an abortion carried out to save the life of the pregnant woman.[58]

ABORTION FOR OTHER REASONS

Once we set aside the very narrow life-of-the-mother circumstance, the line between pro-life and pro-choice positions becomes clearer. People who describe themselves as categorically pro-life reject a rape-or-incest exception to proposed abortion bans, even though a majority of Americans do believe that such an exception is warranted.[59] The argument against these exceptions is straightforward: It is a grave wrong for a man to rape a woman. The man should be apprehended and brought to justice for his outrageous crime. However, the fetus that results from the attack is an innocent child who in no way participated in the sexual assault that brought him or her into being. Just as a woman who is raped may not kill a two-year-old child originally conceived in that rape, so too a woman who is raped may not kill an unborn fetus conceived in that rape.[60]

The argument for a rape-or-incest exception is weaker than the argument for a life-of-the-mother exception because the goal of a lifesaving abortion is (obviously enough) to save a life, whereas the goal of an abortion undergone pursuant to a rape-or-incest exception is to destroy the fetus because the fetus's very existence embodies the violation of the pregnant woman.[61] As in many elective abortions, then, the objective is to bring about the death of the fetus because the pregnant woman does not want him or her in the world, not necessarily because of the physical imposition involved in pregnancy per se. When the woman will die without an abortion, by contrast, it truly *is* the physical imposition of pregnancy that motivates its termination. (We have more to say about the relevance of actual motives in chapter 3.)

Why, then, do many people who generally object to abortion nonetheless draw a line at rape or incest? After all, no one defends the right of the rape victim to kill a resulting child who has already been born, no matter how disturbing or psychologically traumatic the child's existence might be to the rape survivor. Procuring the death of people whose existence is traumatizing to us is simply not a defensible option. Yet many people who think abortion is generally proscribable would accept a rape-or-incest exception to a ban on abortion.[62]

One possibility is that people who favor this exception regard a fetus, at whatever stage of development, as something less than a full person and thus as less entitled to his or her own life than a comparable two-year-old (or newborn) child born of rape. And given that lesser entitlement, perhaps the fact that the existence of the fetus (and the later existence of the child version of the fetus) would traumatize the woman is enough to warrant the fetus's destruction, even if a similar origin would not justify the destruction of a child. If this hypothesis is correct, then perhaps the better question is why people who hold this view do not favor a right to abortion more generally, if the fetus lacks an entitlement to life. The best that might be said in response is that the life of the unborn counts as more than nothing but less than that of a fully entitled person; in this view, destroying a fetus would be justified if its continued existence would inflict sufficient harm, but not otherwise.

If that is the explanation, however, then it is not clear why the fetus must be a product of rape or incest to justify abortion. Shouldn't the psychological harm associated with the fetus's continued existence and birth, whatever the source of the harm, be equally sufficient to justify its destruction? After all, a woman may find the birth of a particular child highly traumatic for a variety of reasons other than the fact that the child was conceived in rape: perhaps the father of the pregnancy *subsequently* raped the woman, and she does not want to give birth to the child of her rapist, even though the sexual act that produced the child was itself consensual; perhaps the woman hates the father of the pregnancy for reasons having nothing to do with rape—maybe he physically or emotionally but not sexually abused her, or maybe he recently murdered one of her family members.

Yet people who favor a rape-or-incest exception frequently refuse to allow a broader exception for psychological trauma. This fact suggests that something about causing a pregnancy through rape or incest may convert the pregnancy into involuntary servitude for the woman carrying the pregnancy.[63] And if an unwanted pregnancy is *ever* to be considered a species of involuntary servitude, then this consideration suggests that *every* pregnancy shares at least some features with such servitude; a pregnant woman and the fetus growing inside her are *not* two independent people who both legitimately exist side by side, with one of them wanting the other dead. Regardless of how one values the moral worth of the fetus, then, the decision to allow fetal destruction when the fetus came into existence through rape has implications for the fundamental meaning of pregnancy—and most clearly of any *unwanted* pregnancy—as an inherently parasitic experience in which one being takes a tremendous amount, in an intimate way, from the other.

This understanding of pregnancy as something different from simple coexistence underlies both the very widespread view that abortion should be available for pregnancies that result from rape or incest and the somewhat less widespread view that abortion should be generally available. Both the limited and the broad view of abortion rights ultimately see abortion as a matter of bodily integrity.[64] If the woman is in the position of giving assistance, of affirmatively sacrificing to provide life support to the fetus growing within her, then it follows that this gift from the woman to her fetus should not be forcibly extracted from her by a third party— whether a rapist or the state—however much we believe that the fetus is a fully entitled sentient being whose existence depends on the woman's profound gift. Viewing pregnancy in this way conceives of a prohibition against abortion as tantamount to coercing a woman to endure the burdens of pregnancy without her consent.

To say that neither a rapist nor the law should be able to force a woman to gestate a fetus is only to say that a woman who has become pregnant through rape or through voluntary sexual intercourse should be able to decide for herself whether to carry her pregnancy to term. It is not to say which decision she *should* make.

Nonetheless, some of the same sorts of considerations that might lead someone to favor a rape-or-incest exception to abortion laws, or to favor the broad legal availability of abortion, could factor into an individual woman's decision about whether she herself should have an abortion. A woman who views her fetus as situated relative to herself like another passenger in a lifeboat might conclude that abortion of an unwanted pregnancy cannot be morally justified. Similarly, a woman who believes that she has strong Good Samaritan duties to render affirmative aid might conclude that even though pregnancy is an asymmetric relationship, she has such a duty to permit the fetus to use her body for his own benefit. And, of course, a woman might conclude that she wants to bring her baby to term for other reasons—a religious conviction that abortion is wrong or a desire to become a parent, for example.

Critically, however, each of the foregoing sorts of reasons for choosing to take a pregnancy to term is consistent with the necessity of abortion's availability to women's bodily integrity. Prior to fetal viability, abortion is always necessary to vindicating a woman's interest in ridding herself of an unwanted pregnancy. When an individual woman concludes that, despite the infringement, she nonetheless will carry her baby to term, she does so because she places less value on her own bodily integrity than she places on something else—her view of pregnancy as nonparasitic, her view of Good Samaritan duties, her religious faith, and so on.

ABORTION FOR DISABILITIES

In addition to exceptions for life-of-the-mother and for rape-or-incest situations, many people take the view that abortion may be justified if the pregnant woman discovers that her fetus would ultimately be born with a severe disability. This exception typically falls into one of three categories. The first involves a disability so profound that the fetus is not truly a being with interests—for example, a fetus that lacks a brain. The second involves a fetus that has disabilities so severe that the baby would live an extremely short and excruciatingly painful life, so that the point of the abortion is to spare that baby the suffering of being born in the first place, a type of involuntary euthanasia. The third, most problematic, category involves a disability that would make life more challenging for the child and for the parent but that might nonetheless offer the child, from his perspective, a life worth living.

This third category of disability-based abortion raises the most serious moral questions of the three because the goal of this kind of abortion is to kill a potentially sentient being (unlike the first category), and to do so in the interests of the would-be parents (but not the fetus himself or herself), parents who believe that they would not be able to love and care adequately for such a child (unlike the second category). In other words, although the fetus might prefer to live if he had a choice, the parents take away that choice because they prefer a world in which he does not exist.

As we elaborate at greater length in the next chapter, most abortions share this feature; they reflect the wishes of the mother or of both parents to end the life of the fetus (rather than simply to end the pregnancy itself). What makes the disability abortion more troubling, we believe, is that the parents are singling out (or targeting) a particular sort of fetus for destruction—one who does not measure up to their standard of a child they would like to have as their own. It is not that they lack the financial resources to care for any child; it is not that they feel emotionally unready for any baby. It is that *this* baby is unwelcome by virtue of his disability.

If a born child (or adult) were killed on account of her disability, this killing would qualify as a hate crime (or eugenic murder), one in which a particular, vulnerable being is singled out for violence and destruction precisely because of her vulnerability. When that destruction occurs during a pregnancy, by contrast, many people view it not only as permissible or tolerable but as reasonable and appropriate. We still recall that during the pregnancy that resulted in our younger daughter's birth, the obstetricians we saw initially were adamant in pressuring us to undergo an amniocentesis, despite the risks of miscarriage that the procedure poses. Their assumption was that, of course, any reasonable person pregnant with a fetus with Down syndrome would want an abortion and would want it so badly that she would risk miscarriage to detect the chromosomal anomaly.[65] Recall that even Sarah Palin, the pro-life, Republican vice presidential candidate in 2008, underwent an amniocentesis and fleetingly considered a disability-based abortion.[66]

Given societal (and medical) attitudes toward abortion of fetuses with Down syndrome, it is easy to understand why groups of people who suffer from such disabilities might feel devalued. After all, many of the people around them believe that killing them would have been justified *prior* to their birth because of their disability. By saying this, we do not mean to minimize the challenges of raising a child with severe disabilities, even if the child is glad to be alive.[67] We mean only to highlight the important moral implications of having a societal judgment that rejects many abortions—due to their violence against innocent life—but exempts from that judgment the cases in which the violence is directed against certain people who fail to measure up to a standard of normality.

One of the many problems associated with abortion prohibitions is that any exemptions for particular sorts of fetuses have significant implications for how our society values differently abled people. Coupled with our view of pregnancy as an affirmative burden on women, this effect of disability exemptions is one reason to reject legal prohibitions against abortion.

In the realm of morality, separate from law, we might (and do) of course make judgments about the rightness or wrongness of particular decisions to grant or withhold aid. You might think that it is selfish of your neighbor to refrain from donating blood out of a squeamishness about needles, even as you simultaneously support the choice of your cousin to refrain from donating blood because her veins are so difficult to find that the technician always has to insert the needle five or six times before succeeding, making the process extremely painful for your cousin. In neither case, however, are you prepared to suggest that anyone should be able to force either of them to donate blood against her will, notwithstanding the lifesaving benefits that would result (and the loss of life that would foreseeably follow a refusal to donate). The decision must remain (and in fact is) that of the donor. And donating blood is a relatively trivial intrusion on a person's bodily integrity by comparison to the hardships involved in enduring a pregnancy followed by labor or surgery.

Similarly, even people who are strongly pro-choice find some reasons for terminating a pregnancy to be disturbing. For example, few Americans are comfortable with a woman's decision to terminate a pregnancy because she has found out that she is having a girl and she believes that girls are worthless. Nonetheless, even the worst possible reason for terminating a pregnancy does not necessarily translate into the proper authority to force a woman to carry an unwanted pregnancy to term.

Answering the question of when an abortion might be deemed "necessary" does not, in any event, require us to sort among good and bad reasons for abortion. When we ask whether an act of violence is justified out of necessity, we ordinarily have in mind the following question: Is it just for A to commit violence against B, given the circumstances that are motivating the violence? The question presumes that there might be some situations in which the motivating circumstances *would* justify the violence while there would be other situations in which they would not.

Killing your neighbor in self-defense is an instructive example. If your neighbor is threatening to rape, kill, or otherwise grievously harm you, and you must kill him to prevent his violence against you, then you are legally and, most people would say, morally justified in doing so. Similarly, in the context of violence against nonhuman animals, if a shark is heading toward you, about to bite off part of your body, then you are justified in killing the shark in self-defense. If, on the other hand, you simply dislike seeing your neighbor each day or you enjoy consuming shark-fin soup, these motivations fail to provide any plausible moral justification for killing your neighbor or the shark (though the legal system distinguishes between the two based on species).

When it comes to pregnancy, however, a woman's reasons— however strong or weak—for wanting to terminate her pregnancy may be less important than the fact that she does not want to continue to provide life support through the onerous process of enduring a pregnancy and labor. Much like a woman who has an offensive reason for refusing to have sex with an unwanted partner (discussed at greater length in the next chapter), a pregnant woman's desire to restore her own bodily integrity is itself enough, on this view of abortion, to justify it. And if the only way for her to terminate her unwanted pregnancy or to stop unwanted intercourse is to kill the fetus or the assailant, respectively, then she ought to be able to do so. It is, in this view, *necessary* for a woman who wants an abortion to be able to have one in order to maintain her bodily integrity.

On the very different view that abortion is an affirmative act of violence, no different from killing a third party who is not doing anything to her, the pregnant woman would never have the right to an abortion because we may not kill a third party who does nothing *to us*, even if killing him or her would facilitate the saving of our own lives. Recall our hypothetical scenario of two people dying of thirst: Joan may drink the water if she can reach it (thereby bringing about John's certain death from thirst), but she may not deliberately kill John to ensure that she reaches the cup before he does.

For the opponent of *all* abortion, then, even a pregnant woman who will die without an abortion is like Joan, and she gets no life-of-the-mother exception to the prohibition against killing an innocent person. For supporters of a general right to abortion, the pregnant woman with a trivial reason for wanting her fetus dead must still have the right to terminate her pregnancy, a termination that—in most cases—cannot be accomplished without killing the fetus in the process.

This brings us, finally, to the case where we might consider the possibility of legally prohibiting a pregnant woman from killing a sentient fetus: the case in which the fetus could be removed from the woman's body without being killed (and without simultaneously causing bodily harm to the woman). Our view is that a woman should have the right to remove the fetus from inside her body, to restore her bodily integrity, but that, after the fetus becomes sentient, she should not have the independent right to procure the fetus's death.

In most cases, removing the fetus from the woman's body will necessarily involve the fetus's death. Despite the fact that fetuses are theoretically viable a few weeks after the halfway point of gestation, the pregnancy needs to progress substantially longer before the fetus has a realistic chance of surviving into childhood without heroic medical intervention (and oftentimes the chance of survival is very low even with such intervention).[68] Therefore, the notion that women might induce labor at twenty-four weeks and then walk away, leaving state-funded medical personnel to take care of the resulting baby, is not a realistic policy program. Effectively, prior to the very late stages of a pregnancy, inducing labor is, in most cases, tantamount to killing the child.

Accordingly, if one conceptualizes pregnancy as we do—as a form of intimate, demanding rescue provided by the woman to her fetus—then one necessarily accepts that a right to stop being pregnant will also involve the death of the fetus, whether the fetus is killed directly during the process or whether the fetus dies because his survival odds are substantially diminished by being outside the womb. Given this fact, we think that selecting one abortion method, induction, rather than another, such as dilation and evacuation, depending on which will yield a live birth, would be arbitrary. Instead, the choice of abortion method should primarily reflect the medical needs of the woman, the only one who can realistically be expected to survive the expulsion of the fetus from her body.

If, on the other hand, fetal life outside the womb becomes a reality—for example, with the creation and low-cost production of artificial wombs—our position on abortion would reflect this change. We do not, in other words, believe that women (or men) have the right to terminate the life of a sentient fetus who can otherwise survive when no one's bodily integrity is compromised by the fetus's continued existence. And we would take this position even in the case in which an abortion could save the life of the mother (by providing an organ for donation, for example). To state it differently, we believe there is a right to abortion so long as abortion (in the sense of killing the fetus) is necessary to terminating an unwanted pregnancy, which we regard as a severe and intimate imposition on a woman to provide internal life support to a fetus. As soon as killing the fetus becomes unnecessary to terminating a pregnancy safely, however—as it would be with the advent of an artificial womb—and killing is no longer an unavoidable feature of terminating a woman's unwanted pregnancy, a sentient fetus should have the same right to live free of human violence as any other sentient being on this Earth.[69]

CODA: ANIMAL EXPERIMENTATION AND FETAL STEM CELL RESEARCH

Embryonic stem cell research provides an opportunity for thinking about the issues of animal exploitation and abortion in an integrated way. Such research typically involves using some of the cells taken from extra human embryos produced in the course of in vitro fertilization treatments.[70] Because many people in the pro-life movement consider such an embryo a full person, they regard embryonic stem cell research as a morally impermissible form of human experimentation.[71]

In contrast to the orthodox pro-life view of stem cell research, many other people find it a very appealing avenue for scientific research. The reason is probably some combination of the fact that (a) most people (like us) consider an early embryo, lacking any capacity to experience the world around it, as also lacking interests and thus lacking rights; (b) stem cell research may offer great promise in treating and someday curing diseases such as Parkinson's and Alzheimer's disease;[72] and (c) the embryos may be discarded by the biological parents, so killing them (even without using them for research) is already a legal option. In these circumstances, bans on embryonic stem cell research may seem affirmatively perverse. As a result of some mix of these rationales, quite a few otherwise pro-life politicians have supported stem cell research, and in 2001, pro-life President George W. Bush issued a compromise approach that would allow research on cell lines that preexisted the date of his announcement.[73]

If one were to assume, however, that an embryo is a person entitled to protection against violence, then stem cell research might present a much more egregious act of violence than abortion.

After all, in having an abortion, a woman is not attempting to *use* the fetus as a means to some further end. She is instead refusing to use her body to provide the fetus with life support (or, in the pro-life view, she is killing the fetus unjustifiably but not as a means of exploiting it as a resource). Whereas pro-life activists in the United States generally seek no penalty against women who terminate their own pregnancies, they do seek penalties against the doctors, whom they view as deriving a financial benefit from killing the fetus.[74] In the case of an embryo in a petri dish used as a source of stem cells for research, there is no one who can claim to be simply terminating her body's use as a means of life support. It is all about using the embryo's cells, and there is therefore no one comparable to the pregnant woman who would be entitled to an "excuse" for her conduct.

If embryos were sentient, then we would agree with the pro-life position on their use in experimentation. We would say that they are entitled to be free of human violence and that that freedom would most certainly include a right not to be killed for the purpose of experimentation. We reject this position only because embryos are not in fact sentient.

When it comes to nonhuman animals used for the many purposes for which billions of animals are used in this country alone—as a food source, as a clothing source, for experimentation—just about all of the violence is exploitative violence. Apart from the rare shark attack or confrontation with a rabid animal, we kill nonhuman sentient beings because we want to use them. In fact, we bring most of the animals we use and kill into existence in the first place precisely because we want to use and kill them. The proper analogy in the context of unborn humans would therefore be the sentient fetus originally conceived specifically to provide organs or an experimental model. Even the embryos used for research, by contrast, were most often conceived for the purpose of bringing those very embryos to life inside a woman experiencing fertility challenges.

Despite their similarities, then, it is here—when we talk about the use of nonhuman animals in lifesaving experiments—that we can truly appreciate how different abortion is from animal exploitation. Abortion is not fetal exploitation, and we suspect that few people would regard a sentient human fetus as a legitimate resource for us to use (whether as a food or clothing source or for organ mining or experimentation). The consumption of animal products is always exploitation, and the question is only whether the purpose for which the exploitation is initiated is utterly trivial (and even counterproductive), as in the case of eating animal products, or whether the purpose is of a more serious sort, as in the case of attempting to save human lives. No matter what, though, no one with a conscience would ever regard any of these forms of exploitation of *persons* as justifiable, which is why people are understandably and especially horrified when they learn about human experimentation, such as the Nazi experiments performed by Dr. Josef Mengele, the Tuskegee syphilis experiments, or the use of African American slaves in gynecological torture by the father of modern gynecology.[75] We would suggest that in the context of exploitation, the category of "persons" ought to include not only born human beings but also unborn sentient humans and sentient nonhuman animals. Use of a sentient being for a "good reason" may be less horrifying than such instrumentalization undertaken for a transparently trivial reason, like palate pleasure or fashion, but it should be horrifying nonetheless.

3

Reproductive Servitude

In chapters 1 and 2 we argued that a pregnant woman needs a good justification for having an abortion once the fetus within her is sentient. We also acknowledged that some people may consider the abortion of even a presentient fetus to be wrong either on religious grounds or on the ground that it wastes potential life. In that prior discussion, we mostly took the perspective of a pregnant woman and inquired into the morality of *her* decision. In each circumstance, we chiefly wanted to know whether abortion would be a morally appropriate choice *for her* to make.

Here we shift perspective and ask when it would be morally permissible for others—the state or private parties—to intervene to stop her from making the wrong moral choice. The two inquiries are not identical. Someone may be acting wrongly, but that does not necessarily mean that you would be acting rightly by forcibly stopping the wrongful act.

Suppose you live in a state that permits parents to use mild force to discipline their own children. You might believe that it is always wrong for parents to hit their children. Yet it does not follow that you would be entitled—legally or morally—to use force against a parent to stop him from spanking his child. The point is not that the question of whether it is right or wrong to spank children is agent-relative. You think that it is always wrong for parents to spank children—not just wrong for you, but for all parents. Nonetheless, you might also think that, within broad bounds, parents are entitled to make vital decisions about how to raise their children, and that this freedom of parenting includes the right to make some bad, even immoral choices, without your justly intervening with force.

Is abortion like spanking? Is it the sort of choice that is some-times immoral for women to make but that they are nonetheless entitled to make without undue interference from the state or pri-vate parties? If so, that surely cannot be because it inflicts only minor harm, in the way that one might think mild spanking does. After all, abortion *kills* the fetus, and—to continue the analogy—the state and private parties are both legally and morally entitled to intervene to stop a parent from killing her own born child.

Nonetheless, in this chapter we provide an argument for under-standing a woman's decision to have an abortion as the sort of sometimes immoral choice that women are entitled to make for themselves. We elaborate a set of concerns about female equality that apply chiefly to humans but that also parallel issues raised by animal agriculture. In so doing, we draw a connection between abortion and animal rights that we have not yet discussed.

Thus far we have been comparing and contrasting abortion and animal exploitation by comparing and contrasting the interests and circumstances of fetuses and animals. But that is not the only salient pairwise comparison. In important respects, women who seek abortions face circumstances similar to those that confront farmed animals, especially female farmed animals, like cows raised for their milk and hens raised for their eggs.

To put the point provocatively, women who are denied the right to have abortions are placed in a kind of reproductive servitude that resembles the reproductive servitude in which dairy cows and laying hens are held. In each case, females' reproductive capacities are used for the benefit of others: abortion prohibitions appropri-ate the bodies of women for the benefit of fetuses; dairy and egg production appropriate the bodies of cows and hens for the benefit of the people who will eventually eat the dairy and egg products.

Admittedly, the circumstances are not identical. Still, thinking about sex-based subordination provides another avenue by which we may gain insights into both the abortion and animal rights debates by considering each in light of the other.

Readers who have followed the public debate about abortion will of course be aware that it is frequently framed as a matter of women's rights. From its inception, the pro-choice movement has organized as part of the women's movement.[1] More recently the pro-life movement has sought to rebrand itself as pro-woman, portraying women who have abortions as themselves victims of abortion. The Supreme Court even credited this line of reasoning by accepting the possibility of "abortion regret syndrome" in *Gonzales v. Carhart*, the partial-birth abortion case we discussed in chapter 1.[2] From both sides, then, seeing abortion as an issue that implicates women's rights and interests is hardly revolutionary.

Nonetheless, we hope to offer a clear-eyed picture of the reproductive stakes that is sometimes missing in the literature. For example, one of the most important pro-choice essays on the subject of abortion is philosopher Judith Jarvis Thomson's 1971 paper in *Philosophy & Public Affairs*, in which she asks the reader to imagine that "[y]ou wake up in the morning and find yourself back to back in bed with an unconscious violinist" who will die of kidney failure if you disconnect him before nine months have elapsed.[3] Thomson's brilliant essay deserves considerable credit for defending a right to abortion even if one assumes for the sake of argument, as she does, "that the fetus is a person from the moment of conception."[4] Yet in relying on the violinist example—and another in which "people-seeds drift about in the air like pollen"[5]—Thomson's essay directs readers to cases so bizarre that their moral intuitions may fail them. Acknowledging our conceptual debt to Thomson and to others who have built on her work, in this chapter we develop an account of pregnancy that relies on more straightforward, albeit no less provocative, examples.

ENDING A PREGNANCY OR KILLING A FETUS?

Abortion entails two simultaneous events: it kills a living fetus (or embryo or zygote), and it also puts an end to the woman's condition of being pregnant. The point is easy enough to see in the case of a forced abortion. When a pregnant woman wishes to remain pregnant until the birth of her child, the forced termination of her pregnancy through abortion results in the infliction of two harms. It attacks both the life of the fetus and the pregnant woman's bodily integrity.

People on both sides of the abortion issue understand this confluence of interests when a woman wants to be pregnant, which is why pro-life and pro-choice advocates can comfortably unite in opposing forced abortions as a profound violation of human rights.[6] For similar reasons, most of us can empathize with the grief that can accompany a miscarriage (or "spontaneous abortion") for a pregnant woman who wanted to remain pregnant. In Japan, people acknowledge and provide a means of commemorating the loss of a fetus or embryo, called a "mizuko" or "water baby," whether through miscarriage or induced abortion (which can itself represent an ambivalent choice).[7]

Sometimes, however, the plans and interests of a pregnant woman plainly conflict with those of the fetus who grows inside her body. When a woman is pregnant but wishes to terminate that condition, the woman's interest in bodily integrity clashes with the fetus's interest (if it is already sentient) in continuing to live. How might that conflict play out?

Suppose that a woman who wants to terminate her pregnancy goes ahead and does so. Let us put aside for the moment the interests of the fetus as such. In that case, the woman succeeds in restoring the physical state in which her bodily processes are no longer involuntarily diverted to the task of providing life support to another living thing. She thereby reestablishes her bodily integrity.

By putting aside the fetus's interests for the moment, we can understand the unhappily pregnant woman's predicament as resembling that of a man who suffers from a tapeworm or a bacterial or viral infection that his body is unable to defeat without intervention. Such a man might restore his physical state, in which *his* bodily processes are no longer involuntarily diverted to the task of providing life support to another living thing, by taking an antibiotic or antiviral medication. Likewise, if the man wishes to eschew treatment (perhaps because remaining ill offers him insights into suffering, or perhaps because he is skeptical of medicine and prefers the illness to all of the available treatments), then his legal right to bodily integrity enables him to refuse medication (again putting aside potentially conflicting public interests in his treatment, such as avoiding an epidemic).

Now consider what would happen if the government (or a private individual) blocked the man seeking otherwise readily available antibiotics to treat his infection from obtaining the sought-after medicine. We would, in this case, describe the government's (or individual's) action as an interference with the patient's bodily integrity. The interference may be warranted (for example, if the antibiotic is dangerous or substantially risks breeding an antibiotic-resistant strain of the pathogen), but it nonetheless seriously interferes with the man's bodily integrity.

For similar reasons, we rightly understand the Tuskegee experiments (briefly discussed in chapter 2) as a deplorable example of human experimentation rather than as a simple omission. The doctors who conducted the experiments did not themselves administer syphilis to the African American victims, but they did stand in the way of the victims' obtaining treatment from others for their condition. The doctors did so by telling the patients that they were already receiving treatment, thereby preventing the patients from seeking an actual cure for their illness.

By contrast to a doctor who simply refrains from treating a particular syphilis patient—someone guilty of an omission—the doctors in the Tuskegee experiment actively blocked their patients from receiving a real treatment, not only from them but from anyone, by deceiving the patients into believing they were already being treated. Stopping someone from ending a condition in which another living organism uses his body to his detriment is thus categorically different from simply stepping aside and choosing not to be the one who helps that someone to obtain relief.

A government or individual might try to stop a pregnant woman from terminating her pregnancy by, respectively, prohibiting abortion or threatening her or her family with violence if she seeks an abortion. In doing so, the individual or government would not simply be refusing to help the woman to terminate her pregnancy (as any doctor might refuse to do).[8] It would instead be affirmatively interfering with the woman's attempt to restore her nonpregnant physiological state, thereby infringing upon her bodily integrity. Like the doctors who blocked the syphilis patients from receiving penicillin, once the antibiotic became available, the individual or government would be compelling the woman to remain pregnant, a state in which another organism is using her organ systems to her detriment and to the organism's benefit, and against her will.

In short, blocking a pregnant woman from obtaining an abortion effectively compels her to remain internally occupied by a physiologically demanding and burdensome organism that she wishes to expel from inside her body. Abortion prohibitions (whether enforced through laws or through private coercion) conscript women, and only women, into reproductive servitude.

To observe that abortion prohibitions conscript women is not to say that such prohibitions cannot be justified. A human fetus is not a viral or bacterial infection. Unlike an infection, many women regard pregnancy as a positive and even joyous condition in which to find themselves, despite the associated burdens. By contrast, it is difficult to imagine a syphilis patient rejoicing at the news that he has contracted the infection. Should these differences matter?

No one considers it wrong to kill a harmful bacterial colony, unless there is some instrumental benefit to be obtained from maintaining the bacteria. That is, everyone engaged in the abortion debate will agree that bacteria lack any foundation for a right to life. To our knowledge, bacteria are not sentient, but even if they were, humans would be entitled to kill attacking bacteria in self-defense, much as we are entitled to kill attacking bears, lions, and humans in self-defense.

When people oppose the use of antibiotics, it is because the antibiotics may interfere with some other instrumental objective, perhaps by breeding antibiotic-resistant bacteria or by failing to give the patient's immune system the opportunity to strengthen itself by fighting an infection without antibiotics. And when an individual objects to taking antibiotics, it is for his own reasons, including perhaps the side effects of the medication that he anticipates; it is not because he wishes to incubate the bacteria so they can live the lives they were entitled to live.

By contrast, from the pro-life perspective, abortion is wrong precisely because the fetus has a right to live; abortion kills the fetus and thus violates its right to live, end of story. To the extent that one's right to take antibiotics is premised in part on the absence of "another side," the analogy between infection and pregnancy breaks down.

BIRTH

From the pro-life perspective, abortion is morally problematic from the "moment" of conception. From the animal rights perspective, a pregnant woman has reason to give moral consideration to the fetus she carries once it achieves sentience. But conception and sentience are not the only lines one might plausibly draw—and to emphasize the point with which we began this chapter, the question of when a woman may herself be under a moral duty to carry her pregnancy to term is different from the question of when (if ever) the government or private parties are entitled to require a woman to carry her pregnancy to term. What other lines might be justified?

One possibility is that no duties are owed to fetuses until they emerge from the pregnant woman's body. This view, along with an associated view of personhood, actually appears in Jewish law, in a portion of the Talmud in which the following question arises: what ought to happen when a woman is in hard labor and will die if she is not released from her labor through an abortion? The resolution in the Talmud is that the person delivering the baby must tear the baby limb from limb to save the woman's life because the woman is a person and the baby is not. Yet this calculus changes if the woman has already delivered more than half of the baby from her body. Once that occurs, the Talmud says that it is no longer permissible to tear the baby apart to save the woman because one must not prefer one human life over another.[9]

Because the Talmud is essentially a theocratic text, it does not generally distinguish between personal morality and legal obligations. Yet that fact makes it all the more remarkable that the Talmud permits abortion (at least to save a woman's life) on the theory that a fetus just short of birth is not yet a person—a legal conclusion *and* a moral conclusion. It is also noteworthy that

Jewish law anticipates the "partial-birth abortion" laws we discussed in chapter 1, laws that make the permissibility of abortion depend on whether a fetus has been delivered to a particular landmark on its body.

Despite this Talmudic provision and the U.S. law that resembles it, it is nonetheless difficult to argue convincingly that the moral status of a fetus or baby truly ought to turn on where in the birth canal it is located. One need not take the orthodox pro-life view that an embryo is a full person in order to question the birth line. Nearly everybody believes that a newborn baby is a person, and it is thus hard to see why a baby who is in the process of being born is something less than a person. We still might want to permit abortion until birth, but that conclusion has nothing to do with the moral status of the fetus/baby just before and just after birth. For moral purposes, it makes little sense to classify a nine-month-old fetus as becoming a person only at the moment of birth.

VIABILITY

Legal personhood may turn on different factors, however, such as the fact that the Fourteenth Amendment to the U.S. Constitution appears to assume that "persons" have already been "born."[10] In *Roe v. Wade*, the U.S. Supreme Court relied in part on the language of the Fourteenth Amendment for its conclusion that fetuses lack constitutional rights.[11] Yet even in *Roe*, and certainly in subsequent cases that cut back on the scope of the abortion right, the justices did not draw the line protecting abortion at birth. Instead they allowed that the government may forbid most abortions after viability, that is, after the point in pregnancy when the fetus is capable of surviving outside of a woman's body.[12] Medical opinion currently places this point at somewhere around six months of pregnancy.[13]

Viability is thus a legally important marker. It also marks an important moment for doctors because it informs how they might go about addressing a number of medical emergencies. For example, if a woman goes into premature labor prior to fetal viability, then doctors know that if labor is not stopped, the fetus will certainly die. That is what viability means. Despite its legal and medical significance, viability does not appear to be a sensible moral line for distinguishing between persons and nonpersons. In saying that a fetus is not a person at point A and is a person at point B, we are necessarily saying that the fetus must have some attribute before it qualifies as a person, and it lacks that attribute at point A but comes to have it by point B. And if the criterion at issue is viability, then we are saying that something about being "viable" gives one the moral status of "person." But what could that be?

To say that a soon-to-be-viable fetus is not yet viable generally means that its lungs have not yet developed sufficiently to take in air from the atmosphere and absorb oxygen into the bloodstream, where it is needed to fuel respiration and bodily functions. Prior to viability, the fetus needs the placenta to supply it with oxygen because it lacks the fully operational equipment permitting it to breathe. But is the capacity to breathe, when one needs oxygen to survive, the kind of attribute or capacity that is necessary to endow a being with moral rights and entitlements? Is it even clear that the capacity to breathe successfully on one's own is of any moral consequence at all? Is a person in the process of drowning no longer a moral person? What about a person on a respirator?

By designating viability as legally significant, the Supreme Court may have had in mind the fact that until viability, the fetus cannot be physically separate from the pregnant woman. Perhaps the justices were thinking that it is medically sensible to consider the woman and fetus as a sort of unit prior to viability, for practical purposes. Once the fetus is viable, on the other hand, the woman can—in theory, at least—decide to stop being pregnant without having to kill the fetus inside her. There is then a way to terminate a pregnancy without killing the fetus. Termination need not entail fetal death. Therefore, if one is worried about protecting the woman's bodily integrity from an unwanted internal occupation, one can do so in the case of a viable fetus without having to violate the fetus's right to life, on the assumption that the fetus has a right to life.

Seen in this way, viability is not a morally relevant fact about the fetus. It is instead a fact that is relevant to how we go about resolving a conflict between the fetus's right to live and the woman's right to rid herself of an unwanted internal occupation. Because a nonviable fetus will necessarily die if removed prior to viability, a woman who has the right to remove the nonviable fetus from her body arguably may kill it prior to doing so, since preserving the fetus's life during its removal will not in fact allow for fetal survival.

In the case of a viable fetus, by contrast, one might resolve the conflict by permitting the expulsion but not the killing of the fetus. Once the fetus is viable, on this approach, killing it may become impermissible (or perhaps may be made impermissible by legislation) because the fetus can survive if it is removed alive.

We believe that this is the most coherent way of understanding viability as a reasonable point at which to permit prohibitions against abortion. In reality, "viability" is something of a misnomer because (as noted in chapter 2) the fetus will in fact suffer serious health problems and run a significant chance of dying if delivered substantially prior to thirty-two weeks gestation. But it may survive, and the ability to survive does matter if we are discussing whether to permit killing in the process of removal.

Yet none of this reasoning bears directly on the fetus's moral status. At most, it assumes that the fetus does have moral value. Only once the fetus has moral value, after all, does its viability translate into an obligation to allow it to live. Viability alone is not sufficient for moral status. Some viruses are "viable" outside of the human organism, but that does not mean that these viruses have the right to continue to exist or reproduce.

SENTIENCE (AGAIN)

As we discussed in chapter 1, we believe that sentience distinguishes an abortion that raises moral concerns on behalf of the fetus from one that does not. Once a fetus has the capacity to have experiences—whether of pain, pleasure, or other subjective states—the fetus has interests and, accordingly, an entitlement to have those interests respected. Once a fetus can feel pain, in other words, others are under an obligation to refrain from inflicting pain on the fetus unless there is an overriding justification for such infliction. Likewise, once the fetus can feel anything, it has an interest in avoiding death, inasmuch as any sentient living being has an interest in avoiding death. For us, then, the difficult question is abortion postsentience. And we are not alone in this perspective.

As we noted in the introduction, a growing number of states have passed so-called pain-capable abortion prohibitions, which ban abortion after the point at which (some) doctors say the fetus is capable of experiencing pain.[14] Notably, these states do not permit "painless" or "humane" abortions of pain-capable fetuses. Instead, they prohibit abortion altogether, thereby manifesting the view that the capacity to feel pain endows a sentient being not only with a right against the infliction of pain but also with a right to life, a view that we share. Once the fetus is sentient, there is a true moral conflict in need of resolution, a conflict between the fetus's right to live and the woman's right to be free of unwanted internal occupation. As each of us has separately described in greater detail, this conflict is difficult to resolve.[15]

In chapter 2, we considered the sorts of reasons relevant to a pregnant woman's decision about how to weigh her own interests against the interests of a sentient fetus she carries. Here we are considering the question from the perspective of the broader society: When may the government (or private actors) intervene to block a woman from deciding to have an abortion? As we have just seen, American constitutional case law draws the line at fetal viability. We think that line can be rendered coherent, and not just as a split-the-difference compromise.

However, the case law pays no attention whatsoever to the vital question of fetal sentience. Now if it happened that fetal sentience corresponded with fetal viability, then perhaps we would have the happy coincidence that the courts had, more or less by accident, drawn the right line. But there remain two reasons to worry.

First, there is no reason to think that viability—which is a function of fetal lung development and the existing state of neonatal medical technology—corresponds exactly with sentience—which is a function of brain development. Like so many matters that touch on abortion, the questions of when a fetus is viable and when a fetus is sentient have become highly politicized, with the pro-life side arguing for early answers to both questions and the pro-choice side arguing for late answers to both questions. In any event, our basic point remains: viability and sentience are different phenomena, so there is no reason why they would necessarily align.

Second, notwithstanding the moral significance that attaches to fetal sentience for a woman making her own choice whether to have an abortion, it may play less of a role in the proper evaluation of the question of when the government (or a private party) may forbid a woman from having an abortion. One might think that the government may legitimately ban abortion after fetal sentience because the fetus's interest in life itself outweighs the pregnant woman's interest in liberty. However, the relation between the woman and the fetus complicates the calculus.

SELF-DEFENSE AND OTHER ANALOGIES

It is possible to argue for a legal right of a woman to abort even a healthy, sentient fetus. We now develop that argument. Following in the footsteps of Thomson, political scientist Eileen McDonagh, and other feminists, we suggest that the best argument for a legal right to abortion begins by analogizing abortion to self-defense, and this argument ultimately justifies such a right even if the fetus is sentient. We believe we break new ground among pro-choice thinkers in taking an unvarnished view of the sorts of reasons for which women typically seek abortions.

The law ordinarily forbids people from killing someone unless that someone is attacking them in a manner that threatens death or substantial bodily harm.[16] We can view the fetus as attacking the woman, and if it threatens the woman's life, then this analogy may be apt. The medieval Jewish scholar Maimonides (who was also a doctor) maintained that a woman may terminate a life-threatening pregnancy without having to consider whether the fetus or baby is a person yet because it represents a "rodef," or someone who is pursuing the woman's life and may accordingly be killed in self-defense.[17] But it may be more accurate to say that the pregnancy—rather than the fetus—attacks the woman, if anything does, and that the attack is generally not fatal. Furthermore, in most instances of self-defense, the chief motivation for the killing is to stop the attacker, but when women decide to terminate their pregnancies, it is often for reasons that have nothing to do with the physical harms associated with pregnancy.

In the typical case, it is not the pregnancy itself that the woman objects to; it is the fact that it will yield a child. Ordinarily abortions happen because the woman (or her partner) does not want to have a child (or this particular child, or a child at this time) and not because she wishes to terminate the physical burdens of pregnancy. In this sense abortion seems different from self-defense since killing the fetus is not simply a means to the end of terminating the pregnancy; it is the true purpose of the abortion, its objective.

The hard truth is that women most commonly choose to have an abortion because they do not want the growing fetus inside them to exist anymore. Self-defense law, in contrast, typically (and quite rightly) gives no weight to one person's interest in the non-existence of another person, in and of itself. Yet once a woman decides she does not want to be pregnant—for whatever reason—requiring her to remain in the state of pregnancy and ultimately to endure labor or surgery at the end, is a form of conscription.

Rape provides another imperfect but useful analogy. When a woman decides that she does not want to have sex with a particular man, the man is morally and legally obligated to refrain from having sex with the woman.[18] A woman has a right to avoid rape even if she has an offensive reason for rejecting the particular man—perhaps she has learned that he belongs to a racial group that she despises. Maybe the reason she does not want to have sex with him is not that she objects to having sex or even to having sex with someone who is exactly like him in every way except for his race. It is only his racial background that leads her to refuse sex. Still, even in these circumstances, it is rape for him to compel her to have sex, notwithstanding her offensive reasons for rejecting him.

Similarly, we believe that even if a woman has a reason for terminating her pregnancy that is not itself linked to the condition of pregnancy but instead stems from her feelings about the existence of the fetus, it is nonetheless a kind of assault on her body for the government (or a private party) to block her from terminating the pregnancy, thereby forcing her to remain pregnant against her will. A forced pregnancy, in other words, is a forced pregnancy, regardless of what truly motivates the woman to seek an escape from her condition.

Now imagine that a pregnant woman has an ultrasound that informs her that her fetus is female. She does not want a female child (for whatever reason), so she seeks an abortion. Many people believe that she should not be allowed to have the abortion, and such abortions are illegal in several countries (where they are, sadly, quite common).[19] Our view is that even when her reason is offensive in this way, the woman has the right to end the internal occupation of her body.

To address the problem of sex-selection abortion, which raises issues beyond the lives of the individual woman and her would-be child, we could accept a prohibition on screening procedures solely designed to reveal the sex of the fetus to a pregnant woman. Although she has the right to terminate her pregnancy if she wishes to do so, it does not follow that she has the right to discover whether her fetus is male or female.

To return to the admittedly imperfect rape analogy, we would likewise distinguish between two men: the man who forces a woman to have sex when her refusal is motivated by racial animus (a rapist), and the man who has consensual sex with a woman after deliberately misrepresenting his racial background to her because he knows that she would reject him if she knew the truth (not a rapist). In another example, a woman might reject a man because he refuses to wear a condom, and his decision to force her to have sex with him anyway would represent a decision to rape her.[20] By contrast, a man who convincingly claimed that he was wearing a condom but was not, would be innocent of rape (though perhaps guilty of fraud and other potential offenses, in virtue of his material misrepresentation). And regardless of her motive for refusing to consent to sex, a woman being raped has the right to kill her rapist if that is the only way that she can terminate what is happening. We would extend that logic to the case of an unwanted pregnancy.

On the other side, however, is the reality that what the pregnant woman does is aimed not simply at refusing to be intimately occupied, as it is in the case of self-defense against rape or medicating an infection. Abortion of a sentient fetus kills an innocent being who appears to be entitled not to be attacked or killed, an entitlement that the sentient fetus has not forfeited in the way that the (also sentient) rapist arguably has. Moreover, if the pregnancy was the result of consensual sex, then the pregnant woman has played an active role in creating the circumstances in which the innocent sentient being grows inside her. We do not believe this fact is dispositive because an act of sex does not, in most cases, yield a pregnancy, and it therefore cannot really be called "consent" to pregnancy. Yet the combination of the woman's consent to sex, the fact that she may be aiming primarily or exclusively at eliminating the existence of the fetus rather than at simply protecting herself from an unwanted physical occupation, and the innocence of her occupying sentient fetus all make the question more difficult here than in the case of self-defense against a rapist.

Our conclusion that the law should nonetheless permit abortion even in the case of sex-selection motivations stems from the fact that pregnant women alone find themselves in the position of having to choose between being a Good Samaritan (by providing internal and extensive life support to a fetus, followed by labor or surgery), on the one hand, and affirmatively carrying out violence, on the other. The rest of us can comfortably ignore the many people who need our help to survive, even if that help would be considerably less demanding than a pregnancy. A blood donation, for example, is relatively easy and painless; yet we are not (and probably could not be, consistent with our system of constitutional rights) forced to donate a pint of blood to save someone else's life. A pregnancy is more like a kidney donation than a blood donation, and each of us is legally allowed to refuse to donate a kidney even when the recipient would be our own child.

What distinguishes the pregnant woman from the rest of us, in other words, is largely the fact that the pregnant woman is physically attached to the being that needs a massive bodily sacrifice on her part to survive. Were the fetus physically separate, the woman could choose not to implant it in her body, even if that choice meant its certain death. Given that fact, we think it unfair to the pregnant woman to routinely make demands of her of a sort that we make of no one else (other than conscripted soldiers in wartime). She, unlike others, cannot decide against being a Good Samaritan without simultaneously engaging in direct harm by killing. We believe that the weight of the unavoidable double choice, unique to pregnancy, is difficult enough for her to bear without a third party such as the government entering in and compelling her to take the path of the Good Samaritan.

SEXUAL SERVITUDE OF FARMED ANIMALS

So what are the implications of our position on abortion for animal rights? In chapter 1 we emphasized the similar interests possessed by sentient fetuses and animals used by humans for food and clothing. In chapter 2 we considered the sorts of reasons that might justify an individual decision to have an abortion or to consume animal products; we found that while there are circumstances in which aborting a fetus may be morally justifiable, even from the woman's perspective, the routine use that humans make of animals is not justified. Here we note that the situations also look different from an external perspective.

A woman seeking an abortion seeks to vindicate her interest in terminating a physically demanding intimate occupation and use of her body and organ systems. By contrast, a man or woman seeking to consume animal products seeks only to vindicate his or her interest in consuming the flesh and secretions of sentient beings. In other words, the interest of the pregnant woman is in terminating her own exploitation, and the interest of the consumer is in perpetuating the exploitation of another.

To appreciate how dramatically different these two interests are, consider a different case involving a pregnancy. Imagine that a woman has a child who has suffered kidney failure and must undergo dialysis several times every week. Assume that she also has no hope of receiving a donor kidney for years, if ever. To help her daughter, the woman intentionally becomes pregnant and, in her eighth month, asks her obstetrician to remove both of the fetus's kidneys for transplantation into her child. The obstetrician tells the mother that the surgery will kill the fetus, but the mother wants to proceed anyway. Is it morally acceptable for the woman to undertake this surgery to help her older daughter? Was it morally acceptable for her to deliberately become pregnant with the aim of having this surgery in the first place?

This hypothetical scenario should give pause to even the most fervent believer in the right of a woman to control her reproductive life. The right to decide whether and when to have children or to continue or terminate a pregnancy does not reasonably contemplate the deliberate creation of sentient fetuses for the purpose of using them as disposable organ donors. Someone with rights has, at the very least, a right against such purely instrumental use (in addition to a right to life).

Now consider what we do to animals—in particular, to dairy cows (and other animals, such as sheep and goats, we bring into the world for dairy). We breed them into existence, like the hypothetical child in the above scenario, with the intention of using them. Unlike even the offensive scenario, moreover, we do so not because we are seeking to provide medical treatment to someone who must otherwise undergo dialysis several times per week. We are instead seeking to consume products that are unnecessary to our health (and that in fact have a deleterious effect on human health) but that we just enjoy eating.

To supply dairy products, the female cow (or other mammal) is first impregnated and then, after she gives birth, separated from the baby with whom she has already bonded, a separation that results in enormous distress and grieving for the mother, a manifestation of a maternal instinct that we all understand well. One way in which we recognize the suffering involved in such a separation and the biological foundation of that suffering is by having laws in the United States that permit human parents who have agreed to surrender a child for adoption to change their minds when the baby arrives.[21] Such laws acknowledge that people cannot always anticipate through the power of reason the intensity of the biologically programmed attachment that will develop between a parent and a child, an attachment that extends beyond the human, "reasoning" species.

In the case of dairy cattle and other animals, this painful separation between mother and baby occurs so that humans—not baby calves—can consume the milk that the cow (or sheep or goat) produces. The baby calf, if he is male, suffers a fate similar to the male chicks we discussed in chapter 1: he has no ongoing use within the dairy industry and will therefore be slaughtered for veal within six months of his birth. If she is female, the baby calf will either become veal or will be raised to be a dairy cow like her mother, losing her every baby soon after birth. Then, after four or five years of repeat pregnancies and loss of her young, she will be taken to the slaughterhouse, just like her mother was before her, and will meet a terrifying and painful death.

Egg-laying hens occupy a similar place of reproductive servitude. We bring them into the world to use them as egg-producing instruments. When egg-layers hatch, professional "sexers" examine each one to determine whether it is a male or a female. We have already discussed the fate of male chicks, but it is not clear that females fare any better. Farmers keep the female egg-laying hens alive for a few years, while they lay enough eggs to be worth feeding, and then they too are killed, often in the same way as their brothers were—that is, by being gassed, suffocated, or ground to death—after they are "spent" from laying more than ten times as many eggs per year as their wild ancestor, the red junglefowl.[22]

The facts behind dairy milk, cheese, ice cream, and eggs are important to consider in our assessment of the relationship between abortion and the consumption of even those animal products that "vegetarians" (but not vegans) typically consume. By examining these facts, we can appreciate how the act of compelling a woman to remain pregnant against her will—as laws prohibiting abortion do—parallels the reproductive servitude in which female animals are held in the dairy and egg industries. Seen in this light, both the pro-choice position on abortion and the pro–animal rights position instantiate an ethic of non-exploitation.

As we have conceded, however, there is another side to the abortion debate, a side that emphasizes the morally salient fact that a woman's refusal to remain pregnant—once she is far enough along in her pregnancy—necessarily also entails the active killing of a sentient fetus. For this reason, one could see both the pro-life position on abortion and the pro–animal rights position as defending the rights of innocent beings. Someone who takes the pro-life/pro–animal rights position would have to concede that far more is demanded of a pregnant woman blocked from having an abortion than is demanded of the male or female consumer blocked from eating dairy or eggs, but she could plausibly maintain nonetheless that actively killing innocents is wrong in both contexts.

In short, we acknowledge that terminating the life of a sentient fetus in an abortion raises a serious moral question, even as we conclude that society ought to leave the decision of how to answer that moral question to the pregnant woman, whose body must otherwise serve as an involuntary incubator, with all that this entails. Regardless of how one resolves the abortion question in the case of sentient fetuses, however, the view that animal slaughter and exploitation is wrong still follows. It is wrong because violence against, and exploitation of, innocent beings must be credibly justified but cannot be justified when the underlying reason for the violence and exploitation is to satisfy culinary and sartorial preferences.

CODA: BANNING ANIMAL EXPLOITATION?

In light of our view that the animal question is so much easier than the abortion question, readers might think that we favor laws banning most exploitation of animals. We do not, but unlike with abortion, we have no reason of principle for opposing the banning of meat, leather, dairy, eggs, and other animal products.

As we have argued in this chapter, the considerations relevant to whether an act is judged immoral may differ from the considerations relevant to whether an act should be illegal. Moreover, some of the latter sorts of considerations are tactical. People who opposed Prohibition or who now favor decriminalization of some drugs do not necessarily think that there is a moral right to drink alcohol or to smoke marijuana (or that the use of alcohol or other drugs is innocuous or even "victimless"). Rather, they may worry that the costs of fighting the social ills associated with the criminalization of alcohol and drugs outweigh any benefits to which Prohibition and the war on drugs may lead.

Our view about protecting animals is likewise tactical. Given current consumer preferences, there is no realistic hope of enacting legislation forbidding the raising of animals for food and clothing.

Indeed, as we explore in chapter 5, even considerably more modest legal reforms—like regulating the size of cages for hens—may prove counterproductive when undertaken in a climate in which the vast majority of the population believes that eating animals and their secretions raises no ethical questions at all.

We must emphasize, however, that these are tactical conclusions in light of existing patterns of human behavior. Someday, in a world in which veganism is very widespread, we might well favor banning all or most forms of animal exploitation. But then we can also imagine a world in which all people—not just pregnant women—are routinely required to sacrifice their bodies to benefit others: a world of mandatory kidney donations, say.

We are not sure we would like to live in a world of legally mandated pregnancy and mandated Good Samaritanism: our objection to the reproductive servitude that abortion bans produce is not simply egalitarian; it is also libertarian. Still, we acknowledge that the abortion calculus could be different in a society that generally enforced strong Good Samaritan obligations. Put differently, it may not be possible to draw a sharp distinction between positions that we take as a matter of principle and those we take as a matter of tactics in light of the facts as they currently exist. Here we have set out our views for the world we know. Should a very different world come into being in our lifetimes, that will be time enough to see whether and how our views might change.

4

Death Versus Suffering

In the introduction and chapter 1 we invoked Jeremy Bentham's question, "Can they suffer?" as the basis for grounding moral rights for animals in sentience. In this chapter we consider a potentially troubling implication of Bentham's criterion: If the capacity to suffer is what establishes that sentient beings are entitled to moral consideration, then what makes it wrong to kill such beings painlessly? How, in other words, does the ability to experience suffering give rise to a right to freedom from unnecessary killing?

As a theoretical matter, that question proves surprisingly difficult to answer persuasively. As we shall explain, however, the difficulty is not unique to nonhuman animals. It is hard to explain why killing *any* sentient being—whether that being is a chicken, a late-term human fetus, or a gifted brain surgeon—harms that being, at least if we imagine that the killing occurs unexpectedly, instantaneously, and painlessly. Attempting to provide an answer is nonetheless useful because the question has implications both for the treatment of animals and for the regulation of abortion.

Some people who think that sentience implies only a right not to suffer take the further view that it is therefore morally permissible to breed and raise animals for food so long as the animals are treated humanely. Meanwhile, if we cannot explain what it is about sentience that grounds a right to continued existence, then we may have difficulty distinguishing between presentient fetuses—which, we have said, do not yet have interests—and people in states of complete unconsciousness, who most people would agree do have interests. We have a strong intuition that there is something about having experienced sentient life that entitles a being to continue that sentient life (so long as that is physically possible), but to answer the objection requires us to interrogate and develop that intuition into something more.

EPICURUS

At first blush the contention that bad treatment of sentient beings is morally impermissible but that killing them is harmless might seem easy to dismiss. Isn't death the ultimate harm to any being? Not necessarily, as both our language and our law recognize. We sometimes refer to various torments as amounting to a "fate worse than death." Meanwhile, American law allows the death penalty but categorically bans torture, even for the most serious crimes. Yet, even if we think torture and some other fates can be worse than death, death is still generally regarded as very harmful.

People who think otherwise rely on an argument given in its most famous form by the ancient Greek philosopher Epicurus. "Death," Epicurus argued, "is nothing to us, seeing that, when we are, death is not come, and, when death is come, we are not. It is nothing, then, either to the living or to the dead, for with the living it is not and the dead exist no longer."[1] We think there is much to be said for the Epicurean view as a guide to how one ought to regard one's own life, which is the context in which Epicurus propounded it. Although modern usage tends to confuse Epicureanism with libertine hedonism, Epicurus espoused a philosophy of personal contentment to be achieved through moderation in all things.[2] In arguing that death does no harm, he aimed to comfort his followers so that they would enjoy life without fearing death. But we—and we suspect most readers—strongly resist what appears to be an implication of the view that death is not harmful: namely, that there is nothing wrong per se with killing another sentient being (human or nonhuman). Let us consider why we properly resist that implication.

To begin, even if we were to concede, for argument's sake, that killing a sentient being does not itself harm that being, such killing generally still leaves behind others to suffer his loss. Human beings are social and interdependent. So are many nonhuman animals, including the ones whom humans use in animal agriculture. Even when raised in atrocious conditions, such animals remain social beings who give evidence of their emotional connections to one another and of the pain they experience when separated from one another, by death or otherwise.[3]

We do not wish to rest the response to the Epicurean argument entirely on the social nature of sentient beings, however. After all, if one really thought that the only harm in death is to survivors, then one might draw the perverse conclusion that it is better to slaughter all members of a family or social group than to leave behind any survivors. Accordingly, in responding to the Epicurean argument, we think it is necessary to explain how death harms not just those who are left behind but the very being who dies as well.

One potentially promising avenue distinguishes between the condition of being dead—which, in the Epicurean view cannot by definition harm the person who was formerly alive—and the process of being killed. Here, too, the Epicurean perspective is defensible in theory: It is possible to *imagine* killings that cause neither physical pain in their execution nor anxiety in their anticipation. The sudden and instantaneous vaporization of the Earth would be a dramatic example, but we can give a more mundane one: A person or animal unwittingly ingests a poison that causes him to fall asleep and then expire peacefully.

In reality, however, killing another being typically causes that being to suffer. That is almost always true of the animals killed for food, even when their slaughter satisfies the minimal legal requirements of humaneness.[4] Many people might imagine that "humane slaughter" is something akin to euthanasia for a beloved ailing pet, but the economic imperative to keep the slaughter line moving quickly, coupled with prohibitions on marketing meat contaminated by barbiturates and other drugs that might be used to make an animal comfortable in dying, ensure that the process of slaughter itself is far from painless.

But suppose it were painless. Still, we would strongly resist the implication that death would then be harmless to the sentient being killed. Perhaps this is just one of our settled convictions for which no further reasons can be or need be given, but we think that murdering another person—even if the victim lives alone, has no friends or relatives, and dies painlessly and completely unexpectedly—harms that person. The most straightforward explanation why also seems like the most persuasive one: Killing someone, whether that someone is a human or another sentient animal, harms that someone by depriving him of something that was his—namely, his life.

Put differently, the Epicurean argument purports to show that death is not a bad state for one to be in because there is no one who is in that state, as death is a state of nonbeing, not a bad state of being. However, the Epicurean argument does not show that the deprivation of life is harmless.

What grounds the moral intuition that we should not kill people? Simply that people have lives that belong to them. And just as the Epicurean argument applies equally to humans and to nonhumans, so does this response. Sentient animals' lives belong to them. Just as humans do, likewise nonhuman animals experience their own lives.[5]

THE (IR)RELEVANCE OF A "LIFE PLAN"

Some philosophers who have expressed sympathy for this sort of response to the Epicurean view nonetheless resist the conclusion that all sentient beings own their own lives because they doubt that all sentient beings experience their lives *as* lives, rather than as a series of unconnected sensations. As one would expect, opponents of animal rights express this view in the hopes of distinguishing between humans and most or all other animals.

More surprisingly, even champions of animals' well-being have sometimes expressed a version of this idea. For example,

Tom Regan argues that the moral entitlement to continue living extends to beings who are the "subject of a life," a term he uses to encompass most but not quite all sentient beings.[6] Stranger still, Peter Singer has argued for humane slaughter of farmed animals instead of arguing for the abolition of animal agriculture because he believes that killing animals painlessly inflicts no harm on them.[7] Singer contends that humans (and perhaps some of the other "higher" animals, such as great apes and dolphins) have life plans that include preferences regarding the distant future, while "lower" animals do not. He says it is wrong to frustrate the "higher" animals' life plans (by killing them and thus cutting short their plans), but it is not immoral to kill those who lack the capacity to form such long-term plans.

Within the group of thinkers who endorse the idea that only continuity over time justifies a right to life, the difference between opponents and supporters of animals' right to live depends in part on a factual question: To what extent do various animals in fact experience their lives as continuing over time rather than living simply "in the moment"? There is also a theoretical disagreement over just what sort of experiences and capacities ought to count as establishing continued existence. We briefly consider these disagreements together.

Some of the more ambitious opponents of animal rights have articulated stringent criteria for establishing that members of a particular species of animal conceive of themselves as persisting over time, asking, for example, whether members of the species keep diaries.[8] We find these to be transparent efforts to select criteria simply for the purpose of distinguishing humans from other animals—and they do not even work for that purpose. After all, most humans do not keep diaries, and it is not clear why belonging to a species that includes some members who do keep diaries entitles one who does not keep a diary to the privileges that supposedly go with diary keeping—other than the very prejudice against members of unfavored species—which the resort to objective criteria is supposed to justify, not simply assume.

In any event, we need not question the good faith of the thinkers who espouse life planning as a criterion for an interest in avoiding death because the argument fails on its own terms. Why should moral entitlements flow from keeping a diary or making a life plan—much less from having the *capacity* for such activities or, while lacking the capacity as an individual, belonging to a species whose members generally do have the capacity, which some of them exercise? Pointing to such activities does not appear to respond to the Epicurean challenge. Certainly Epicurus himself did not think so. The lineage of arguments about the value of a life plan can be traced back to Aristotle, who was already in his forties and a renowned philosopher when Epicurus was born.[9] Undoubtedly familiar with the Aristotelian claim that a life well lived follows a plan, Epicurus evidently did not regard that claim as preempting his own argument that death does no harm.

Did Epicurus have good reason to think that beings who formulate life plans are as unharmed by death as those who do not? It would appear so. Suppose someone formulates and begins to live out his life plan but then dies suddenly and painlessly. He will not actually *experience* frustration of his life plan, so on the Epicurean logic, death for him is no worse than it is for a human who lived day to day, or for a "lower" animal who was incapable of formulating a life plan.

To be sure, such activities as diary keeping and life planning could provide evidence that a being continues across time, but even then they are hardly necessary to establish continuity of the self. Animals of the sort that humans exploit and kill, as well as their wild cousins, typically manifest behaviors that, taken at face value, pretty clearly indicate an internal sense of continuity over time: They act excited in anticipation of a meal or agitated in anticipation of an unpleasant experience; they express joy upon reuniting with kin and companions; and they undertake tasks that will bring them rewards only in the future (as when birds fashion sticks as special-purpose tools for obtaining a meal or when squirrels who have buried acorns for later use dig them up if a potential competitor witnessed the burial). Whereas animal behavioralists might, in the past, have dismissed some of these observations as "anthropomorphizing" and described the underlying behaviors as merely instinctual, scientists have increasingly come to recognize that the best explanation for animals' behaving in ways similar to how humans behave relative to their future selves is that the animals are experiencing the world and themselves in much the same way that humans do.[10] And given our shared evolutionary history, Occam's razor suggests that, absent some better explanation, animal behavior that appears future-oriented in some of the same ways as human behavior does probably *is* future-oriented.

To be sure, one can never know exactly what it is like to experience the world as a member of another species experiences it.[11] But then one can never know exactly what it is like to experience the world as a different member of one's own species. Each of us is ultimately trapped in his or her own perspective.

IDENTITY OVER TIME

Indeed, no one can even be sure that he himself persists as a continuing being over time. English philosopher John Locke's influential 1690 *Essay Concerning Human Understanding* argued that memory establishes continuity over time, but memory looks like a problematic criterion in both directions.[12] False memories occur, and the philosophy of personal identity literature is riddled with science-fiction stories of the implantation of one person's memories in the mind of another.[13] Thus, memory is not a sufficient condition for identity over time.

Nor does memory work well as a necessary condition for identity over time. A person with amnesia might still be said to be the same person that she was before the amnesia struck even though she can no longer remember events that occurred during the prior period. Or consider a person suffering temporary amnesia. On the Lockean criterion, she is person X before the amnesia, then a different person Y when she has amnesia, and then X again when she recovers her memory, which seems quite counterintuitive.

Moreover, even without any failure of memory, it is unclear why the memory of past experiences makes the rememberer the *same* person as the person who had those experiences. Scottish philosopher David Hume, writing in the first half of the eighteenth century, described the notion of a continuing self as a kind of illusion that our minds create to make better sense of the world.[14] Hume wondered whether our lived experience might really be closer to the "living in the moment" that contemporary opponents of animal rights claim is the lot of most nonhumans.[15]

In expressing doubts about the continuity of the self over time, Hume echoed a very old set of concerns. We can find similar ideas in the fragmentary records of the thought of the pre-Socratic philosopher Heraclitus of Ephesus, whose aphorism *one can never step in the same river twice* has been understood by some as a metaphor for constant change of living beings, not just bodies of water.[16] Likewise, Buddhists have attributed to the Buddha (who was roughly a contemporary of Heraclitus) the notion that all things, including ourselves and our consciousness from moment to moment, are impermanent (or *anicca* in ancient Pali).[17]

Consider a famous example in the philosophical literature concerning the puzzle of identity over time—addressed in one form or another by Plutarch, Aristotle, John Locke, and Thomas Hobbes (as well as by contemporary philosophers): the so-called Ship of Theseus problem. The basic problem contemplates a ship consisting of wooden planks that, over time, wear out and are replaced one by one. Eventually, all of the planks are replaced. Is the resulting ship the *same* ship as the original one? If not, at what point did its identity change? Would the answer change if (as first suggested by Hobbes) the worn-out planks had been saved and were reassembled?[18] Examples like this one reveal that our everyday notions of identity over time—even for simple objects like wooden boats—may not withstand critical scrutiny.

Nonetheless, we do not mean to endorse the skeptical view of identity. With the philosopher John Perry, we worry that "[t]o deny the reality or importance of identity," as the Heraclitian/Buddhist/Humean view appears to do, "seems self-defeating at best, psychotic at worst."[19] The question whether a ship with all of its planks replaced is the *same* ship as it was before the planks wore out feels like a semantic question: The answer ultimately depends on what we mean by "same." But the question whether the person who will move to Tokyo in three years is you or merely some future person connected to you through memory, physical continuity, and so forth, *feels* like a question to which the answer expresses a truth about the world as it is. Either that future person really is you, in which case you have special reason to worry about what befalls him, or it is somebody else, in which case you may have altruistic reasons to care about him but no *personal* reasons.[20]

The puzzling cases that expose the fuzziness of identity over time are so challenging in part because the stakes are so high. If our continuity over time really is no more than an illusion, then nearly everything we do, including but not limited to our moral decisions, is built upon a lie. When we punish John Doe for murder, we necessarily and inevitably punish the wrong person, for the murderer by hypothesis no longer exists. This seems intuitively wrong, and yet no account of personal identity we have encountered appears fully up to the task of refuting the skeptical view of Heraclitus, Buddha, and Hume.

Still, life goes on. Thus, rather than attempt to referee a millennia-old debate about the nature of the self, we would leave the puzzles over personal identity more or less where we left the puzzles over the Epicurean view of death that sent us down this road in the first place. Earlier we said that if Epicurus is right that death is no harm, then by the terms of his argument that is true for humans no less than for nonhuman sentient beings. Here we add that if the Heraclitian/Buddhist/Humean skeptics are right that continuity of existence is an illusion, then it is also, by the respective terms of their argument, an illusion for humans no less than for nonhuman sentient beings. Or perhaps, as Perry suggests, the "watered-down vulgar sense of identity" that we all use in our everyday lives is sufficient; but here too this conception would be sufficient for sentient nonhumans no less than for humans.

Within that commonsensical framework, it is nearly impossible to imagine sentience—a subjective perspective—that exists only in a moment rather than across some substantial increment of time. Maybe a dog chasing a ball does not think about a distant-future winter, but he certainly envisions the near-future moment when he will catch the ball. And just that small extension forward into time is all that is necessary to escape the radically skeptical view of identity. If we can trust our common sense to tell us that it harms a person to kill him—notwithstanding the fact that we lack a philosophically airtight reply to the skeptical view of personal identity espoused by Heraclitus, Buddha, and Hume—then we can equally trust our common sense to tell us that it harms a cow, a sow, or a hen to kill her.

EPICURUS IN THE OTHER DIRECTION: DEAD VERSUS NOT YET BORN

Earlier we said that the following is the best response to the Epicurean implication that the unexpected, instantaneous, and painless killing of a being does that being no harm: Such a killing nonetheless deprives that being of future life. But who exactly, the Epicurean might fairly ask in response, is being deprived of life by being killed? Not the dead person because that person does not exist anymore. And not the person when he was alive because when he was alive he had not yet been deprived of anything. So perhaps this most persuasive answer to Epicureanism is not very persuasive at all. Indeed, it is arguably not even an answer, much less a persuasive one.

In order to make more sense of the response we have proposed, one must suppose that a current being stands in a certain sort of relationship to his future self, such that preventing that future self from existing wrongs the current being. In the discussion thus far, we were comfortable to leave the matter there because it seemed to us that, whatever sort of relationship between a present self and a future self suffices to make the future self the *same* self as the current self, that relationship is roughly equivalent for humans and most nonhuman animals. Thus, our answer either works or it does not, but it stands or falls equally for humans and for other animals.

We cannot simply leave matters ambiguous on this point, however, because how we specify the kind of relationship that establishes continuity of the self over time may have ramifications for how we think about abortion. In particular, if we imagine that killing living person P_0 at time 0 harms P_0 because P_0 would have been the same person as P_1 at later time 1, but for the killing, then what grounds do we have for saying that aborting presentient Fetus F_0 at time 0 does not harm F_0, which, but for the killing, would have become sentient fetus F_1 at time 1 and eventually sentient person P_2 at time 2?

We might think that the answer is simple: If Fetus Fs is sentient at time 0, then yes, of course aborting Fs harms Fs in exactly this way. Pursuant to the sorts of considerations we addressed in chapters 2 and 3, a pregnant woman may have sufficient reason to inflict that harm on Fs, but with respect to the question of harm, the sentient fetus stands in the same relationship to his future self as an already-born person (or other sentient being) stands in relationship to her future self. Meanwhile, the abortion of a presentient fetus Fps does not harm Fps even though it prevents Fps from becoming the sentient person that he would otherwise become because Fps is not the sort of entity that is capable of having interests and thus not the sort of entity that is capable of being harmed. In short, current sentience is a necessary condition for having an interest in continued sentience.

But is it really? What about killing a person in a coma from which she is likely to recover? Assuming we sufficiently overcome the Epicurean objection to be able to say that the sudden, instantaneous, and painless killing of a conscious person harms that person by shortening his life, do we not also want to say that killing an unconscious person harms that person by shortening her life? To be sure, people in comas sometimes remember what transpired around them once they "wake up," suggesting that they were never fully unconscious, so we might be tempted to say that the person in the coma is sentient even during the coma.[21] But we can choose a different example.

In 1999 Swedish radiologist Anna Bågenholm fell into icy water while skiing in Norway. When rescuers found Bågenholm fully submerged in the icy water over an hour later, her blood had stopped circulating and she was, by all appearances, dead. Her brain and all of her organ systems were frozen. Nonetheless, by administering CPR and then slowly thawing Bågenholm, a team of over one hundred doctors working for nine hours brought her back to life. Eventually she made a nearly complete recovery.[22] Her story, while unusual, is hardly unique. Cases like hers form the basis both for promising new medical treatments for patients who appear to be dead and for (essentially religious) claims about life after death.[23]

Let us put aside the medical and religious implications of Bågenholm's story. What does it tell us about the relationship between sentience and interests? To answer that question we will treat her case as a kind of thought experiment in which the actual facts are less important than the moral intuitions they provoke. We thus assume that Bågenholm was not sentient—that is, that she was *completely* unconscious—for some period of time while she was frozen. Would failure to revive her have caused her no harm? If so, the reason would have to be because, after Bågenholm froze but before she was unfrozen, "she" did not exist. She was then something, not someone, and things lack interests.

We cannot speak for all readers, but our own fairly strong intuition is the opposite: We think that Bågenholm continued to have interests even while she was frozen. Put differently: during that period, she was an unconscious someone but still someone. In what way, however, was she different from a presentient fetus? The only possible answer is that, although Bågenholm was not sentient while frozen, she *had been* sentient, and she retained the capacity to become sentient again under the right conditions. So if a frozen or comatose nonsentient person has an interest in being revived but a presentient fetus does not, it must be because past-but-revivable sentience makes someone a *someone* with an interest in continued existence, but a (non)being that has not ever been sentient is still only something, even if it could develop into someone in a relatively short time in a properly supportive environment.

Does *that* description jibe with our moral (and other) intuitions? We confess to some genuine confusion because we lack experience with revivable frozen people, so we are not sure we can trust our reactions to a case like Bågenholm's. Asking whether presentient fetuses have interests by interrogating our intuitions about frozen-but-revivable people is a bit like asking the questions Judith Jarvis Thomson posed about violinists and "people-seeds," discussed in the preceding chapter: It feels like an analogy going in the wrong direction, attempting to shed light on a subject about which we have some grounding for our moral intuitions by imagining bizarre circumstances about which we lack clear moral intuitions.

Nevertheless, to the extent that we do have intuitions that may be shared by readers, we think they warrant interrogation. Our intuitions are as stated earlier: a presentient fetus lacks interests while a frozen-but-revivable skier has interests; thus, it does not harm the presentient fetus to abort it but it does harm the skier to thaw her in such a way that she can no longer be revived. It also harms the skier to leave her frozen for sufficiently long that she can no longer be revived, but that harm may not be attributable to any actor if it results from an omission rather than an act. As discussed in chapter 1, the act/omission distinction is vitally important to many moral questions, and we shall return to it momentarily. For now, however, we want to ask only whether it is possible to reconcile our intuitions that presentient fetuses lack interests while frozen-but-revivable skiers have interests.

THE ENDOWMENT EFFECT

These intuitions appear to track a well-known psychological phenomenon called the "endowment effect," which is closely related to "loss aversion." The basic idea—for which there is a substantial body of empirical support—is that people value things that they already have more highly than things that they do not yet have.[24] You will be more upset if you lose $100 than if you fail to acquire $100.

Part of the endowment effect might be attributable to the decreasing marginal utility of wealth. If you have only $100, then losing $100 wipes you out, whereas if you have $100 but fail to gain another $100, then you still have half of what you might otherwise have had. But the experiments showing an endowment effect cannot be explained simply as a consequence of the decreasing marginal utility of money. For example, one leading study gave people either mugs or candy bars and then asked them whether they wanted to trade the one they had for the other; regardless of whether they were originally given (i.e., endowed with) a mug or a candy bar, subjects were unlikely to want to trade.[25]

Does the endowment effect successfully reconcile our respective intuitions about presentient fetuses and frozen skiers? In other words, can the fact that the presentient fetus has not yet had (i.e., been endowed with) subjective experiences while the frozen skier has had such experiences account for the line we draw between them? One objection concerns the size of the effect. Some recent research casts doubt on the very existence of an endowment effect, but even if one accepts the body of work showing the effect to be real, it remains only a relative phenomenon.[26] People may value what they already have more highly than what they hope to acquire, but they still place *some* value on what they hope to acquire. If it hurts more to lose $100 than to fail to gain $100, failing to gain the $100 is still worse than actually gaining the $100. Likewise, if—in the logic of the endowment effect—it is worse to die than never to be born, that does not mean that never being born is harmless.

But who, exactly, is harmed by never being born? It is one thing to say that a gambler who loses $100 feels worse than a gambler who, having temporarily won $100, then loses that $100 but does not feel so bad because it was only "house money" and therefore conceptualized by the gambler as money not gained rather than as money lost. The gambler exists as a being with interests in each case, so we can compare his frame of mind in the various scenarios. However, the "person" who is never born has no well-being of which to speak; he is not in a state of "zero" well-being or some such—he is not in any state at all.[27] It makes no sense to talk about whether a nonexistent-but-potential person would be better off existing, unless one has already assumed the conclusion that the nonexistent-but-potential person is already a being with interests.

Suppose you accept that the endowment effect explains your intuitive sense that the skier but not the presentient fetus has a stake in future life. Even so, we need to do more if we are to maintain that taking away is also *morally* worse than not giving. The endowment effect is a psychological phenomenon, a *fact* about how people experience the world. In seeking to reconcile our intuitions, however, we are not seeking a psychological explanation; we are seeking a *normatively* attractive principle. Although some pragmatist philosophers and postmodernists deny it, we basically side with Hume and the rationalist tradition in thinking that one cannot derive a normative proposition from a descriptive one, an *ought* from an *is*.[28] And so, by itself, the endowment effect cannot tell us that we are justified in thinking that frozen-but-revivable skiers have interests but presentient fetuses do not.

And yet the endowment effect does feel normatively relevant, not just psychologically relevant. In distinguishing between "taking away" and "not giving," the endowment effect parallels a vitally important feature of deontological morality that we discussed at length in chapter 1: the act/omission distinction. After all, we are not concerned simply about whether one is better or worse off losing or not gaining various items. Our concern is ultimately about how moral agents must *act* upon others. And for that purpose the endowment effect—or rather, its moral analogue, the act/omission distinction—is often an all-or-nothing matter.

Absent some compelling justification, it is wrong for A to steal $100 from B but blameless for A to choose not to bestow a gift of $100 on B. Indeed, that absolute distinction remains in place even if the valuations change dramatically so that B would value the gift more than he values avoiding the loss: A wrongs B by stealing $1 from B while A acts blamelessly by choosing not to bestow $1 million on B. In the moral domain, taking away is a presumptively forbidden act, whereas not giving is an innocent omission.

Does the act/omission distinction enable us to explain our conflicting intuitions about a presentient fetus and a frozen-but-revivable hiker? Not exactly. As we discussed in chapter 3, abortion is in some respects an act, not merely an omission. Conversely, potential rescuers who come across a frozen skier but do not take steps to revive her have merely failed to take supererogatory actions; that is, they have engaged in an omission. Thus, one might even invoke the act/omission distinction to say that our moral intuitions about the two cases are backward.

However, we would use the act/omission distinction somewhat differently. A presentient fetus has never been a someone; thus, for a woman to gestate the presentient fetus past the point of sentience and then give birth to the resulting infant is, in an important sense, to bestow a gift. It is an odd sort of gift, to be sure—in that the giving of the gift of life simultaneously creates the recipient of that gift. Nonetheless, there remains a palpable sense in which abortion of a presentient fetus is simply a failure to bestow life rather than a taking away of life.

Meanwhile, when the frozen skier remains frozen past the point of revivability or thaws in a way that is inconsistent with her revival, we have a corresponding sense that the skier's life has been lost. Whether the frozen skier's death results from an act (such as incompetent rescue) or an omission (such as indifference by passersby), the skier has lost something rather than having merely failed to gain life.

In short, the principle that we have invoked to explain our pair of intuitions about the presentient fetus and the frozen-but-revivable skier is a kind of moralized version of the endowment effect. It is not exactly the endowment effect, which is a psychological phenomenon rather than a moral proposition. Nor is it exactly the conventional act/omission distinction that gives moral content to the otherwise merely psychological phenomenon of the endowment effect. Nonetheless, the resulting psychological/moral hybrid that distinguishes between losses and nongains does appear to do the work necessary to make sense of the pair of intuitions.

Accordingly, and to return—finally—to the problem with which we began, we can resist the Epicurean claim that death itself harms no one without having to sacrifice the view that it does no harm to presentient fetuses to fail to bring them into existence.

CODA 1: EUTHANASIA

Before concluding this chapter, we need to address two loose ends: euthanasia and laws banning abortion of pain-capable fetuses. In addressing the Epicurean claim that death does not constitute a harm to the one who dies, we made three sorts of arguments: First, we pointed to harms often associated with death, such as suffering for those left behind and the pain associated with the killing or dying process, especially when animals are killed for food; second, we suggested that death is harmful to sentient beings because they persist over time, so killing them deprives them of their future lives; and third, we explained that, to the extent that Epicurus was right, he was equally right about humans and nonhumans. Indeed, Epicurus made his point specifically about humans, and yet no one seriously argues on Epicurean grounds that murder of humans is harmless. Certainly Epicurus himself never said any such thing.

Might attitudes about voluntary euthanasia nonetheless demonstrate that people hold views that credit the Epicurean idea of death for animals but not for humans? Consider the fact that our society generally treats a human's decision to euthanize a very sick companion animal as a laudable act of mercy while most jurisdictions in the United States criminalize physician-assisted suicide. Does this pair of attitudes suggest that, as a society, we think that animals have an interest in avoiding suffering but not in continued living, whereas humans have an interest in continued life?

The short answer is no. For one thing, physician-assisted suicide is legal in four American states: Montana, Oregon, Vermont, and Washington.[29] Moreover, public opinion polls show that there is substantial, if not quite national majority, support for the practice.[30] At the very least, there is no universal consensus that physician-assisted suicide is wrong. More directly to the current point, even though proponents of legal physician-assisted suicide frequently do argue that the same mercy we extend to our companion animals should be extended to humans seeking death in similarly trying circumstances, opposition to the practice does not rest on the species-selective Epicurean claim that death harms humans but not animals. When opponents of physician-assisted suicide attempt to distinguish humans from companion and other animals, they typically rely on other grounds.

What are those grounds? Much of the opposition to physician-assisted suicide can be traced to the religious view that God alone may decide when a person's time on this mortal coil has ended. In this view physician-assisted suicide is sinful for the same reason that any suicide is sinful: It arrogates to people a decision that is not theirs to make. And because, in this view, only humans have immortal souls, they alone commit a sin in hastening their own deaths.

We are not now interested in the theological merits of the religious arguments against physician-assisted suicide, or even in whether those arguments properly bear on the collective decision to forbid physician-assisted suicide by law. Instead we would simply note that the religious argument does not rest on specifically anti-Epicurean grounds. Persons who have religious grounds to think that they may euthanize a suffering animal with advanced

cancer but that they may not end their own lives in similar circumstances most certainly do not hold these views because they
think that people have continuing lives that belong to them while
other animals live only in the moment, so that death harms people
but not other animals. Quite the contrary, they believe that the
soul, and thus the life, of a human being belongs to God, not that
human being.[31] Religious opposition to voluntary euthanasia thus
does not rest on anything like the view that a human owns his own
life but an animal does not have a continuing life.

To be sure, there are other, secular grounds upon which some people oppose physician-assisted suicide and euthanasia more broadly.
Some people worry that if physician-assisted suicide is legal, doctors, relatives, and others will exert subtle or not-so-subtle pressure on patients to end their lives. A *right* to die will thus become
a de facto *duty* to die, on this view.[32] Moreover, these opponents
of physician-assisted suicide do not raise the same alarms about
euthanasia for pets—even though pet owners make the judgment
about whether to end a pet's life for the pet, and often do so under
the very pressures (including financial pressure) that people worry
about with respect to voluntary euthanasia for humans. Does that
juxtaposition of concerns reflect the view that Epicurus was right
about nonhuman animals but wrong about humans?

That supposition seems far-fetched. We think it is much more
likely that people who oppose physician-assisted suicide for
humans but do not oppose euthanasia for pets thereby display
the general tendency of humans to place much greater value on
humans' lives and well-being than on the lives and well-being of
nonhumans. What would opponents of physician-assisted suicide
say in response to the question of why they (or most, or at least
some of them) nonetheless countenance euthanasia for ailing pets,
notwithstanding the likely greater risk that pet owners make their
euthanasia decisions on the basis of financial and other considerations rather than just their pets' best interest? We have not conducted the relevant public opinion research, but we strongly suspect they would say something like the following:

Euthanasia for an ailing companion animal is generally a
mercy in exactly the same way that voluntary euthanasia

for an ailing human can be a mercy. In the circumstance in which cost is the decisive factor motivating someone to opt for euthanasia rather than expensive surgery for a companion animal, that results in a harm to the animal, just as it is a harm to a human to pressure her to end her life prematurely, but because human life is more valuable than nonhuman life, the risk of pressure cannot be tolerated for humans, even though it is tolerable for other animals.

We reject the categorical assumption that human life is of greater value than animal life, but we certainly recognize the fact that many people make that categorical assumption. Our point here is that this broad view that humans are superior to animals—rather than the view that Epicureanism is correct for animals but not humans—underwrites the inconsistency in attitudes toward humans and animals held by secular opponents of physician-assisted suicide.

CODA 2: FETAL PAIN

If attitudes toward physician-assisted suicide and euthanasia for pets end up shedding no real light on views about the Epicurean claim, attitudes toward fetal pain turn out to be more relevant—and in a way that provides surprisingly strong support for our overall argument.

As we noted in the introduction, a number of states have enacted statutes forbidding the abortion of fetuses capable of experiencing pain. These laws forbid abortions after twenty weeks of pregnancy based on an explicit legislative determination that from this point forward a fetus can experience pain.[33] Although we explained in the introduction that the most passionate members of the pro-life movement do not regard sentience as a crucial marker in fetal development, we nonetheless think that these laws say something very significant about what the broader public thinks. They reflect a view that fetal sentience marks a critical boundary in pregnancy.

To be sure, we disagree with the policy judgment that underlies laws banning abortion of pain-capable fetuses. As we explained in prior chapters, we believe that abortion of a pain-capable (i.e., sentient) fetus harms that fetus, and that, therefore, a pregnant woman generally ought not to choose to abort a sentient fetus absent some very good justification; however, the *law* need not and should not command people to satisfy all of their moral obligations, especially not when doing so places duties of affirmative assistance uniquely on pregnant women. Thus, there are abortions of sentient fetuses that we would regard as immoral but that we would nonetheless wish to see remain legally permissible.

Nonetheless, we regard the enactment of laws banning abortions of pain-capable fetuses as highly significant for two reasons. First, it shows the salience of the sentience line in the eyes of the public. And second, it aligns sentience with interests generally. The relevant laws typically say that once a fetus is capable of experiencing pain, the fetus is entitled not only to be protected against pain—in the way that a law requiring the use of anesthesia for abortion of pain-capable fetuses would—but that the pain-capable fetus is entitled to live.[34]

In short, laws banning abortion of pain-capable fetuses rest on the very proposition that we have invoked against the Epicurean claim: Sentience—the ability to have subjective experiences—grounds an interest in continued existence; it does more than merely ground an interest in avoiding suffering.

PART II

MOVEMENTS

Thus far, our discussion of abortion and animal rights has focused on arguments. We asked questions about the moral obligations people have to unborn humans and to born nonhuman animals, and about the extent to which those obligations should be given the force of law.

Arguments can play a crucial role in bringing about social and political change. For example, the growing support among Americans for legal recognition of same-sex marriages over the last decade resulted in substantial part from the evaluation of arguments. Prominent court cases, state referenda, and legislative battles put the question of same-sex marriage on the public agenda and, at that point, many people came to understand the weakness of the reasons for forbidding gay and lesbian couples from marrying. People who formerly opposed same-sex marriage scrutinized the contention that it would somehow undermine traditional opposite-sex marriage, and they found that there was nothing to the claim.

But it would be a mistake to conclude that arguments alone shifted attitudes. The campaign for same-sex marriage and the broader struggle against homophobia succeeded (to the extent that they have) because of interactions between movement activists and ordinary citizens. Thousands of lesbian, gay, bisexual, transgender, and questioning individuals and couples "came out," thus putting sympathetic, familiar faces on the movement. Meanwhile, strategically minded activists (on both sides of the issue) chose battles that they thought they could win or battles that, even if lost, would serve the larger cause. One can make similar observations about movements to secure the rights of racial minorities, women, the disabled, and others.

In short, arguments matter, but they only operate in a context—what political scientist Sidney Tarrow and the late sociologist Charles Tilly aptly labeled the "political opportunity structure."[1] For an argument to succeed in changing hearts and minds, movement activists must successfully appeal to the broader public in light of the possibilities open to them. There is a critical place in any movement for arguments, but there is an equally critical place for considerations of strategy and tactics.

The three chapters in this part of the book consider common strategic and tactical questions faced by the pro-life and pro-animal movements. Chapter 5 looks at broad strategic issues. It explores efforts by pro-life and pro-animal activists to secure reforms that not only fall short of the movements' respective long-range goals but that are in some fundamental sense inconsistent with those goals. For example, the pro-life campaign against "partial-birth" abortion could be taken to imply that the named method of abortion is somehow worse than other methods of abortion, and that therefore other abortions are morally preferable or even acceptable. Likewise, animal welfare campaigns for larger cages for egg-laying hens or for bans on gestation crates for sows could be taken to imply that there is nothing wrong with consuming eggs or pork produced using the allegedly more "humane" methods.

Chapters 6 and 7 address tactical questions. In chapter 6 we consider the use of images by both movements. Do displays of mangled aborted fetuses and suffering animals at feedlots, auctions, and slaughterhouses yield converts? Or do they simply evoke a temporary disgust response? And are there hidden costs to such displays?

Chapter 7 discusses violence. The pro-life and pro-animal movements each have violent wings. We unequivocally reject violence both on principle and because we think it is often likely to be counterproductive—especially for justice movements.[2] Nonetheless, understanding the reasons why some people in each movement turn to violence sheds light on the nature of the movements.

Just as we foreswore any effort to provide a comprehensive account of the arguments for and against animal rights and fetal rights in the first part of this book, so the chapters in this second part do not aim to provide anything like a full history of the animal rights and pro-life movements or their respective countermovements. Instead, by looking at some of the similar strategic and tactical choices faced by pro-life and pro-animal activists, we uncover important tensions within each of the movements. In the end, we conclude that strategic and tactical questions cannot be cleanly separated from questions of principle.

5

Strategy

Activists in many areas frequently face a strategic choice: Should they seek ameliorative reforms that fall short of their ultimate goal or should they "go for broke" by adopting an "all-or-nothing" position? The question has at least two dimensions, one principled and the other pragmatic. The question of principle is whether support for ameliorative reform measures will implicate the activists in the very practices they aim to eradicate. The pragmatic question is whether reforms that fall significantly short of the movement's ultimate aims will be counterproductive because they will signal to the public that, as reformed but not eradicated, the challenged practices are acceptable, or whether they will nonetheless move society closer to those ultimate aims.

The questions of principle and practicality may intertwine. Consider a famous, albeit almost certainly apocryphal, example. The Russian revolutionary communist Leon Trotsky supposedly never tipped waiters because he feared that doing so would ease their plight just enough to delay or wholly prevent the revolution of the working class. If this story is true, Trotsky may have been right. German chancellor Otto von Bismarck's policy of deliberate co-optation of some of the left's policy agenda played a key role in sapping the strength of more radical movements.[1] American president Franklin Delano Roosevelt's New Deal reforms had the same effect, which is why some people say that Roosevelt "saved capitalism from itself" by reforming it just enough to stave off true revolution.[2]

Should Bismarck and Roosevelt therefore be celebrated as heroes or condemned as villains? Should Trotsky's alleged ill-treatment of particular waiters be celebrated as revolutionary discipline or reviled as callous calculation? We do not think it is possible to answer such questions without engaging the facts and values in play. Today we know that every large-scale attempt to implement communism failed, bringing death and misery to millions of people. Accordingly, it is easy to condemn the Trotskyite approach both as callous to individuals and as serving a terribly misguided long-term goal. But in Bismarck's time (although perhaps not as late as in Roosevelt's time) it was possible for a person of good faith to believe that the projected benefits of a communist revolution outweighed the costs of temporarily making some people worse off. We and our readers likely find it easy to condemn Trotsky's the-worse-the-better approach, but we might not be so quick to condemn a similar attitude in different circumstances.

Consider the case of Christian slavery in the antebellum United States. People may associate the phrase "Christian slavery" with the efforts of white southerners to justify slavery using Biblical passages—for example, by reference to the "curse of Ham."[3] However, alongside Christian apologists for slavery there existed before and even during the Civil War a smaller but apparently sincere group of Christian clergy who sought to reform slavery to make it more humane.[4] Were abolitionists wrong to distance themselves from the efforts of the advocates of Christian slavery on principled grounds? If one could somehow show that the Christian slavery movement served as a kind of gateway to abolition, would that mean that abolitionists ought to have cooperated with the Christian slavery movement in order to chip away at slavery's foundation? And even if it is possible to make such a judgment after the fact, could one ever confidently predict the aggregate impact of ameliorative reforms in advance? Will they set the stage for, or will they instead preempt, more substantial revolution?

In looking at just these two sets of examples, we see a complicated mix of empirical and normative issues. Will the pursuit of radical change end up simply making modest ameliorative reform look more palatable by contrast—what sociologist Herbert Haynes dubbed the "radical flank effect"?[5] Conversely, what will efforts to achieve piecemeal reform do to efforts for more far-reaching change? Will they pave the way for such change? Delay it? For how long? By how much? Are the piecemeal reforms worth pursuing in any event? How much better, if better at all, would the postrevolutionary world be than the modestly reformed world? And so on. The questions of principle and of strategy governing the choice between reform and revolution cannot be addressed in the abstract.

That said, we do think that we can gain meaningful insights by comparing movements because all movements face the potential tradeoff between principle and pragmatism, between short-term and long-term goals, and between reform and revolution. Moreover, comparisons of movement strategies can elucidate movement goals because the mix of strategies adopted by any particular movement may say as much about that movement's ultimate aims as it does about the means for achieving those aims. In turning our attention to how the animal rights and pro-life movements have approached the question of reform versus revolution, we hope to shed further light on the nature of each movement.

WHAT IS EACH MOVEMENT?

In assessing the strategic choices of a movement, we need some account of what the movement is. But how do we know who counts as part of a movement or what the movement's position is? Someone who supports (or opposes) the movement for animal rights, abortion rights, fetal rights, gay rights, environmental justice, an individual right to bear arms, or any of countless other causes might donate money to one or more official groups, but she might not. She might attend rallies frequently, occasionally, or not at all. She might attach bumper stickers to her car, write letters to her representative in Congress, or repost articles on Facebook and Twitter—or she might not. She will likely agree with other people who self-identify as supporting or opposing the particular cause on most issues but disagree with some of those people on other issues. Although particular organizations associated with a movement typically formulate official policy positions, movements as such do not issue policy statements or membership cards. A movement is a collection of organizations and somewhat likeminded individuals acting somewhat in concert. Its boundaries can be vague and fluid. Accordingly, any statement about the ends that a movement seeks or the means that it uses to pursue those ends necessarily oversimplifies. Movements, by their very nature, are diverse and dynamic.

Nonetheless, we can often make sufficiently general statements about particular movements to allow us to identify the movement, at least in relation to its chief antagonists, for a specific period. For example, in the United States in the last two and a half decades, political activists seeking broader legal recognition for same-sex marriage could be readily understood as part of the lesbian, gay, bisexual, transgender, and questioning (LGBTQ) rights movement—even though there were also some people in that same movement who opposed devoting resources to fighting for expansion of an institution (marriage) that they regarded as fundamentally repressive (or at least "heteronormative").[6] That point of disagreement occurred *within* the broader LGBTQ rights movement. By contrast, socially conservative political activists who campaigned to retain marriage as a strictly opposite-sex institution on the ground that they considered homosexuality to be immoral could not fairly have been regarded as part of the LGBTQ rights movement in any way.

Likewise, with respect to animal rights and abortion, we can distinguish debates *within* each movement from public debates between each movement and its adversaries. But with respect to both the animal rights movement and the pro-life movement, the task is complicated by the fact that many people who are best understood as standing outside of the movement hold views that are in some respects sympathetic to the movement's goals. At the risk of providing merely stipulative definitions, we would distinguish each movement from its sometimes-fellow travelers in order to bring analytical clarity to our coming discussion of the strategic choice between reform and revolution.

We begin with the animal rights movement. Many people who say (and no doubt believe) that they "love" animals or that they wish to act "humanely" toward animals also regularly consume—and may not see anything fundamentally wrong with consuming—products made through the suffering and death of animals. They may frequently buy "cage free eggs," "free-range beef," and other animal products that suggest that the animals who gave rise to these products led good lives. Such people also may support laws restricting what are regarded as some of the worst practices within animal agriculture—such as California's Proposition 2, a 2008 ballot initiative that, beginning in 2015, set minimum cage space requirements for veal calves, egg-laying hens, and gestating sows in California. While 63 percent of California voters supported Proposition 2, it would be inaccurate to classify any but a small fraction of them as part of the animal rights movement. If these people should count as part of a movement involving animals at all, it would be the animal *welfare* movement rather than the animal *rights* movement.

"Pure" animal welfarists believe that human beings should try to reduce the suffering of the animals we use but that there is nothing morally objectionable in itself about using animals for our own ends. The best-known American organizations aiming to prevent or remedy gratuitous cruelty to animals—such as the American Society for the Prevention of Cruelty to Animals (ASPCA) and the Humane Society of the United States (HSUS)—are welfarist. They focus much of their attention on protecting companion animals (mostly dogs and cats) while addressing what they regard as abuses within industries that use animals as sources of food and fiber. By contrast with animal rights activists and organizations, welfarists do not necessarily see animal agriculture or animal exploitation more generally as inherently problematic.

Should someone who cares about the plight of animals donate money to or otherwise work with welfarist organizations like the ASPCA or the HSUS? If he shares the welfarist orientation—that is, if his ultimate goal is a world of somewhat reformed animal exploitation—then yes, doing so would be perfectly logical. But suppose instead that you agree with us that nearly all animal use is unjustified. Suppose, in other words, that you take what Gary Francione has dubbed the "abolitionist" approach.[7] In your own life, you avoid purchasing animal products and, as an activist, your aim is a vegan world. Should you nonetheless partner with, work for, or otherwise support welfarist organizations or welfarist campaigns like California's Proposition 2 as a means of gradually working toward abolition and ameliorating suffering in the meantime? Or should you distance yourself from welfarist organizations and campaigns? We consider this issue momentarily, but first we draw a similar distinction with respect to the pro-life movement.

Many Americans are ambivalent about abortion. They regard early abortions as morally permissible, or at least as less morally problematic than late abortions. They think that some reasons for abortion are better than others. They may sympathize with a woman who chooses to terminate a pregnancy resulting from rape or a woman who aborts a fetus who would otherwise grow into a child who would have a severe disability, but they have less sympathy for a woman who chooses abortion because of economic constraints on her ability to raise a child. They may also think that a minor lacks sufficiently developed judgment to make a decision to have an abortion without first consulting with her parents.

People who hold mixed views about abortion are roughly analogous to animal welfarists. Such "abortion welfarists" may support laws banning abortion on "pain-capable" fetuses and "partial-birth" abortion, laws imposing waiting periods on women seeking abortion, and laws requiring that minors consult with one or both parents before having an abortion. We put the term "abortion welfarists" in quotation marks because we recognize that some half measures regarding abortion are designed not to promote the welfare of particular fetuses slated for abortion but to forbid some, but not all, abortions. People who support such abortion restrictions may be analogized to supporters of the Nonhuman Rights Project, an organization that litigates to end the exploitation of some sentient animals—such as great apes, dolphins, and orcas— but not others—such as pigs, cows, and chickens.[8] Nonetheless, for ease of comparison, we will refer to supporters of pro-life half measures as abortion welfarists. Such persons support measures falling short of abortion bans because they think that abortion should be regulated so that women have abortions only under the right circumstances; their support does not necessarily reflect opposition to all abortion.

Now suppose that you are staunchly pro-life in the following sense: You believe that human life begins at conception, that all or nearly all abortions (including via contraceptives that work as abortifacients) are immoral, and that the law ought to forbid all abortion (except perhaps those truly necessary to save a pregnant woman's life). Should you nonetheless cooperate with or promote abortion "welfarist" campaigns to regulate or restrict some but not all abortions on the ground that these campaigns will bring our society closer to the day when we ban all abortions and that, in the meantime, they may prevent some abortions? Or should you distance yourself from such campaigns?

The questions we have raised with respect to the relation between long-term goals and short-term tactics for the animal rights and pro-life movements clearly parallel each other. However, the answers may differ. Accordingly, we must consider not only the general dimensions of the reform-versus-revolution question but also how the relevant considerations operate in their respective contexts.

THE ACTIVIST'S DILEMMA

People who hold strong views are more likely to be activists than people who support a cause more weakly. But weak supporters broaden the base of an organization and may provide crucial financial support. Consequently, one finds that the people who actually work for merely reform-oriented organizations may themselves be committed to more far-reaching change than the organizations formally espouse.

The foregoing dynamic (which sociologist James Jasper calls the "extension dilemma")[9] affects how outsiders perceive reformist organizations. People working for or otherwise supporting the animal agriculture industry may suspect that abolitionists are using the welfarist organizations as a Trojan horse—as when Humane-

Watch, an industry-backed entity, collects abolitionist quotations from current HSUS president Wayne Pacelle and others from their prewelfarist days.[10] In doing so, the self-styled watchdogs aim to expose the supposed hidden abolitionist agenda of officially welfarist officials and organizations.

Meanwhile, some abolitionists worry about the opposite problem. They might be pleased to discover that welfarist officials and organizations were secretly implementing a plan to achieve abolition, but they see little evidence of that. These abolitionists say that the need to raise money from the general public and the constant imperative to achieve what look like legislative victories ensure that abolitionists who go to work for welfarist campaigns eventually become co-opted by the organizations and their imperatives.[11] Moreover, the welfarist organizations themselves become co-opted by the animal-using industries that they seek to reform but not abolish as they end up cooperating with those industries.[12] In this view, Pacelle changed his tune when he went to work for HSUS because his views actually changed when he became answerable to a welfarist constituency; he did not simply alter his rhetoric to deceive the public.

We think it is unfruitful to speculate about whether abolitionists who work within welfarist organizations co-opt the organizations, vice versa, or something in between. Instead we are interested in looking at the issue from the perspective of a good-faith activist. Suppose an animal rights activist wants to further the cause. He could try to start his own abolitionist organization or join an existing one, or he could make a career in some other field and devote his spare time to promoting abolitionism. But what if he wants to work full-time on behalf of animals? The largest pro-animal organizations are welfarist in their orientation, and even the major organizations that may promote veganism to some degree—like Vegan Outreach, Mercy for Animals, and People for the Ethical Treatment of Animals (PETA)—also devote much of their energy and resources to sponsoring and participating in welfarist campaigns. Should our hypothetical abolitionist accept a job working for a welfarist organization?

A debate between two prominent animal rights activists at the 2013 Animal Rights Conference in Washington, D.C., nicely captured the competing considerations.[13] Both Bruce Friedrich and Gary Francione are vegans who oppose virtually all use of animals as resources for humans. Friedrich is currently the senior director for strategic initiatives at Farm Sanctuary, and he formerly held a senior position at PETA. Francione is a law professor at Rutgers University, an author of many books and articles on animal rights, and an activist. During their debate (and in other venues), each did an excellent job of explaining his respective position.

Friedrich's argument has two central pieces. First, he contends that the best should not be the enemy of the good. Thus, even as he acknowledges that laying hens raised under the conditions mandated by Proposition 2 in California will still suffer terribly, he argues that it is better for those particular hens to be treated a little bit better than for them to be subject to the even greater suffering that they would endure without the mandated reform.

Second, Friedrich argues that piecemeal welfarist reforms serve a consciousness-raising function. People who find themselves supporting better conditions for hens or for gestating pigs will come to see themselves as concerned about the well-being of animals, and some of them will then take further steps that will lead them eventually to understand that if they really do care about the well-being of animals, they should not be consuming animal products at all. Friedrich and others cite studies that, they say, show that welfarist campaigns lead to reduced consumption of animal products, and they point more generally to other justice movements that achieved their aims gradually.[14]

Francione agrees that less suffering is better than more suffering, but he challenges Friedrich's contention that welfare campaigns in fact lead to less suffering. For one thing, Francione contends that the sorts of reforms that are enacted are so minimal that abolitionists cannot in good conscience support them at all. Second, he argues that supporting an "improved" form of animal exploitation practice necessarily implicates the supporter in the violence perpetrated by the animal exploitation industry. Francione offers a provocative analogy that suggests that animal rights advocacy for larger cages for farmed animals is like Amnesty International campaigning for padded waterboards. Yes, Francione says, if you are going to be tortured, you might be slightly less tortured if you are strapped to a padded waterboard than if you are strapped to a bare wooden one, but organizations that oppose torture would not and should not dilute their message by cooperating with torturers or by praising torturers who have implemented slightly less torturous methods of torture. Yet animal welfare campaigns do the equivalent, he says, when they praise firms like Whole Foods or KFC for sourcing their animal products from suppliers who (perhaps) treat their animals slightly less horrifically than some of their competitors treat their animals.[15]

Francione also contests Friedrich's claim that welfarism leads to abolition. Francione explains that welfarism is not a new movement. Anticruelty societies already existed in the first half of the nineteenth century; yet, despite welfarist efforts, global demand for animal products has steadily increased. And predictably so, Francione argues: welfarist measures assure the public that abusive animal practices are aberrant rather than inherent in animal exploitation.[16] To similar effect, Sandra Higgins, the director of Eden Farm Animal Sanctuary in Ireland, cites evidence that Irish egg consumption *increased* after the European Union banned "barren" battery cages in favor of "enriched" cages, contending that, as a result of the false assurance implied by that measure, "the conscience of the public has been assuaged by the notion that the hens who lay the . . . eggs are living in enriched, furnished luxury."[17]

Who is right? The question is partly normative: Is support for measures like cage-size regulation a sell-out that reaffirms the status of animals as property? Francione is not alone in answering yes. For example, communications scholar Carrie Freeman criticizes the most common animal welfare and animal rights campaigns for their emphasis on particularly cruel practices; she proposes instead that activists should make the more straightforward and authentic argument that animals simply should not be used as commodities.[18]

But the question is also strongly empirical. Setting aside questions of principle, which strategy (vegan education alone, as Francione, Freeman, and other abolitionists advocate; or vegan education combined with support for welfarist measures) is more likely to lead to a reduction in, and ultimately the abolition of, the use of animals as resources for humans?

We return to the empirical question later in this chapter, but to summarize our analysis, we do not think that Friedrich, Francione, or anyone else has marshaled sufficient data from which one could definitively conclude that one or the other strategy is clearly superior as a factual matter. Nonetheless, we do think that we can gain some useful insights by comparing the position of animal rights activists relative to animal welfare campaigns to the position of antiabortion activists relative to abortion welfarism.

PHILOSOPHICAL CONTRADICTIONS

Just as mainstream animal protection organizations like HSUS, PETA, and Mercy for Animals regularly promote welfarist measures, so too the leading pro-life organizations regularly promote legislation that prohibits some abortions or that limits some people (such as minors) from, or some reasons (such as sex-selection) for, terminating a pregnancy.[19] From the perspective of their impact on the general public, such laws could be expected to have one of two competing effects. They might focus any existing public discomfort about abortion on particular prohibited or limited practices and thereby relieve people of any qualms about the remaining, permissible abortions. Alternatively, abortion welfarist laws might acclimate people to abortion limitations and to the notion that abortion is a harm that ought to be curtailed, thus paving the way for acceptance of more and broader abortion restrictions. In other words, just as Friedrich argues that animal welfarist regulations can trigger cognitive dissonance and what he calls the "consistency principle," leading people to see consumption of all animal products as wrong, likewise laws limiting some abortions might generally accustom people to laws that limit abortion and thereby ultimately allow for outright prohibitions in the future.[20]

Regardless of their strategic efficacy, however, abortion measures that prohibit some abortions based on fetal development clash fundamentally with what we have identified as the pro-life movement's core commitments. While the pro-life community identifies conception as the moment at which a person with the right to live has come into existence, bans on late-term abortions have as their premise the notion that later terminations are worse than earlier ones because later-term fetuses have more rights and a higher moral status than embryos—by virtue of their developmental stage.

This conclusion seems most consistent with the view that abortion on the whole is something less serious than the killing of a person who has already developed sufficiently to be delivered. After all, if late abortion is worse than early abortion, then killing a baby may be worse than killing a fetus. Yet the pro-life movement rejects this approach and holds that a preference for early abortions over late abortions is no more principled than a preference for killing a two-year-old rather than a four-year-old child. Once a person has come into being, he or she may not be ranked as more or less worthy of life by virtue of her age or the extent of her development. Laws such as the federal Partial Birth Abortion Ban Act (PBABA) that we discussed in chapter 1 and other prohibitions and regulations that turn on—or emphasize—developmental stage endorse a view of the developing embryo and fetus inimical to the pro-life movement's core commitment.[21] The PBABA treats *birth*, rather than conception, as the significant demarcation line, while laws banning abortions of pain-capable fetuses treat the ability to endure pain as the relevant line.

Likewise, at a philosophical level, Francione and Freeman appear to be right that animal welfare laws contradict the animal rights movement's core commitments. That does not necessarily mean that Friedrich is wrong when he says that the movement should support such laws strategically. We are speaking now only about whether the logic of welfarist measures is consistent with the philosophy of animal rights that Friedrich shares with Francione, Freeman, and us. At that level, there is a strong parallel with the abortion welfarist measures. Such measures implicitly rank objectionable practices (that all involve inflicting captivity, suffering, and premature death on animals) differently based on what the movement considers morally irrelevant facts.

For example, one premise of welfarist animal cruelty laws is that an animal's entitlement to be free of human-inflicted torture and death turns on the particular uses to which that animal is put. The law tolerates more violence when the human purpose for keeping the animal is for slaughter and consumption, such as in the case of a pig, a cow, a chicken, or a turkey, than when the human purpose for keeping the animal is companionship or recreation, such as in the case of a cat, a dog, or a horse.[22] In the case of "food" animals exploited for their flesh and hormonal secretions, permissible regulations tend not to disrupt the business of hurting and killing the animals for profit. Thus, the slaughter of horses is prohibited in various states because Americans do not conceptualize horses as "food" animals, whereas the slaughter of cows, chickens, turkeys, pigs, and sheep is permitted.[23] And even laws that govern the treatment of "food" animals distinguish between inflicting pain that is unnecessary to the business (and therefore not a routine practice of the industry) and inflicting pain that is part and parcel of bringing animal-based food to market.[24] In that sense, many welfare-oriented regulations can be said to assume and even to entrench a vision of animals as commodities to be exploited and disposed of by humans.

DOES WELFARISM "WORK"?

Earlier we presented the debate between Francione and Friedrich as reflecting something like a down-the-middle split within the animal rights movement. But as Freeman's research shows, in terms of institutional reach, Friedrich's position is dominant partly because it draws support from animal welfarists who do not seek abolition as a long-term goal at all.[25] Likewise, although some pro-life activists oppose abortion welfarism on grounds that parallel Francione's opposition to animal welfarism, as a whole, the pro-life movement appears to be comfortable with the philosophical inconsistency in banning what people outside the movement view as "worse" abortions (those later in pregnancy and those for objectionable reasons, such as sex-selection) even though the movement is united in viewing the distinctions the larger public draws between "worse" and "better" abortions as morally irrelevant.[26]

How shall we evaluate the fact that many activists in both movements pursue short-term goals that, in some sense, contradict their core beliefs? One factor we might use to decide whether compromise is a wise choice is whether compromise has been effective in pursuing the goals of each movement. If one measures success by the proliferation of legislation, then both pro-life and animal rights groups can celebrate victories because we now have a great many laws regulating abortion and animal use. It is tautological, however, to designate legislation as a measure of success if the legislation is intended not as an end in itself but as a means of bringing about embryo rights or animal rights, which—for people who support these two objectives—is, by hypothesis, the goal.

What about actual numbers? The rate of abortion has decreased in the last few decades, and perhaps some of that change can be attributed to the legal reform strategy of the pro-life movement during that period.[27] Meanwhile, in very recent years American meat consumption has dropped, a trend that some attribute to consumer choices, which in turn could be partly a product of animal advocacy, including the public awareness generated by welfarist campaigns.[28] But the picture is hardly clear. For one thing, these are fairly modest declines from very high peaks.[29] For another, Americans appear to be substituting dairy cheese rather than plant-based foods for meat.[30] And some of the legal reforms address practices in the animal industry that were developed and expanded only relatively recently.[31]

To complicate matters, we do not know what the world would look like in the absence of abortion limits and animal welfare measures. Perhaps we would see a greater drop in abortions if pro-life advocates had been more consistent and clear in their message opposing all abortions rather than supporting legislation that draws distinctions among different abortions that the movement finds morally equivalent.

To the extent that the pro-life movement has embraced abortion welfarism as a means of nudging society toward the movement's view that all postconception human lives are sacred, the growth of the fertility industry in the last several decades must count as a notable failure of the strategy. Since the first test-tube baby was born in 1978, millions of babies have come into existence through fertilization that occurs outside of the human body, with such procedures accounting for roughly 3 percent of live births in developed countries.[32] The orthodox pro-life view opposes in vitro fertilization (IVF), which routinely involves the creation of surplus embryos to maximize the odds of eventually achieving a successful pregnancy for each patient. Many of the surplus embryos are either discarded or frozen, but even frozen ones eventually decay and die.[33] Some of these embryos, moreover, become a source of embryonic stem cells for research, a project that itself enjoys support from a clear majority of the public.[34] And even in a period during which the pro-life movement has succeeded in enacting various abortion restrictions, most Americans view IVF itself favorably.[35]

The popularity of IVF shows that the pro-life movement has been unsuccessful in persuading people that embryos and newborn babies have an equal entitlement to life. We do not have the kind of evidence from which we can draw firm causal conclusions, but the evidence we do have is at least consistent with the hypothesis that campaigns for legal measures that emphasize later abortions further entrenched the view that the morality of abortion lies along a continuum based on fetal development, and that early abortions are either moral nonevents or less morally troubling than later abortions. At the same time, it is also possible that things might have gone even worse were it not for the abortion welfarist campaigns. Perhaps in a counterfactual world of unregulated abortion, IVF would be even *more* popular.

Similar counterfactual hypotheses might be offered with respect to animal welfare campaigns. Maybe such campaigns have moved society closer to the abolition of animal exploitation than we would have been in their absence. Or maybe Francione is right, and in the counterfactual world, some of the time and money that has been devoted to welfare campaigns would have gone to vegan education and outreach, thereby decreasing demand for, and thus ultimately the supply of, animal products.

Whether animal welfare and abortion welfare reforms will lead, respectively, to abolition of animal exploitation and abortion are complex questions that can only be truly answered empirically—and even then, our limited ability to run controlled experiments means that we will probably never know the full story. Nonetheless, we can point to particular features of the animal rights and pro-life arguments that make the welfare-to-abolition strategy likely to be more or less effective in each particular context. We next consider two questions that seem relevant to that inquiry: First, how receptive is the general public to each movement's message? And second, how does each movement position itself relative to its respective countermovement?

AUDIENCE RECEPTIVITY

Both the animal rights movement and the pro-life movement aim to change minds. But the audience for their respective messages has different investments in their current practices. A look at the statistics gives us a snapshot. According to the Guttmacher Institute, by the time a woman reaches the age of forty-five, she has a one in three chance of having had an abortion.[36] Each year roughly 2 percent of women between the ages of fifteen and forty-four have an abortion.[37] In total, that amounts to approximately 1.3 million abortions per year.[38] This may seem like a lot of people, but a comparison with animal consumption puts that number in a different light. By conservative estimates, about 98 percent of the United States population consumes animal products. Americans each consume, on average, over two pounds of animal ingredients each day.[39]

What difference does this make? If you actively and comfortably engage in a practice as part of your daily life, you are naturally going to resist information that suggests that you should stop engaging in that practice. People resist the idea that their behavior is unhealthy or dangerous.[40] They also resist the idea that their practices are morally wrong.[41] People who willingly and regularly engage in a particular activity want to be able to continue to do so without feeling either guilty or frightened as a result. It is much more comforting to hear that something you are doing is either good (for you or others) or innocuous than it is to hear that you really ought to stop doing it.

A thought experiment illustrates what research confirms. Suppose that you drink coffee every day and enjoy it very much. If a friend were to tell you that you add substantially to your risk of developing Alzheimer's disease by drinking coffee regularly, this (completely fictional) statement would immediately induce anxiety and cognitive dissonance.[42] You do not want to develop Alzheimer's disease, but you also do not want to give up drinking coffee. You might resist accepting what your friend has told you, trying to find competing evidence that is consistent with your not developing Alzheimer's disease while continuing to drink coffee every day. You might even resort to irrational arguments—you know someone who drank coffee every day and never became sick with Alzheimer's disease, and so you conclude from this single data point that coffee is not harmful.

Likewise, if someone were to tell you that you harm others when you drink coffee, you would likely be similarly unreceptive to this message. Suppose that human slaves were used to grow coffee beans and that the money that went into the purchase of coffee helped sustain the institution of human slavery. If a coworker brought this information to your attention, you would be discomfited, but you would still want your coffee. You do not want to participate in and contribute to human slavery, but you also do not want to stop drinking coffee. The natural reaction is for you to try to figure out a way to reject what your coworker has told you and thereby restore your feeling that you can both drink coffee and think of yourself as a moral person who does not participate in the institution of human slavery. Accordingly, with respect to animal products, we would predict that a typical American—who every day consumes almost two pounds of food derived from animal torture and slaughter—will resist the suggestion that consuming animal products is morally wrong.

Contrast abortion. If you are an average American woman, then you are somewhat more likely *never* to have had an abortion than you are to have had one or more abortions. And regardless of whether you have had an abortion in the past or will have one in the future, you are very unlikely to have had one this year, not to mention *today*. Further, if you are a man (and do not work as an abortion provider), you will *never* participate directly in the killing of an embryo or fetus.

If someone tries to persuade you that abortion is immoral, you might be somewhat uncomfortable (perhaps because you have previously had an abortion or because you have considered abortion an option that you could pursue if you were to become pregnant and did not want to have the baby). But it is unlikely—if you are not personally or professionally committed to the reproductive rights movement—that you would experience intense cognitive dissonance upon encountering arguments against abortion that seem compelling to you. For example, if someone told you that a newborn baby can immediately recognize the sound of her mother's voice and prefers it to the voice of a stranger—a fact that suggests fetal consciousness at some point during pregnancy—your mind is unlikely to revolt and insist that this cannot be true.[43]

If you became convinced that abortion is wrong, in other words, your life would probably not change dramatically. The idea that abortion is wrong is simply not that threatening to most people, even if they disagree with this idea at the moment. Stated differently, even people who are currently pro-choice are likely not that intensely and deeply invested in being pro-choice if they are not themselves abortion providers or advocates.[44]

Contrast these circumstances to people's investment in the morality of exploiting animals for food. Almost everyone who has not specifically decided to step out of the animal-consuming process and become vegan is daily and actively involved in eating and otherwise using the products of animal harm and slaughter and thereby supporting, sustaining, and demanding further harm and slaughter. Most parents induct their children into supporting animal exploitation before the children are even old enough to speak. By the time they learn that "chicken is chicken," children have been eating slaughtered chickens for quite some time and may therefore already be deeply invested in believing that it must be morally acceptable to do so.[45]

While women who have abortions are at least old enough to ovulate, children begin eating animal flesh and hormonal secretions before knowing and understanding that all such foods come into being through violence against living, breathing, and feeling beings. And even after a woman has had an abortion, she cannot plausibly be characterized as having become "used to" having abortions, such that she would feel deprived of a daily comfort or familiar activity if she were to come to view abortion as wrong. No child has an abortion, and though minors sometimes terminate pregnancies, they do so at an age when they are at least quasi-adults and capable of moral reasoning and decision making (sufficient to permit severe punishment for crimes). Indeed, the Supreme Court has acknowledged their quasi-adulthood by requiring parental-notification laws to include a provision for a judge to allow sufficiently mature pregnant minors to make their own decisions about abortion.[46]

This comparison suggests that regardless of how compelling a case one makes to call into question the morality of abortion and of the consumption of animal products, the listener will be inclined to resist the behavioral implications of the animal rights argument—and therefore the argument itself—much more strenuously than she will be to resist the pro-life argument. The investment in believing that the particular behavior is morally acceptable is much greater for someone engaged in the behavior every day, several times a day, from childhood than it is for someone for whom the prospect of engaging in the behavior is likely to be a rare-if-ever occurrence. Stated differently, most people can question the morality of abortion without disrupting their lives very much, whereas questioning the morality of animal consumption is necessarily disruptive.

As a result of this difference in the psychological investments of the target audience for each movement, the challenge of inducing people to reconsider their beliefs about farmed animals is formidable in a way that challenging people to reconsider their beliefs about abortion is not. One might therefore think that the pro-life movement could afford to be uncompromising and to advocate for laws that genuinely reflect their true position—that fully entitled life begins at conception. By contrast, one might expect a greater need to support compromise measures in the animal rights movement because the world seems unready for the whole truth. Legal measures that seemingly endorse harm by regulating and thereby implicitly endorsing wrongful behavior—whether abortion or animal product consumption—might, in other words, seem pragmatically more advisable for the animal rights movement than for the pro-life movement.

And yet both movements have embraced strategic "welfarism." Indeed, although opposition to welfarism is a minority position within both movements, such opposition appears to be more robust in the animal rights movement than in the pro-life movement. Does such opposition simply reflect naïveté on the part of abolitionists like Francione? Or is there another factor at work that may make strategic welfarism less likely to succeed as a pathway to abolition in the animal rights context than in the pro-life context?

DIFFERENT OPPONENTS

Social and political change movements do not choose their strategies solely in anticipation of, or in response to, how the audience of the general public will respond. Movements operate in a dynamic "political opportunity structure" that includes not just the public but also countermovements.[47] Thus, to understand the strategic positions of the pro-life and animal rights movements, we also need to consider their respective relationships to the pro-choice and pro-animal-use countermovements. What narrative does each countermovement promote, and how does each counternarrative constrain the opportunity structure of each movement?

Let us begin with abortion. The pro-choice narrative has included two strains—one of which holds that an embryo is "not a person" and the other of which holds that a woman is entitled to sovereignty over what (or who) is allowed to grow inside her body.[48] Abortion "welfare" regulations—though philosophically inconsistent with the pro-life position in the way we described earlier—nonetheless also fundamentally challenge both of these pro-choice narratives. To the claim that an embryo or fetus is not a person, the pro-life movement offers mandatory ultrasound prior to abortion (which shows the woman the uncanny resemblance between her fetus and a baby) along with a gut-wrenching description of what the fetus undergoes in a "partial-birth" abortion, clenching and unclenching his fists in full view of the medical staff as the doctor drives a pair of scissors through his head.[49] Such regulations thereby necessarily call the public's attention to physical realities that appear to contradict the pro-choice countermovement's "not a person" narrative.[50]

Along the same lines, mandatory "informed consent" sessions about abortion require women to confront some combination of facts and philosophical views about what happens to an embryo or fetus when termination occurs.[51] Such a simple conveyance of information stands as an apparent rebuttal to the pro-choice claim that nothing of moral significance happens when a woman chooses to terminate her pregnancy. If abortion were just a medical procedure with no greater moral import than an appendectomy, then mandatory information sessions would not be as upsetting as people on both sides of the issue understand them to be.[52]

To the "my body, my choice" narrative, abortion welfare regulations present a different but equally powerful challenge. Sex-selection abortion prohibitions (and people's overwhelming support for them)[53] demonstrate to the public that they do not *truly* believe that a woman can do whatever she wants to a fetus so long as it is inside her body. Interestingly, in its case before the U.S. Supreme Court in the 1991 term, the Philadelphia-area chapter of Planned Parenthood declined to challenge the provision of the Pennsylvania abortion law prohibiting sex-selection termination precisely because the notion that a woman has the right to kill her fetus for being the "wrong" sex is unappealing to most Americans and would doubtless have been offensive to a majority of Justices on the Supreme Court as well.[54] To challenge such a provision and then lose (as undoubtedly would have happened) would be to highlight the unease that both legislatures and courts apparently feel in taking "my body, my choice" to its logical conclusion.

Abortion welfare restrictions cross-examine the pro-choice narrative. They say: "Not a person? Then why are you turning away from the ultrasound picture?"; "let's talk about the details of late abortions and see whether people are prepared to accept them as nonevents." "Isn't it true," such laws ask, "that you really think that this is more than just 'tissue' growing during a pregnancy, and isn't it also true that you don't really believe that women should have complete autonomy over whether or not to terminate their pregnancies?"

When people answer "yes," as they do by supporting various abortion welfare measures, they deal a serious blow to the pro-choice countermovement.[55] Even if abortion welfare regulations tacitly concede that some abortions are worse than others—a position that is inconsistent with the pro-life movement's core commitments—perhaps that effect is substantially outweighed by the impact that such measures have on the pro-choice account of abortion. The invisible violence of abortion thus becomes visible—and accordingly objectionable—to the general public, the audience for both pro-choice and pro-life advocacy. In the competitive environment of pro-life versus pro-choice messaging, pro-life support for abortion welfare measures that are inconsistent with the pro-life movement's view of abortion but that do even more to undermine the pro-choice counternarrative is a bit like sacrificing a pawn for the opponent's queen.

For consumers of animal products and for the animal-using industry, however, the anti-animal-rights narrative operates in a somewhat different way. There are, of course, elements of "not a person" and "it's my choice" here as well, a kind of food libertarianism that sees vegan advocacy as akin to similarly meddlesome nanny-state measures like former New York City mayor Michael Bloomberg's quixotic campaign against sugary drinks sold in large containers. Nonetheless, the fundamental underlying idea that producers and consumers of animal products use to justify their practices is that animals are here for our use.

That idea—that animal exploitation is just and natural—has no clear analogue in the abortion debate. People who support access to abortion regard an unwanted pregnancy as more akin to a threatening intruder than to a resource for potential exploitation. This is why nearly everyone who is pro-choice would be horrified to learn that a woman deliberately became pregnant so she could abort the fetus and use its tissue or organs to make shoes or lotion.[56] We do not view human fetuses as material resources to be "farmed," and a scenario in which one is treated in this way would likely inspire revulsion.

But the countermovement to the animal rights movement—consisting of the multibillion-dollar animal exploitation industries and the many millions of their customers—views animals in just that way. The most numerous animal victims of human violence are those we "farm" by forcibly inducing reproduction in female animals and breeding their offspring into existence so we can use and slaughter them. Rather than viewing animals as "potential persons"—as even people who are pro-choice view embryos—most of us view farmed animals as potential and actual resources. For animals, death and utilization are the point. Indeed, people sometimes argue against animal rights by pointing out that the whole reason that we brought "food" animals into existence was to slaughter and eat them (an argument that would sound monstrous if carried over to the fetal context).[57] Or they say that we do domesticated animals a favor by eating them because their species' DNA "thrives"—through its large numbers of live exemplars in existence—by virtue of our demand.[58]

People who believe that humans are entitled to use animals for human purposes have long accepted in principle a coordinate obligation to use the animals humanely.[59] That is, simultaneous with the growth of animal agriculture developed an "ethic" that said that we should cause no more suffering or distress than is necessary for carrying out the intended use of the animal. Humans are not monsters, according to this logic, because we use the animals—who after all exist to serve us—with kindness and restraint.

Such considerations have not, of course, prevented humans—even in the days before "factory farms"[60]—from castrating "our" animals without anesthesia, even once anesthesia became available, because it would be prohibitively expensive; from branding them with hot irons (also without anesthesia); from removing their babies from them (as separate commodities whose destinies would likely take them to a different slaughterhouse); from tying them up; or from cutting their throats. But the people who directly do the exploiting of the animals in person profess, and the people who do the consuming believe, that animal exploitation is fully consistent with animal welfare.

Thus, whatever the reality, reforms that aim to improve the welfare of farmed animals do not seriously challenge the fundamental premise of animal exploitation. Whereas a law banning late abortions or requiring fetal ultrasounds challenges the "not a person" pro-choice narrative, laws regulating cage sizes and access to fresh air for farmed animals reinforce the pro-animal-exploitation narrative. Animal welfare is the reassuring complement to animal use. Like the proverbial velvet glove over the iron fist, animal use and animal husbandry/animal welfare work together, the latter (or the illusion thereof) softening the violence of the former. Where acknowledging the personhood of the fetus and the limited nature of reproductive autonomy are currently not part of the pro-choice position—and in fact pose a threat to it—animal welfare is and has been a part of the industry's theory of sanctioned animal use, even if (and perhaps because) it means so little in practice. In short, animal welfare laws fit quite comfortably into the "use them, but use them humanely" paradigm that has consistently been a part of animal exploitation.

Before concluding that animal welfare will necessarily fail as an incremental means of achieving the abolition of animal exploitation, we should note that the animal-exploiting industry could be said to disagree with our analysis. How else to explain the fact that the industry routinely resists animal welfare laws?[61] If such laws simply reinforce the dominant view of the animal exploitation industry, why doesn't the industry welcome them?

The tacit premise of that question is wrong. The fact that any particular industry resists regulation does not mean that the regulation at issue in any way fundamentally threatens the long-term viability of the industry. Regulation may simply raise costs and therefore cut into profits. One must therefore take industry claims that animal welfare measures serve a radical vegan agenda with a gigantic grain of salt. That sort of claim may be rhetorically powerful, but the real concern of the industry may simply be with cost, or perhaps it manifests a reflexive impulse on the part of industry to resist regulation.

Furthermore, the animal exploitation industries do not in fact uniformly oppose animal welfare regulation. Savvy industry leaders (in the animal agriculture industry and other industries) may support regulation because they are better positioned to comply with the regulations than are some of their less efficient competitors. They may support relatively unobtrusive regulation because doing so prevents the enactment of more substantial regulation. And they may support such regulation because doing so is good public relations. All of these factors could have been in play when the United Egg Producers—whose members account for 95 percent of egg production in the United States—agreed to join some animal welfare organizations in supporting draft legislation that would result in modestly improved conditions for laying hens.[62] Whatever the complete explanation, one cannot seriously maintain that any large industry groups would support an animal welfare measure if they thought that it could lead to the abolition of their business.

LESSONS FOR ACTIVISTS

Our analysis suggests that pro-life activism stands a better chance of succeeding than does pro-animal activism. Pro-life activists can afford to be uncompromising and can afford to use half-measures as a means of advancing their long-term agenda. It would be practical for pro-life activists to reject abortion measures that draw lines between "better" and "worse" abortions based on such matters as fetal development. Mainstream Americans may be inclined toward a pro-choice view, but their inclination is likely to be somewhat weak, given the relative insignificance of abortion in the daily lives of most Americans. Thus, they are at least potentially receptive to the pro-life message even if stated in uncompromising terms. Meanwhile, pro-life activists can, alternatively or additionally, embrace compromise measures because—though at odds with pro-life commitments—such measures undermine the core commitments of the pro-choice countermovement to an even greater extent than they undermine the pro-life view.

The animal rights movement, by contrast, confronts a mainstream audience with an enormous investment in exploiting animals. The movement might therefore view compromise measures as unavoidable given that abolition might appear utterly inconceivable to most people. Yet animal welfare reform measures are unlikely to lead to abolition because they do not fundamentally challenge the narrative of the animal-exploiting industries, which agree in principle with the view that animals can be and should be used and slaughtered "humanely." Therefore, though seemingly inevitable, incremental animal welfare legislation might also seem pointless in a way that analogous antiabortion measures do not.

Should animal rights activists therefore give up? Hardly. To begin, we can draw distinctions among different kinds of incremental change. The animal industries' existing ethic of "humane" care might counsel against collaboration through efforts to reform standards of animal husbandry. But abjuring such campaigns of collaboration still leaves open important avenues for incremental advocacy, including (1) pressing for laws and social norms that protect people who want to opt out of participating in animal harm, including accommodation of prisoners who seek a vegan diet while they are incarcerated, providing vegan options at public school cafeterias, and a norm of supplying vegan options at communal meals more generally;[63] (2) advocating for laws that reduce governmental support for harmful practices, including farm subsidies that artificially lower the prices people pay for animal products;[64] (3) providing uncompromising animal rights educational outreach; and (4) seeking legal protection for people engaged in animal advocacy, for example, by opposing so-called ag-gag laws that constrain the free speech of investigators seeking to expose animal industry practices. (In the next chapter, we have more to say about the tactic of rendering abortion and animal exploitation more visible.)

Although each of the foregoing steps is incremental in the sense that it will not abolish animal exploitation, such measures do not betray the underlying view that farming animals represents unjustified violence because they do not embrace reforms that identify the problem as one of *how* we use animals as commodities rather than *that* we use them.[65]

Notably, the pro-life movement has engaged in various parallel sorts of incremental-but-uncompromising activism. It has secured laws that accommodate providers, including pharmacists, who do not wish to participate in the termination of postconception human life and who wish accordingly to "opt out" of customary practices.[66] The pro-life movement has also attempted, with some success, to restrict government funding for abortion, including funding for discussions of abortion as an option.[67] And it has engaged in advocacy that emphasizes and unequivocally defends the pro-life view that protected human life begins at conception.[68] The pro-life movement has also encouraged couples thinking about expanding their families to consider adopting "snowflakes," frozen embryos that would otherwise have been discarded.[69] Although the latter operates noncoercively, in that it does not compel anyone to carry an unwanted pregnancy to term, it nonetheless effectively promotes the pro-life view that an embryo is no less a full person entitled to a "loving home" than is a baby born to parents who cannot keep him.[70] In order to pursue incremental change without betraying its core values, the animal rights movement apparently has much to learn from the pro-life movement, in spite of the relative luxury and flexibility that the pro-life movement enjoys in pursuing its goals and in spite of the many differences between the substantive commitments of the two movements.

Why, then, do animal rights advocates continue to press for animal welfare regulation? One answer may have to do, again, with the audience to the animal rights message. The audience consists of people who like to think of themselves as caring about and for animals. If they eat animal products, as most people do, they want to see the resulting animal suffering as the fault of the people directly inflicting that suffering—that is, the people who earn their living by exploiting animals—rather than as the fault of consumers who pay the exploiters to produce their products. When shocking video footage of animal torture on farms emerges, as it does every so often, there is an outcry by people who want to continue consuming animal products but experience discomfort with the idea that their consumption choices may be causally connected to such suffering.[71] They then support laws that purport to order the industry to be "kinder" to the animals whom they use and slaughter, laws that permit people to imagine farmed animals living in peace in the way they do in the children's stories that many of us remember fondly.

Animal rights advocates want to reach that audience, but it is difficult to persuade them that it is wrong to use animals and that the horrendous suffering in the videos will end only when they themselves stop using animals as a food source. It is therefore much easier to allow the audience to set the agenda, and the audience in this case wants to believe that passage of welfarist measures "helps the animals," even if the people who support such measures continue participating in and supporting those and other cruel practices by purchasing the products that result.

By aiming their criticism at firms and people who supply animal products rather than at people who demand those products, animal welfare organizations and activists let consumers off the hook. *It's not my fault*, the typical consumer can tell herself; *it's the fault of the farmers who don't give the animals enough space or beat them or shock them*. In some ways this scapegoating (to use a speciesist figure of speech) of the people involved directly in slaughter mirrors the stigma that traditionally attached to executioners—those who carried out the death penalty—notwithstanding the fact that, like farmers of animal flesh, skin, and secretions, executioners were and are doing precisely what the larger society has authorized and entrusted them to do.[72]

As we noted earlier in this chapter, financial imperatives can also skew organizations' missions. Most people who think of themselves as pro-animal also consume animal products, and thus most potential donors to pro-animal causes also consume animal products.[73] The need to avoid alienating donors favors a welfarist message that does not challenge the basic fact of animal exploitation.

Even if compromise measures are not a path to abolition, perhaps some of them do some limited good in their own domain. To use Francione's analogy, other things being equal, maybe a padded waterboard is better than an unpadded one. One might acknowledge that "happy meat" is a lie but still believe that "slightly less miserable meat" is better than "slightly more miserable meat."[74] High-profile efforts to make conditions for farmed (or otherwise exploited) animals slightly less terrible could, of course, further entrench the practice of consuming animal products, and so slightly less terrible on a per-animal basis—even assuming that this is what welfarist campaigns produce—could result in more total animals being treated terribly. As we have explained, although the empirical question is complicated, there are reasons to think that animal welfare campaigns could have this effect.

In our view, the fundamental problem with the "humane exploitation" approach—both as a pathway to abolition and for its own sake—is that it focuses on the wrong side of the economic equation. Modern factory farm practices reflect the quantitative demand for animal products. So long as huge numbers of people continue to demand large quantities of animal products at affordable

prices, mass production is inevitable, and the predictable consequence of mass production that involves live animals is crowding
and relentless suffering. Campaigns for "happy" animal products
therefore motivate cosmetic alterations (such as "free range" and
"cage free") that still leave animals in horrific conditions.[75] When
people who favor abolition of animal exploitation endorse such
campaigns, they tacitly encourage consumers to continue to consume animal products (while allowing them simultaneously to feel
virtuous about their conduct).[76] As a result, the people who want to
"do something" when they become aware of what consuming animals really entails end up doing next to nothing. Because so much
of the energy of the pro-animal movement is now devoted to welfarist measures, we very much hope that Friedrich is right and that
Francione is wrong, but our analysis leads us to think otherwise.

6

Graphic Images

Both the pro-life and animal rights movements have at times presented the public with violent imagery in an effort to change hearts and minds about the morality of abortion and animal exploitation, respectively. In the anti-abortion movement, *The Silent Scream* is an iconic film that shows an abortion via ultrasound in utero, with narration by an obstetrician who tells the audience that the fetus is manifesting suffering during the procedure.[1] Within the animal rights movement, *Earthlings* is a similarly well-known film that shows graphic footage of the violence that saturates the five common ways in which animals endure exploitation: for food, clothing, entertainment, scientific research, and the breeding and sale of pets.[2] Many people active in each movement promote the use of these and other similarly graphic material as a means of exposing the broader public to what might otherwise remain hidden from consumers of abortion services and animal products.

Most Americans (and others) have seen at least some of the violent imagery made available by both the pro-life and animal rights movements. When one of us (Sherry) was a college student, she spent a summer doing an internship as a counselor in a mental health outpatient center. The office where she worked was located inside a building that also housed an abortion clinic. As a result, each day, upon arrival at work, Sherry faced a group of protesters holding up large posters with photographs of bloody fetuses (ostensibly the products of abortion), handing out literature, and urging Sherry and other young women entering the building not to kill their babies. The images were disturbing and gave rise to a visceral sense in the viewer that abortion raises serious moral issues.

At other times, both of us have encountered posters with photographs of the violence committed against cows, pigs, chickens, and other animals who are farmed for their flesh and secretions. In addition, we have encountered live footage of the trapping of fur-bearing animals and of the farming and slaughter of captive animals.[3] Long before either of us considered becoming vegan, we found such imagery disturbing, and our tendency was (as it continues to be) to look away.

In this chapter we consider the proper role of graphic imagery in a movement for social justice. We examine the principled arguments that people make for and against the display of graphic images, and we analyze the tactical efficacy and shortcomings of distributing such material.

WHY DISTRIBUTE THE IMAGES?

For anyone who counts herself a part of either of the two movements we discuss in this book, one obstacle to progress is the disjunction between the violence involved in creating the product being consumed, on one hand, and the apparent similarity between consuming the product at issue and consuming other products that involve no similar violence, on the other hand.

Consider abortion. When a woman goes to a hospital or clinic for an abortion, absent regulations that might require her to hear about her fetus's age or to see an image of her fetus on ultrasound, the woman could in theory undergo the procedure and experience it as no different from a surgery to remove fibroid tumors. From the perspective of the consumer of abortion services, in other words, there is nothing inherent in the process of undergoing an abortion that would alert her to the graphic reality of violence involved in terminating the life of a fetus.

From the perspective of those involved in performing the abortion, by contrast, things look very different. In chapter 1, we quoted the Supreme Court's description of a "partial-birth" abortion in *Gonzales v. Carhart*, which in turn quoted a nurse's testimony for the Senate Judiciary Committee before the latter approved the federal law at issue in the case. There we noted how the testimony made plain the nurse's view that the fetus was sentient—that the fetus was *someone*, capable of having experiences, rather than an insensate *something*. Here we emphasize the further point that both the nurse and Justice Anthony Kennedy, the author of the Supreme Court's opinion, were undoubtedly trying to make: that the abortion procedure is gruesome. The nurse recounts that the "baby's little fingers were clasping and unclasping, and his little feet were kicking. Then the doctor stuck the scissors in the back of his head, and the baby's arms jerked out. . . . The doctor opened up the scissors, stuck a high-powered suction tube into the opening, and sucked the baby's brains out."

Although Justice Kennedy does not provide an actual visual depiction, his apparent objective in providing a graphic quotation, and the goal of the nurse who originally testified about the procedure, was to highlight with descriptive language the violence that a woman who undergoes an abortion solicits but ordinarily has no occasion to witness. In reflecting on this hidden violence, Justice Kennedy proposes that many women who have undergone an abortion will later learn what was entailed and will then come to regret their choice. He states for the Court: "It is self-evident that a mother who comes to regret her choice to abort must struggle with grief more anguished and sorrow more profound when she learns, only after the event, what she once did not know: *that she allowed a doctor to pierce the skull and vacuum the fast-developing brain of her unborn child, a child assuming the human form.*"[4]

In one sense, this discussion of notice in *Gonzales v. Carhart* was beside the point. That decision was about whether the Constitution permitted Congress to ban one particular method of abortion consistent with other Supreme Court decisions recognizing a right to abortion. A patient's knowledge or ignorance of the particular violence entailed really had nothing to do with the decision before the Court because the statute at issue did not provide for disclosure or informed consent. It was a straightforward prohibition. In another sense, however, it was understandable that in deciding whether to grant constitutional protection to the abortion procedure at issue, the Court would consider the invisibility of the abortion from the woman's perspective. In considering the particular late-term abortion, Justice Kennedy might well have felt it necessary to carefully ponder the violence involved precisely because he thought that the people exercising their rights—the women authorizing their doctors to kill their fetuses—likely did not fully realize the mechanics of what they were asking their doctors to do. A woman who later learned what those who witness such abortions already know—that it is a bloody affair in which the fetus appears to be suffering—could regret not only that she authorized the act but also that she was empowered by the law to do so.

A related thought process drives many animal rights advocates to display the cruelty and violence of animal "raising" and slaughter for audiences, in films as well as in video clips and pictures available on the Internet.[5] Consider how this idea works in the context of animal rights advocacy. People who consume animal products like dairy cheese ordinarily have little or no occasion to witness the violence necessary to bring such a product to their tables. They might have a sanitized image in their minds of cows "giving milk," but they likely have never even contemplated, let alone watched, what is actually entailed in producing dairy, whether on a "factory" or a family farm: the forcible insemination of cows to make them pregnant and give birth so that they lactate; the great distress and vocalizing of a cow when her young baby who wants to nurse is ripped from her side to divert her milk to humans; or the ugly slaughter of male calves and "spent" dairy cows who no longer produce much milk by the age of four and therefore are no longer worth feeding, even though cows can live to be twenty if they are cared for instead of killed.[6]

Even most vegans were once ignorant of these and myriad other cruelties that purchasing animal products inherently demands. Many of us imagined that farmed animals live relatively peaceful lives until the "one bad day" on which they are killed in a painless fashion. Reflecting on our prior conduct, we find ourselves feeling grief and sorrow—of the very sort that Justice Kennedy describes—as we regret the utterly unnecessary and tremendous violence that we authorized by consuming animal products, along with the legal option we had to authorize it.

A scene in the popular Netflix original television series *House of Cards* is inadvertently very revealing on this point. In the first episode of season 2, Freddy, a sympathetic character who owns and operates a small restaurant that sells pork ribs, responding to a customer's question, explains to the main character, Frank, why the ribs that day taste so unusually good.[7] Freddy says that these ribs came from a butcher who performs the "slow kill" method of slaughtering pigs, which requires soundproof walls to obscure the screaming of the pigs as they endure the horrific process. Freddy adds that he probably will not use that butcher again, observing that the "humane" way to slaughter a pig is to put a bowl of slop in front of him and then shoot him in the head so that he never knows what hit him.[8] This short segment of the show, undoubtedly meant as a metaphor for Washington politics, effectively exposes the fantasy that most people seem to nurture if they contemplate the slaughter of pigs at all; they fantasize that it is quick and painless, and that only merciless deviants use a "slow kill" method that requires soundproofing.

In reality, however, the ordinary slaughter of pigs is extremely violent and cruel. The animals know what is coming because they can smell the blood of other pigs, and they can hear their cries as the animals resist and scream in terror and pain. Conventional slaughterhouses are in fact effectively (and often actually) soundproofed, kept far away from where kind people like Freddy (and the typical consumer of animal products) could witness (and object to) what is going on.[9]

When animal advocates ask people to watch footage of what happens on farms and in slaughterhouses, their goal is to awaken the moral outrage and horror that many will experience upon seeing the truth about flesh, dairy, and eggs (as well as leather, wool, and other nonfood animal products that people purchase).[10] The implicit premise of displaying the images, to paraphrase Sir Paul McCartney, is that if slaughterhouses had glass walls, then everyone would be vegan.[11] Violent imagery is thus intended to awaken conscience and shatter the myth that one can coherently oppose unnecessary violence against animals while simultaneously consuming animal ingredients, the products of unnecessary violence.

To unite the two subjects, we observe that absent opponents' intervention, a woman who has an abortion and a man or a woman who consumes animal products can do so without having any real consciousness of the violence that they thereby authorize and solicit. A woman can visit her doctor for an abortion and experience something not very different in kind from the parallel experience of a woman undergoing a morally neutral surgery involving her reproductive organs. A person who consumes a tuna salad sandwich can likewise have an experience of eating that differs little from the experience of a parallel consumer who eats a chickpea-salad sandwich.

This failure of the consumer's sensory experiences to detect or reflect any measurable difference between violence and nonviolence in engaging in these consumption practices seems to call for enlightenment and education. That education can take the form of books, articles, blog posts, and lectures in which ethical vegans let the public know that the common expression "a little chicken soup couldn't hurt"—a depiction of chicken soup as a soothing and harmless product—is a lie.[12] The logic of actually exhibiting the violence at issue (rather than simply describing it) is that what leads us to stop committing acts of violence goes beyond cognitively knowing that violence occurs and requires that we emotionally and viscerally appreciate the morally relevant impacts of our choices in a way that sights and sounds help us to do.[13] Put differently, the adage "a picture is worth a thousand words" understates the value of powerful imagery. Pictures communicate in a way that cannot be replicated in any number of words.

MORAL OBJECTIONS TO DISPLAYING VIOLENT IMAGES

People within and outside of the two movements in question have voiced objections to the display of graphic images of violence in abortion and animal exploitation. The basic moral claim behind the objections is that presenting people with such images inflicts a harmful experience on the viewer, an experience that may interfere with the viewer's life in undesirable and unjust ways.

On the pro-choice side of the aisle, critics argue that publicly displaying graphic photographs of mangled, aborted fetuses coercively confronts an audience that rightfully prefers not to witness such images. Similarly, critics of animal suffering displays suggest that showing pictures and films of tortured animals on farms, in slaughterhouses, and in other venues of animal exploitation can traumatize the viewer and inflict psychological distress. Given that both pro-life and pro-animal-rights advocates purport to favor a more peaceful world in which we minimize suffering, it might appear inconsistent with that vision to be subjecting viewers to a potentially traumatic visual (and sometimes audio) experience.

In the context of abortion, Professor Carol Sanger offers a subtle variant on this argument in her critique of regulations that require a woman undergoing an abortion to be shown ultrasound images of her fetus in utero prior to the procedure.[14] By requiring that a woman be confronted with a picture of her own fetus, Sanger contends, the government coercively turns the woman into a "mother" against her will, a status vis-à-vis the fetus that she has specifically rejected by choosing to terminate her pregnancy.

Superficially, one could respond that any time the government speaks to the public in a manner that displays a preference for childbirth over abortion, it thereby "imposes" its view that a pregnant woman is already a "mother" to the fetus she carries inside her body.[15] Indeed, the preference for childbirth—whether expressed in words or in a mandatory ultrasound—signifies the view that, unlike a woman considering whether to conceive a pregnancy, the already-pregnant woman is in an existing, morally weighty relationship with her unborn child. When the government urges women not to have abortions, it expresses the view that, regardless of what women may wish to believe, the choice of whether to have an abortion is not a decision whether to avoid commencing a relationship that has yet to begin (for example, by undergoing a tubal ligation) but instead a decision whether to terminate one that is already in progress.

Yet Sanger is right, we think, to propose that displaying a mandatory ultrasound does something to the pregnant woman that is qualitatively quite different from what the government does in stating its viewpoint regarding pregnancy and abortion. As with graphic images of violence, a graphic image of a live fetus moving around inside a woman's body viscerally—and potentially traumatically—conveys to the woman her (undesired) connection with that fetus. A woman may be fully aware of the pro-life position on her decision, but directly witnessing the living evidence of her unborn child's life can potentially trigger a change of heart or, at least trigger future regret that would otherwise have never come to pass.

The question that Sanger's argument raises, then, for both the abortion and animal rights contexts, is this: Do people who make a choice that is legally theirs to make necessarily have the right to avoid the moral reluctance or regret that can result from an unwanted, direct, and visceral emotional exposure to images of what they are actually doing? This question is highly relevant to the animal rights context as most people who consume animal products in legally permissible ways would likely prefer not to see (or potentially to feel remorse for) the animal suffering and slaughter that their choices necessarily solicit. Their preference is to remain unaware of their own relationship to the animals whose flesh and secretions wind up on their plates.

To answer this question about an entitlement not to see, it is useful to think about the ways in which the division of labor in modern societies has altered the relationship between those who commit legally sanctioned violence and the victims of that violence. When people were gatherer-hunters in the distant past (though only a moment ago, if one considers time as a proportion of humans' presence on earth),[16] a person who wanted to consume the flesh of an animal would need to kill the animal and watch him or her suffer, bleed, and die before his or her eyes before doing so.[17] Even after the domestication of "food animals," once animal agriculture had begun in earnest, families tended to "raise" and slaughter their own animals rather than delegating the job to a professional slaughterer.[18] This meant that people generally lacked the option of seeing only the disembodied and burned corpses of their animal victims; they saw with their own eyes and heard with their own ears the sights and sounds that accompany slaughter.

Regarding abortion, women have long known how to terminate unwanted pregnancies, even before medical doctors became the primary abortion providers.[19] Women knew about herbs and other natural medicinal substances that would induce uterine contractions and cause a woman to lose her pregnancy.[20] Presumably, the woman taking the herbs in question would have gone on to see the so-called products of conception as they emerged from her body, and she would accordingly experience viscerally the bloody physical evidence of her choice.

The fact that we often experience discomfort, regret, and guilt when we participate in violence that we directly witness is a very useful mechanism for curbing our violent impulses. Dave Grossman has written extensively about people's innate resistance to carrying out violent acts, noting, for example, that many soldiers in World War I appeared to have deliberately fired their weapons so as to miss their targets.[21] One might say that it is "natural" for humans to experience psychological distress when seeing themselves carry out acts of violence; the distress is a psychic cost that motivates people to refrain from violence unless there are strong countervailing factors that favor it.

The division of labor in our more developed society, however, permits people who wish to solicit violence to enjoy the gain that results from the violence without having to pay the psychic cost of that violence. Consider a schematic hypothetical example involving unlawful violence. John Doe might find himself very uncomfortable in the presence of suffering and bleeding but might wish to be rid of a business competitor, James Roe. If Doe can hire an assassin to kill Roe, then (so long as he is not apprehended, prosecuted, and convicted) he can "have his cake and eat it too": he avoids the visceral experience of his relationship to his victim (as the one who brought about the victim's pain and death) while nonetheless profiting from the fruits of having eliminated a business rival.

If we are naturally programmed to avoid violence when feasible, then the division of labor—in addition to all of the advantages that a modern economy confers—also enables violence on a massive scale by peaceful people who are generally averse to causing suffering and death, and would go to great lengths to avoid the psychic cost of such violence. "Protecting" people from seeing the black and white (and color) realities of the violence they solicit may thus increase the amount of violence in our world by artificially preventing internal, antiviolence mechanisms from operating as they have evolved to do. When we solicit the commission of violence with our money (or, if someone else pays, with that someone else's money), we in fact enter a relationship of violence with our victims, whether or not we want to think about it, and facilitating our denial may potentiate violence without internal accountability.

In concrete terms, some women who seek to terminate a late-term pregnancy might choose instead to take their pregnancies to term if they had to watch the process of abortion and then see the bloody remains of what would have otherwise been their son or daughter, disposed of in a metal basin. And some people who dine on the flesh and reproductive secretions of tortured cows, pigs, chickens, and fishes would eagerly switch to consuming a vegan diet if eating a cheese sandwich entailed watching footage of nursing calves taken from their bellowing and inconsolable mothers, along with footage of the "spent" mothers dragged to slaughter, eyes wide with terror, at the young age of four.[22] From this perspective, exposing people to images of the violence in which they actively participate simply restores the ordinary (and self-correcting) course of moral decision making that operated throughout most of human history.

To understand more fully the moral implications of allowing people to offload the direct experience of the violence that they solicit, consider the fact that when we delegate violence, there is generally another person or other people who consequently will have that direct experience of violence. In the case of abortion, there is the abortion provider and his or her staff, people who carry out the potentially disturbing acts that they perform on behalf of the women for whom Sanger claims a right to be insulated. And in the case of animal products, the people who consume these products and prefer not to see the slaughter of the animals whose flesh and secretions they demand, have offloaded the violence to people who work in hatcheries, dairies, and slaughterhouses, people who do not have the luxury of protecting *their* senses from the direct impact of viscerally knowing the violence of animal exploitation.

What costs do the people in such industries bear? We are unaware of evidence of systematic trauma among most abortion providers and their staffs.[23] However, there are anecdotes of providers who apparently find their experiences so disturbing that they alter their line of work and ultimately become activists for the anti-abortion movement. One noteworthy example is the obstetrician and gynecologist Bernard Nathanson, the founder of NARAL Pro-Choice America, who left his profession and ultimately decided to narrate *The Silent Scream*.[24]

The impact on workers of killing animals in slaughterhouses is, by contrast, well documented and profound. In her book *Slaughterhouse*, Gail Eisnitz discusses the soul-crushing effect of slaughterhouse work on its laborers' psyches.[25] During in-depth interviews, current and former slaughterhouse workers tell Eisnitz that they found themselves becoming increasingly sadistic toward the animals during the workday;[26] they report engaging in domestic violence and alcohol abuse as a consequence of working in a slaughterhouse.[27] Others have reported statistics showing that introducing a slaughterhouse into a community corresponds with an increase in the crime rate in that community, especially crimes of violence committed against vulnerable victims, such as rape and domestic violence.[28] The prevalence of antisocial behavior that follows such work does not excuse an individual who engages in this behavior, but it does strongly suggest that slaughterhouse work results in post-traumatic stress disorder that can help explain the predictable uptick in violent and criminal misconduct.

As in the pro-life movement, moreover, so too the animal rights movement includes people who have "switched sides"—former farmers and others who slaughtered large numbers of animals but who eventually rebelled against the violence in which they had participated. The film *Peaceable Kingdom: The Journey Home* tells the stories of several such farmers, including a small family goat farmer, a large-scale cattle rancher, and a farmer who worked in several fields of animal husbandry.[29] One of the farmers describes his own experience as a child being inducted into animal farming as a trauma akin to child abuse.

Part of what happens when large numbers of people delegate the direct experience of violence to a relatively small number of people is that the trauma of direct exposure is multiplied many times over for those unlucky enough to be in close proximity to the blood and death. Where, in the past, a family might have confronted the trauma of slaughtering one animal relatively infrequently—once in a few months or every year (depending on the size of the animal), a person who works in a slaughterhouse on behalf of the many millions of people who demand flesh, dairy, and eggs regularly finds himself or herself knee-deep in blood. As we learn from Timothy Pachirat's undercover exposé *Every Twelve Seconds*, slaughterhouse workers witness and participate in violence against animals on an almost unimaginable scale.[30] The title of Pachirat's book refers to the rate at which workers slaughter cattle at the unnamed meat packing plant at which he worked undercover and which he describes in great detail.[31]

Needless to say, not everyone who provides abortions becomes a pro-life activist, and not everyone who works in animal agriculture becomes a vegan. Most do not. But the fact that foes of abortion and animal exploitation want to reveal the gory details to the public, and the fact that defenders of abortion and animal exploitation want to shield the public from those gory details, show that both sides on each issue recognize the potential of an up-close look at these practices to dramatically alter perspectives.[32]

There are therefore two undesirable features to offloading direct confrontation with the violence that we solicit. First, insulation from the visceral reality of violence can disinhibit violent conduct by removing the psychic cost otherwise associated with inflicting suffering and slaughter on a sentient being. For most people, it is far easier to order a chicken sandwich than it would be to slaughter a living, breathing chicken. And second, the visceral impact from which consumers protect themselves leads to the concentration of such experiences in a small number of people who must do the "dirty work" for a living, and they consequently pay very high psychic costs for someone else's gain. In economic terms, this would represent a paradigmatic case of externalizing harm. In the language of economics, showing people disturbing images of what they are actually soliciting may represent a salutary intervention that begins the process of addressing such externalities.

TACTICAL QUESTIONS

Some methods of showing people the consequences of their choices go too far. For example, Virginia legislators were appropriately criticized for a 2012 bill that would have required a woman contemplating an abortion to undergo a transvaginal ultrasound.[33] This is a kind of state-mandated medical rape that is wholly improper on grounds having nothing to do with any putative right to ignorance. A North Carolina law requires a doctor to perform a (conventional) ultrasound on a woman seeking an abortion and to describe the fetus, even if she covers her ears. That law was found invalid by a federal appeals court on the ground that it infringes the doctor's free speech rights.[34]

However, putting aside extreme measures, we conclude that simply exposing people to the violence that they solicit with their choices as consumers is morally appropriate and perhaps even beneficial given our natural psychological processes for inhibiting violence. Nonetheless, whether to expose people to violent images is not exclusively a moral question. It is also a tactical question. Viewed strictly as a matter of tactics, we are less confident in the wisdom of exposure than we are in its moral legitimacy.

Consider again the nature of what happens to slaughterhouse laborers when they are traumatized by their exposure. Many of them report becoming numb to (or even enthusiastic about) the suffering of the animals on whom they are inflicting torture and death, as a means of protecting themselves from the pain of empathy that they might otherwise experience.[35] Forcing a person to witness the violence in which she is engaged can therefore backfire. It can make the viewer more callous and therefore better able to tolerate the violence, thus further disinhibiting violence rather than keeping it in check.

We suspect that slaughterhouse workers come to tolerate—and numb themselves to—the suffering of the animals in their "care" in part because such workers likely perceive themselves as having

few other options than to do the work that they do.[36] They therefore can either feel guilty and sickened about what they are doing
and eventually refuse to keep doing it and become unemployed, or
they can recruit psychological defenses that allow them to survive
and continue on a path that they view as inescapable. By classify-
ing the animals as "other" and as adversaries (whose resistance to
dying makes the slaughterhouse workers' job more difficult), the
workers enable themselves to keep going without completely losing their minds.

One of the former animal farmers interviewed in *Peaceable Kingdom: The Journey Home* attests to the normal process of desensitization to the suffering of animals on the farm. Willow Lyman talks
about how her young son once expressed sadness at witnessing the
family's cows being branded with hot irons. Willow's response at the
time was to think that he would later toughen up with repeat experience, and, "unfortunately," as she describes it in the film, he did
toughen in this way, and came to no longer take in the suffering of
the cows undergoing branding or the many other routine mutilations
in a farmed animal's life. People can and regularly do "get used to"
the violence they commit rather than decide to stop committing it.[37]

The same process of desensitization can occur for the general
public, and if it does, that will render gory images counterproductive. People who may have previously been shocked by photographs and videos of animal exploitation and abortion can look at
such images without feeling anything. For example, in *The Omnivore's Dilemma*, Michael Pollan describes challenging himself to
kill a pig as a precondition to continuing to eat animals.[38] Then,
invested as he plainly was in continuing to enjoy consuming animal flesh, Pollan finds that he is able to eat the meal composed
of the corpse of the pig he has killed; his joy in eating overcomes
his disgust in killing.[39] Rather than serving to discipline the violent conduct, exposure to the visceral reality of violence can thus
have the perverse consequence of persuading the actor that "I can
watch this animal suffer and die, so it must be permissible for me
to order more such deaths so I can consume animals' flesh and
reproductive secretions in perpetuity with a clean conscience."

We observe a paradox about the age of factory farming in which
we are currently living, a paradox that we believe is a direct product

of insulating consumers from the violence that they solicit. With the farming of animals largely hidden from our view, consumers on the whole have become better able to empathize with the animals whom they consume because they need not suppress their compassion in the way that those directly engaged in the violence may need to do. When such consumers do come across violent footage, they are disturbed and outraged because they have not yet had to numb themselves to these images in order to overcome a resistance to slaughtering sentient beings by hand and otherwise mutilating them in person. Today's consumers of animal foods are accordingly more "reachable" by the animal rights movement because they have not built the emotional callouses that people build when slaughter is a visible and accessible part of their everyday lives.

Yet, because of consumers' insulation from the violence—an insulation that enables the capacity for empathy to develop—consumers have been enabled to participate, through demand, in cruelty against farmed animals on a scale and to an extent that dwarfs what came before. It might therefore be thought useful to show the naïve consumer (who chooses not to see or think about the violence) the reality of what he or she is funding. But people who feel strongly about continuing to consume the animal foods that they presently consume may actively resist the discomfort associated with brutal imagery. And the consequence may be the very numbness that characterizes the slaughterhouse worker, stuck in a violent habit but preferring to use coping mechanisms like desensitization rather than make what may appear to be terrifying changes to his or her life. After witnessing enough footage, consumers could ultimately become as numb as slaughterhouse workers.

For people using imagery within the pro-life movement, we think that the tactical dilemma may be less clear. As we noted in chapter 5, people who consume animal products typically consume them at least three times every single day: the average American consumes more than two pounds of animal-derived food daily.[40] Accordingly, they may actively resist feelings that could motivate them to become vegan, eagerly recruiting coping mechanisms as an alternative to change. Women who have abortions, by contrast, represent a minority of the population (approximately one in three women by the age of forty-five)[41] and even those who have had more than one abortion have never had several of them per day. Therefore, from the perspective of people who are not themselves abortion providers or active advocates within the pro-choice movement, the possibility of feeling something in response to an image of an abortion and of consequently changing one's mind about abortion is not nearly as threatening.

Pro-life advocates can therefore hold up photographs of aborted fetuses and pass laws that require women to view images of their fetuses in utero prior to an abortion, and these measures may effectively inhibit the practice of abortion rather than numbing the public to the issue. For animal rights activists who want to inhibit violence against animals, by contrast, the outcome of exposure is far less clear. In our view, it may be wisest to expose consumers only occasionally to the violence of animal exploitation but generously and repeatedly to the beauty and serenity of farmed animals who have been rescued, while letting everyone know how healthful, delicious, and nourishing a vegan diet can be. Accordingly, we conclude that using violent imagery about animal exploitation as an advocacy tool should be a relatively rare and carefully selected tactic.

7

Violence

On May 31, 2009, Dr. George Tiller was shot and killed by an anti-abortion activist while Tiller was attending church in Wichita, Kansas.[1] He was not the first person to die as a result of anti-abortion violence, and he probably will not be the last.

An FBI official, speaking in 2005, identified "the eco-terrorism, animal rights movement" as the top "domestic terrorism threat" in the United States.[2] That was undoubtedly an overstatement. With one possible exception, no human being has died as a result of illegal acts by animal rights activists who aim to free captive animals from laboratories and farms or otherwise inflict damage on such institutions.[3] Still, the animal rights / animal liberation movement includes a violent fringe, and because the tactics of some activists have included firebombing, the fact that no one has yet died at their hands is partly just a matter of good luck.[4]

The mainstream pro-life and animal rights movements condemn violence, even though violence and intimidation could sometimes advance their respective goals, at least in theory.[5] In practice, the two movements have behaved quite differently from each other. Since the Supreme Court decided *Roe v. Wade* in 1973, the anti-abortion movement has used political violence on a much larger scale and, arguably, more effectively than has the animal rights movement.[6] Pro-choice organizations make a fair point when they argue that doctors' and other providers' fears of violence have reduced the availability of abortion.[7]

To be sure, some scientists and others who perform experiments on animals report similar fears, leading them to consider other lines of work.[8] Relative to the pro-life movement, however, the animal rights movement produces less political violence, the political violence it does produce is less lethal, and it does not appear to have had a substantial impact on the numbers of animals killed for food, science, or other human projects.

Whatever the relative prevalence and efficacy of violence within the pro-life and animal rights causes, the perceived association of either movement with violence represents a major public relations problem. Any highly publicized violence generates public sympathy for each movement's respective opponents and may lead to the enactment of laws inimical to the causes that the perpetrators of the violence seek to advance. Examples of such legislation include the federal Freedom of Access to Clinic Entrances Act and state buffer zone laws as well as the federal Animal Enterprise Terrorism Act and state "ag-gag" laws, the latter of which make it virtually impossible for animal rights activists to gain access to farms to document animal torture and abuse.[9] Although their proponents seek to justify such laws as necessary to prevent violence, once in effect, the laws impede the work of peaceful activists and protesters as well.[10]

To be sure, the view that violence generates adverse publicity that undermines a movement may be based more on wishful thinking than careful empirical analysis. In his landmark study, sociologist William Gamson questioned whether "the recipients of violence rouse the public sympathy with their martyrdom, rallying to their cause important bystanders who are appalled at their victimization," and found, surprisingly, that "violence users ... have a higher-than-average success rate," at least as judged by some methods.[11] Violence might be counterproductive, but it might not be.

Moreover, the fact that violence can be counterproductive as a matter of public relations is only a *tactical* consideration. Are there reasons of *principle* for people who are committed to the pro-life or animal rights cause to reject violence categorically? Can we say that it is not only counterproductive for a pro-life activist to kill a doctor who performs abortions but actually wrong? Can we say that it is wrong for an animal rights activist to use force to break into a laboratory or a farm to liberate animals who are routinely subject to torture and slaughter there?

Both of us unequivocally and categorically oppose violence in both of the movements that we discuss here. Nonetheless, we attempt in this chapter to take seriously the arguments that one might make in favor of violence, which have at least a superficial logic to them. After all, if you really believe that abortion is murder or that animal suffering and slaughter have moral weight, then you might conclude that, notwithstanding the law, you are morally justified in using violent means to rescue or protect human fetuses or animals. To examine what might be wrong with this inference requires us first to acknowledge its seeming appeal. Accordingly, this chapter explores the arguments for violence as a means of advancing the respective goals of the pro-life and animal rights movements.

BEYOND CIVIL DISOBEDIENCE

To evaluate the legitimacy of activist violence, we must first define the sort of law breaking we have in mind here. We focus on violence, not on illegal conduct as such. Some of the laws that would shield the targets of activism—like the state ag-gag laws and over-broad restrictions on protests at or near abortion clinics—are unconstitutional infringements on the freedom of speech.[12] In our legal system, there is generally not even a *legal* duty, much less a *moral* duty, to obey such invalid laws.[13]

Moreover, there is a long tradition of activists violating even generally valid laws as a form of protest against injustice. Mainstream opinion celebrates such champions of civil disobedience as Henry David Thoreau, Mohandas Gandhi, Rosa Parks, and the Reverend Dr. Martin Luther King Jr., notwithstanding the fact that they all spent time in jail—indeed, partly *because* they all spent time in jail—to manifest the depth of their commitment to their ideals. In many circumstances principled, nonviolent law breaking will be the best tactic for achieving some aim, whether the aim is dramatizing opposition to a war, gaining independence for a country, or fighting racial oppression. Civil disobedience, though illegal by definition, does not in our view raise the moral issues that surround the use of what we would call "violence": namely, acts that include the infliction of injury, death, or terror on one's adversaries.

But civil disobedience typically appeals to the conscience of the oppressor. What if the oppressor has no conscience—or has a conscience but utterly rejects your view of what morality requires? A categorical pacifist will stick with nonviolence nonetheless. Most people, however, are not categorical pacifists. Most believe that deadly force is morally permissible in self-defense or in justifiable defense of others. And so, if you have reason to believe that appeals to conscience will inevitably fail, then you might conclude that violence is in some instances both necessary and morally justified.

The stakes of the question appear in an exchange between Gandhi and the philosopher Martin Buber. In a 1938 essay Gandhi addressed the question of whether he thought nonviolence was the answer to Nazism. After disavowing all war, he said yes, even if the expected result would be what eventually occurred—the murder of nearly all of the millions of Jews who lived in Europe.[14] Buber, a Jew who had at the time only recently fled Germany for what was then Palestine, replied that "[a]n effective stand in the form of non-violence may be taken against unfeeling human beings in the hope of gradually bringing them to their senses; but a diabolic universal steamroller cannot thus be withstood."[15]

We think that Buber had the better of this argument. While it may sometimes be morally permissible—and perhaps even laudable—to turn the other cheek to aggressors, there are other times when violence may not only be legitimate but may even be morally obligatory.[16] We regard the need to stop Hitler to have represented one such moral imperative.

The fact that violent resistance to Nazis was justified does not mean that violent resistance to abortion providers or vivisectionists is justified in contemporary America. For one thing, democratic means of struggling against injustice are available to modern activists in this country. Surely before one turns to violence, one must take advantage of nonviolent methods of affecting change. And, as we have noted, that is the approach of the mainstream pro-life and animal rights movements. Violence is justifiable only in the absence of nonviolent alternatives—that is, in cases comparable to self-defense or defense of others against an imminent threat of death or injury. Can violent activists within either the pro-life or the animal rights movement plausibly claim that violence is "necessary" in this sense?

GLASS HOUSES

As an initial matter, the answer depends on how narrow or broad a view we take of the activist's conduct. In particular, we think it necessary for the activist to consider how his or her own conduct may be part of the problem of violence against animals or fetuses that he or she opposes. To mangle a metaphor, activists who live in glass houses should not throw stones at laboratories or abortion clinics.

Before turning to coercive violence that aims to change the behavior of others, an activist ought to ensure that she herself is not, through her own conduct, part of the problem. For that reason, we have little patience with self-described animal rights activists who engage in violence—even violence that aims to cause only property damage—while they themselves eat or wear animal products.

For one thing, as we note in chapter 2, although most animal experimentation is unnecessary, the case for the moral permissibility of some medical research on animals is stronger than the case for the moral permissibility of exploiting and slaughtering animals for food and clothing. Hence, targeting animal experimentation for violence—as some do—while leaving the producers of animal food and clothing unmolested seems morally backward.

More importantly, engaging in *any* violence against people who harm animals as part of their business while voluntarily purchasing animal products and thus supporting those or indistinguishable businesses reeks of hypocrisy, or at best confusion.

We might level a related sort of criticism against those anti-abortion activists (violent or otherwise) who oppose government programs that aim to make contraception more widely available. Some forms of contraception prevent uterine implantation of a zygote and, for that reason, are regarded by some abortion opponents as an abortifacient, objectionable in itself.[17] But there are also people within the pro-life movement who oppose all forms of contraception because contraception licenses (heterosexual) sexual pleasure without the "penalty" of pregnancy and, depending on the method of contraception, the penalty of sexually transmitted disease.[18] Much of this opposition is fueled by conservative religious teaching, but regardless of the source, the impact is the same: By working to decrease the availability of contraception that would prevent unwanted pregnancies, these pro-life activists increase the number of unplanned pregnancies and thus increase the demand for abortion, which is the primary driver of supply.

In both contexts, resort to violence is unjustified, given that there are nonviolent measures the activists themselves could take—or refrain from taking—in their own lives that would reduce the same sort of harm that they purportedly aim to impede by violence.

Accordingly, let us imagine the strongest case for movement violence, one that will be unrealistic as a description of many actual activists. If our hypothetical activist is part of the animal rights movement, she is a vegan. If she is in the pro-life movement, she also promotes contraception and generous child-care subsidies. In either case, suppose that she works tirelessly to change hearts and minds. She writes to her elected representatives, she tables, she demonstrates, she festoons her body and her possessions with movement messages. She undertakes all of these activities with the aim of making long-term change, which she agrees is a possibility in our democracy. She accepts the lessons of the Gandhi/Buber exchange and acknowledges both that her fellow citizens have consciences that can be reached and that our system of government provides her with opportunities to reach them.

Nonetheless, the activist says, such efforts at persuasion aim to bring about long-term changes in individual behavior and in the law. For the animals now being held captive or for the fetuses about to be aborted, the long term is too late. She has very good reason to believe that stopping the torture and killing of these *particular* animals or the abortion of these *particular* fetuses can be accomplished, if at all, only through violent means. Put differently, with respect to these particular individuals, the use of violence really is the only hope, and thus it is a last resort. What can we say in response to that sort of argument?

WHEN TO ELEVATE SPECIFIC VICTIMS

As we discussed earlier, most people think (and the law accepts) that violence is morally permissible in the face of an imminent threat of death or substantial bodily harm, if the only way of repelling the threat is through the use of violence. But the use of force in self-defense or defense of others when born humans are involved differs in some key ways from activist violence on behalf of nonhuman animals or fetuses.

Consider one distinction. At the present time, the law (in the United States and most other democracies) permits the killing of fetuses through abortion, and the law (virtually worldwide) not only permits but condones and (in the United States) heavily subsidizes the killing of animals through the production and consumption of animal products. As a result, an enormous number of human fetuses and an almost incalculable number of nonhuman animals (worldwide, over 1 trillion per year) constantly face imminent violent death.[19] By contrast, because the law generally prohibits the killing of born humans, far smaller (though not inconsequential) numbers of born humans face imminent violent death.

These facts have important implications. Suppose that you see a gunman preparing to kill your next-door neighbor. If there were no time to call the police, you would be legally and morally justified in using violence. But this experience is likely to be highly unusual. Unless you are a vigilante or live in an especially crime-ridden neighborhood, it would present a once-in-a-lifetime opportunity to use violence to save a human life. If you wanted to save a different born human from imminent violent death, you could not simply walk a block and expect to encounter another neighbor also facing an imminent violent death and try to save her instead. In situations of violence against born humans, when you have the opportunity to use violence to intervene (and where nothing short of violence will work), you are accordingly *not* in a "triage" situation in which you must decide "will I save this person from violence, although it involves my using violence, or will I walk away and save another person, whose rescue may not require that level of (or perhaps any) violence?" You are not like a firefighter who must make a tragic choice of which stranded person to save from a burning building; there is just one person in the burning building whose life you have the opportunity to save right now.

Even when you face a triage situation of this sort, of course, you might see fit to refrain from rescuing the victim either because you categorically oppose violence in all circumstances or because you hope to avoid the risk to yourself or innocent bystanders if you attempt a rescue. It is therefore fair to describe the circumstances, when one could rescue an innocent through the use of violent force, as presenting a choice between permissible violence and permissible nonviolence (perhaps in a way that we would not describe the circumstances of countries deciding whether to enter World War II to stop the Nazis).

By contrast, no one ever really has the opportunity to rescue *just one particular* fetus or *just one particular* animal but no others. Doctors are performing—and women are undergoing— many abortions every day, and most people are individually consuming animal products, thereby participating in the infliction of suffering and slaughter on animals, several times each day. To intervene to prevent violent death in these two contexts is therefore necessarily to make a choice: which individual fetuses or animals will you endeavor to rescue or save and what means will you deploy in your efforts?

Consequently, even though violence may be the only means available to save any one particular fetus or animal (or any one group of fetuses or animals), there is generally no reason to decide to favor the lives of the particular fetuses or animals threatened in one context rather than the lives of those threatened in a different context. Why, then, would anyone choose to do violence to a fellow human in an effort to save particular innocent victims rather than employ some other, nonviolent, method of rescue to save different—and equally worthy—innocent victims? Violence against any particular person harming fetuses or animals, or in favor of any particular fetuses or animals, is arbitrary. The huge number of victims therefore provides a reason to choose peaceful rather than violent means of serving the cause because the victims whose rescue requires violence are no more or less worthy than the victims whose rescue does not.

An advocate of violence might challenge this conclusion by asking how you might peacefully rescue victim A from violence rather than violently rescue victim B from similar violence. In the context of both abortion and animal rights, the obvious answer is through nonviolent advocacy and education. By reaching out with information to the population generally—those people who use abortion services and consume animal products—advocates can reduce the demand for what they regard as unjust consumer products.

A pro-life advocate can convince women through speeches, literature, and perhaps even graphic footage (as we discussed in detail in chapter 6) to refrain from having an abortion. She can also offer women alternatives to abortion, given the fact that at least some number of women might prefer to take their pregnancies to term if only they had financial support for raising a child or if only they had the option of co-raising a child with an open adoption rather than giving birth and then having to say goodbye to their newborns forever. In other countries where people oppose abortion, the pro-life movement does not appear to engage in the sort of violence we see in the United States but instead offers financial aid as an alternative to women seeking to terminate a pregnancy.[20] Each time a woman decides not to have an abortion, the advocate who influenced her has nonviolently rescued a fetus from death.

Similarly, in the animal rights movement, one can save animals by providing education about why those of us who are ethical vegans decided to give up animal products. We can talk about the nutritional adequacy and, indeed, superiority of the vegan diet,[21] we can offer delicious vegan food samples, and we can discuss the environmental benefits of boycotting animal agriculture. On average, each person who becomes vegan due to our advocacy efforts results in over one hundred fewer animal deaths annually due to consumer demand.[22]

If one wants to rescue specific, identifiable fetuses or animals, one can do so. Advocacy that addresses particular pregnant women necessarily aims to rescue particular fetuses: namely, the ones gestating inside those women. Animal rights activists also can rescue particular, identifiable victims. They can provide sanctuary to one or more of the many animals who have been discarded and have been slated to die not to serve any human desire but as the garbage of industry. Such animals include the millions of dogs, cats, and other companion animals—and "racing" or "performing" animals—abandoned and surrendered by owners who have lost interest in the relationship.[23] In the food industry, one can find similarly discarded lives at stockyards and slaughterhouses, where large numbers of animals are left to die on the ground, or at hatcheries where male chicks are killed.[24] And at least some of the animals exploited in scientific experiments are available for adoption once their utility in the laboratory has run out.[25] One need not use force or violence to take in these animals because no one is generally fighting to hold onto them. And their lives have as much inherent worth as those of the animals whose rescue might require violence. The sheer numbers of animals in need of rescue—and the corresponding impossibility of saving them all (or even a significant proportion of them)—liberates those who wish to rescue victims to concentrate on the ones who may be saved peacefully.

A proponent of violence still might counter that some fetuses (those gestating in women who have firmly made up their minds to have abortions) and animals (those whom the industry has not discarded) cannot be rescued by nonviolent means, but, to reiterate, the activist has no morally nonarbitrary reason for focusing on those particular fetuses or animals rather than on the ones who can be rescued through peaceful means. Thus, violence is not *necessary* to rescue fetuses or animals or even to rescue particular fetuses or animals. In the absence of necessity, vigilante violence is not only tactically dangerous but also morally unacceptable.

ANOTHER WAY IN WHICH VIOLENCE IS ARBITRARY

Anti-abortion violence typically targets doctors and other medical staff who provide abortions rather than women seeking abortions. Indeed, in recent years, even the mainstream pro-life movement has sought to portray women who have abortions as victims of the abortion "industry," as evidenced by the supposed "abortion regret syndrome" that we discussed in chapter 6. Likewise, animal liberationists tend to vilify "vivisectionists" and, more rarely, slaughterhouse workers rather than the people who demand food, cosmetics, and apparel made from animal products.

At one level, the activists' focus on supply rather than demand makes sense. A pro-life activist who prevents one woman from entering an abortion clinic saves (at most) one fetus from abortion. But an activist who kills or intimidates the one doctor in the region who performs abortions may save thousands of fetuses. Focusing violence and intimidation on providers rather than suppliers has a larger payoff in the abortion context.

The calculus differs somewhat for animal activists, but it may lead to the same tactical conclusion. Unlike a woman who may have at most a handful of abortions in her lifetime, most people consume hundreds or thousands of animals over the course of a lifetime. Thus, targeting consumers for education could be more effective than targeting particular animals for liberation. Yet consumers do not *directly* kill or harm the animals; they demand the animal products that others must kill or harm animals to create. An animal rights activist who hopes to liberate animals may believe that he can do so only by targeting the people who are exploiting them directly on farms, in laboratories, and in other settings where they endure human-inflicted suffering and death.

We are not persuaded by these arguments on their own terms, as we explain shortly. However, even granting for now that the foregoing sorts of reasons explain why pro-life or animal rights activists might think that they have good tactical reasons to target supply rather than demand, they raise a broader problem. In attacking suppliers, activists send the tacit but unmistakable message that the suppliers, rather than the consumers, are the bad actors. Indeed, as we have noted, in portraying women who have abortions as victims of abortion providers, the pro-life movement more or less sends this message expressly.

A policy of attacking supply without addressing demand will likely be ineffective over the long run. So long as there is demand for abortions and animal products, there will be incentives to supply them. Indeed, even legal prohibitions that target supply without substantially dampening demand often fail, as the American experience with Prohibition and the "war on drugs" illustrates.

Moreover, even beyond the likely inefficacy of attacking supply but not demand, the practice is morally arbitrary. Just as an activist generally will have no sound reason to rescue some particular fetuses or animals violently rather than some other fetuses or animals nonviolently, so she lacks a sound moral reason for targeting suppliers rather than consumers.

The people who provide abortions and animal products are no worse than the people who demand them. Indeed, they may not be as bad. Much of the work in the animal exploitation industry—especially in slaughterhouses—pays poorly and traumatizes workers.[26] The people who do this work do so because of limited economic opportunities. By contrast, people who consume and thereby demand animal products generally have real alternatives. Meanwhile, medical staff who perform abortions despite the personal sacrifices it entails frequently do so because of a moral commitment to women's reproductive autonomy. It is one thing for pro-life activists to reach a different conclusion about the morality of such work; but it is hard to say that someone who performs abortions to help others is worse than a woman who decides to abort her own fetus for reasons that pro-life activists would likely regard as insubstantial, such as to avoid the economic burden of raising a child.

PRACTICAL CONSEQUENCES INFORM PRINCIPLE

We now return to a point we foreshadowed earlier. We said that we are not persuaded by the claim that an activist can do more for his movement through violence than through nonviolence, but the reader may be wondering whether that is really an objection *in principle*. We think it is because, as we noted in chapter 5, matters of practicality and principle can often intersect.

Suppose that an animal rights activist is considering sabotaging a farm or a laboratory. Even if the activist takes steps to minimize the risk of death or serious bodily harm to the human beings who work at the farm or laboratory, the sabotage might be unjustified if it ends up doing more harm than good for the cause. Even assuming that the benefit to the particular animals at the farm or laboratory could justify the risk of harm to the humans holding them captive, if the net impact of sabotage is counterproductive to the animal rights movement, then a lesser-of-the evils approach to morality would consider it unjustified.

In other words, the practical objection that pro-life or animal rights violence is counterproductive is also a reason of principle why such violence is wrong. Even a deontologist cannot ignore the consequences of her actions in making a moral judgment, especially when the violence is itself deployed with the intention of having an impact on the public rather than just on the specific animals who might be rescued.

Someone might object to this line of reasoning on the ground that it is too demanding. One who wants to rescue captive animals or fetuses slated for abortion (typically) aims to do so because she believes that the animals and fetuses have a *right* to their own lives, just as already-born human beings have a right to their lives. By comparison, we would not say that a particular act of self-defense is unjustified if it turns out that it sets in motion some chain of events that later ends up causing more harm than would have resulted from submitting to injustice. Likewise, one might conclude that pro-life or animal rights violence is either justified or not based on its immediate projected effects without consideration of its likely long-term consequences.

Yet that response makes too much of the analogy to self-defense or defense of others. As we have already noted, in the usual circumstances, a claim of justifiable self-defense or defense of others will arise when a person is suddenly confronted by a wrongdoer. An activist, by contrast, goes out to look for the good he can do or the wrongs he can combat. In deciding how to spend each marginal increment of his activist time, a consideration of the aggregate impact of his activities does seem highly relevant because he has the luxury of deliberation in a way that an actor confronting a sudden attack does not.

Of course, even if we are right that counterproductive violence is therefore objectionable on principle, a particular activist might disagree with our empirical assessment that violence will be counterproductive for the movement as a whole. And we acknowledge that pro-life violence may not be counterproductive, on net. Perhaps the intimidation of doctors and other medical staff ends up so reducing the number of abortions that are performed as to outweigh the other, counterproductive, effects of pro-life violence. The consequential calculus is, we recognize, complex.

Accordingly, acknowledging that counterproductivity is partly a matter of principle does not necessarily provide a categorical objection in principle to pro-life violence because any given activist might argue that such violence is, on net, beneficial to the cause. And to the extent that an animal rights activist reaches a similar conclusion about the costs and benefits of violence, she too might reject our objection, although the scale of violence against animals is such that it is hard to imagine activist counterviolence making a dent in either the supply of or the demand for the products of animal exploitation.

MORAL CONSIDERATION OR MORAL EQUALITY

The arguments we have thus far considered against violence should apply to all activists, regardless of the reasons for their activism. But the pro-life and animal rights movements are diverse, encompassing people with a variety of views. Depending on their underlying philosophical beliefs, some activists may have an additional reason for opposing violence.

Our argument for veganism in chapters 1 and 2 can be rephrased in the form of a syllogism: (A) Because sentient animals have interests of their own, they are entitled to moral consideration; (B) the primary purposes for which people use animal products—palate pleasure and fashion—are not sufficiently weighty to override the interests of sentient animals; and therefore (C) humans generally have a moral duty to avoid creating demand for the exploitation and slaughter of animals.

Put differently, the syllogism establishes that animal interests in their own lives generally outweigh the interests that humans have in exploiting or taking those lives. But it does not necessarily follow that vindicating the interests of animals outweighs the interests of humans in continuing their own lives or in remaining free of violent attack. It is one thing to say, as we do, that we are morally obligated to make the relatively modest personal sacrifice of becoming vegan (especially as we no longer regard it as a sacrifice at all). But in order to justify killing (or taking actions that create a substantial risk of death or serious injury to) the people who work in the animal exploitation business, would appear to require more. That further step would appear to require that one believe that animals and humans have an equal right to their own lives so that, as between the animal victim and the human perpetrator, judgments about innocence and guilt may justify violence against the latter to stop the harm he is doing to the former.[27]

The same sort of consideration could also be relevant to an anti-abortion activist's decision whether to engage in violence. After all, many people who oppose abortion nonetheless believe that an abortion to save the mother's life is morally permissible. Why? One possibility is a syllogism that goes something like this: (A) Fetuses are entitled to moral consideration; (B) most of the reasons why women have abortions are not sufficient to overcome the fetus's interest in life; and therefore (C) abortion is usually immoral; but (D) when carrying a pregnancy to term would threaten a woman's life, then she is justified in having an abortion.

The final step in the foregoing reasoning chain could be based on the view that in a situation of unresolvable conflict, it is permissible to prefer one's own life to that of another full rights-bearing person.[28] Or it could be based on the view that, while fetuses are entitled to moral consideration, they are not entitled to quite the same moral consideration as people who are already born. To the extent that someone holds the latter view, she could conclude that she would be unjustified in committing acts of serious violence to prevent an abortion. As with animal rights, so too the reasons for not having an abortion do not necessarily justify killing (or taking actions that create a substantial risk of death or serious injury to) the people who provide abortions.

How effective are these arguments? We note first that many, perhaps most, animal rights and pro-life activists would not regard the arguments as relevant to evaluating the case for or against violence in their respective domains. Many activists in fact believe that animals or fetuses are entitled to the same moral consideration as already-born humans are. For them, violence to stop unjustified violence against animals or fetuses, if wrong, must be wrong for reasons that do not diminish the moral status of nonhumans or fetuses relative to born humans.

Furthermore, we are not even confident that the inequality/disproportionality argument would be persuasive for those activists who take a narrower view of the rights of animals or fetuses. After all, defensive violence can be morally justified even when it does more harm to the perpetrator than the perpetrator threatens to do to the victim. The law of self-defense provides a potentially helpful analogy.

In all American jurisdictions with which we are familiar, the law permits the use of deadly force in self-defense or in defense of a third party, even to stave off an attack that threatens only to cause serious bodily injury but not death. Suppose that a Good Samaritan observes a man attempting to rape a woman. The Good Samaritan knows this rapist's history and knows that he never kills or threatens his victims' lives. U.S. constitutional law recognizes that killing is a greater deprivation than rape by categorically barring the death penalty as a punishment for rape even as it allows capital punishment for some murders.[29] Nonetheless, the Good Samaritan is legally entitled to use deadly force to stop the attack. In other words, the law permits killing to prevent "merely" serious bodily injury.

We should be clear about how we are and how we are not using the foregoing example. We are using the law to illustrate a particular widely shared moral intuition—namely, that violence against aggressors and in defense of innocents can be justified even when the defensive violence results in a *greater* harm than the violence it aims to avert. This may be in part because people who threaten to inflict grave injury on innocents have perhaps forfeited some of their own right to be free of violence, a principle that complements the retributive case for violence we discussed earlier. Thus, even if one regards the interests of animals or fetuses in their lives as somewhat less important than the interests of already-born humans in their lives, one could still think that it is morally justifiable to kill a person who is attacking an innocent animal or fetus. The fact that the killing in defense of another (here an animal or a fetus) averts a lesser harm than the one it causes does not necessarily render the other-defending killing unjustified.

Of course, we are not arguing that the law itself already acknowledges that violence is justified to prevent voluntary abortion or the exploitation or killing of animals. Plainly, the law generally denies any such right. Nonetheless, the law of self-defense and defense of others reflects a general moral principle that authorizes violence against aggressors even when the violence is not exactly proportionate to the harm that the aggressors themselves are perpetrating. One could then invoke that general principle in support of an argument to justify anti-abortion or anti-animal-exploitation violence, even by people whose commitments are rooted in moral respect for fetuses or animals but not in full equality for fetuses or animals.

In short, the disproportionality objection to violence against abortion providers or animal exploiters may fail, even if one views fetuses or animals as morally inferior to already-born humans. Someone who believes that fetuses or animals are equal to already-born humans would find the objection irrelevant, and even someone who thinks that fetuses or animals are entitled to somewhat less moral consideration than (already-born) humans can respond that violence remains justified.

A SOMEWHAT CONTINGENT
CASE AGAINST VIOLENCE

It may be that nothing we have said here would persuade a pro-violence activist to change course because we recognize that most of our arguments are contingent in some way or another. If one thinks that violent law breaking is ever morally justified, then arguments about its justification in any particular circumstances will tend to turn on particulars.

Indeed, even one of our strongest points—the arbitrariness of attacking producers but not consumers—is contestable. Consider antislavery violence in the antebellum United States. Was such violence wrong because it attacked slaveholders but not the people, including many north of the Mason-Dixon line and in Europe, who consumed the products of slave labor? We think it was wrong, but we suspect that people who today condemn slavery (as nearly everyone does) will likely have a variety of views on the question. Likewise, it should not be surprising that people who regard abortion or animal exploitation as an evil comparable to slavery also divide on the question of the legitimacy of violence as a means of attacking these institutions.

Thus, although we continue to think that neither pro-life nor animal rights violence is justified, given the stakes, we are not surprised that some people in each movement disagree. We are simply grateful that the leadership of each movement opposes violence, and we wish that the pro-life movement's leadership were as effective in discouraging violence by its radical fringe as the animal rights movement's leadership has apparently been with respect to its radical fringe.

Conclusion

When friends and colleagues learned that we were writing a book about abortion and animal rights, some of them were confused. They thought we might be writing about whether animals should have a right to abortion. The confusion was at first amusing, but as we thought more about it, we realized that it points to a serious issue. As we explained in chapter 3, the reproductive servitude of dairy cows and egg-laying hens bridges the animal rights and pro-choice movements. But even though the immorality of dairy and eggs are clear, other questions about animal reproduction are more complex. Human beings, including humans like us who oppose treating animals as things, routinely control animal reproduction.

In this conclusion, we raise questions about human control over animal reproduction. Our discussion points to one final link between (human) abortion and animal rights: Moral decision making with respect to both abortion and animal rights will often be fraught because it occurs in a damaged world. In a perfect world, humans would never have selectively bred animals who are dependent on humans to reproduce and many of whom suffer serious health problems when they live more than a few months. In a perfect world, every human pregnancy would be planned and wanted. But we do not live in that perfect world, and so we face some difficult choices. Focusing on one such choice— whether to neuter a companion dog or cat—serves to illustrate the broader phenomenon.

STERILIZATION: THE LESSER EVIL

We live with our two human daughters and three dogs we adopted from shelters. Our dogs were surgically sterilized before we adopted them, but even if they had not been, we would have had them surgically "fixed" to prevent them from procreating, as we did for our earlier generation of dogs. We would not dream of doing anything like this to our human daughters, so why do we think that it is permissible—indeed, even morally obligatory—to neuter or spay dogs and cats?

The short answer is that we do not regard companion-animal sterilization as an unalloyed good. Rather, it is a choice in favor of the lesser of two evils, much as "pet ownership" itself raises difficult questions even if the animals are adopted from shelters. We focus here on human limits on companion-animal reproduction, but we recognize that other ways in which humans limit the freedom of even beloved companions may be problematic as well.

Involuntary sterilization of animals harms their interests in three principal ways. First, it inflicts pain. Animals exploited for their flesh and bodily products suffer unanesthetized mutilations because farmers derive no economic benefit from paying for anesthesia. Thus, for example, millions of male piglets raised for meat are routinely castrated without anesthesia. As one would expect, they scream bloody murder.[1]

By contrast, companion animals receive anesthesia when they undergo spaying or neutering. Our first two dogs, Scooter and Mandy, were unconscious for their surgeries, for instance, and we gave them pain medication postoperatively. Nonetheless, they clearly experienced discomfort, which they manifested by attempting to lick the surgical sites for days. In the interest of avoiding infection and to prevent them from ripping out their stitches, we stopped them by attaching cones to their collars, thus generating frustration on top of their discomfort.

Second, in addition to causing suffering, neutering an animal deprives that animal of the opportunity to enjoy sexual pleasure. Although some neutered animals continue to manifest what appear to be sexual urges, the surgery prevents them from satisfying those urges in the way that unaltered animals can.

Third, other than in the unusual circumstance in which a companion animal adopts another animal's biological offspring, neutering deprives an animal of the opportunity to experience a strong emotional bond with her young. (We say "her" in recognition of the fact that in most species kept as companion animals, females play a larger role than males do in caring for young.) Anyone who has ever observed mother hens with their chicks, or a dog or cat grooming her puppies or kittens, understands that nonhuman animals form intense parent–young bonds. Science confirms that the biochemical mediators of such bonds are remarkably similar in humans and other vertebrate animals. Oxytocin, the so-called love hormone, plays this role among mammals while similar chemicals can be found in other vertebrates.[2] Animals deprived of the opportunity to parent young thus miss an important piece of what it means to thrive.

Despite the foregoing deprivations, we nonetheless agree with the conventional wisdom that dogs and cats (and other animals) kept as companions should be neutered because we agree that, left unchecked, "pet" reproduction would cause even greater harms. The supply of puppies and kittens created by breeders and by dogs and cats who reproduce on their own (either because they are strays or because their human caretakers do not spay or neuter them) exceeds the demand for companion animals. Although outreach can increase the number of available homes, thus reducing the number of healthy animals killed by shelters, the demand almost certainly cannot be brought to the level of an unmediated supply; consequently, each additional puppy or kitten brought into the world will likely take his or her place in a home that would otherwise have gone to some existing animal. Accordingly, we sterilize our companion animals—even though it harms them—in order to spare other animals an even worse fate.

Is that judgment consistent with a commitment to animal rights? The decision to spay or neuter any particular dog does not at first appear to be for the benefit of that particular dog. It may not even seem to benefit the puppies to whom that particular dog would otherwise have given birth or sired. Have we fallen into a crude utilitarianism that simply trades off the interests of one dog against those of another?

To make the problem concrete, imagine an example. Suppose that Sally (a human) shares her loving home with two healthy young, unrelated dogs, Rex and Ginger. Suppose further that Sally's neighbors offer to open their homes to any puppies whom Rex and Ginger might produce. If Sally neuters Rex and spays Ginger, assume that those same neighbors would go to the local animal shelter to adopt dogs, but if she instead refrains from altering them, and they reproduce, the resulting puppies will be adopted by the neighbors instead. The displaced dogs in the shelter will not be adopted but will be killed. Is it permissible for Sally to neuter Rex and spay Ginger—to harm them—in order to confer a benefit on other dogs even though Rex and Ginger are not responsible for having put those other dogs in their current circumstances? If so, how do we reconcile that conclusion with treating animals as individuals?

Our answer begins by questioning whether sterilization really is contrary to the interests of Rex and Ginger or to the interests of their puppies. Wolves—the wild animals from whom domesticated dogs descend—spend their entire lives in packs of related animals. Thus, not surprisingly, most canine mothers experience a loss when a breeder or purchaser takes their puppies from them at an early age, often as young as seven weeks old.[3] If we could ask Ginger whether she would rather have puppies but have them taken from her at an early age or be spayed and thus not have puppies at all, it is hardly obvious that she would choose the former.

Moreover, even if Ginger would prefer to have loved and lost than to have never loved at all, failure to neuter Rex and spay Ginger will create new problems—and not just fail to address existing problems. Sally may have commitments from her neighbors to adopt the first generation of offspring from Rex and Ginger, but she cannot be certain that there will be homes for the puppies'

puppies, much less the puppies' puppies' puppies. Failing to neuter Rex and Ginger thus does more than merely prevent the rescue of dogs in shelters who would otherwise be adopted; it will likely lead to the creation of puppies (one or two or more generations down the line) who themselves will face an early death at a shelter because insufficient numbers of homes can be found for them.

Might the failure to spay or neuter nonetheless be characterized as a permissible omission, whereas spaying or neutering is an affirmative, and thus culpable, act? Although earlier parts of this book relied on the act/omission distinction in a variety of contexts, we also acknowledged that that distinction is less salient when moral agents have special agent-relative duties. In particular, we acknowledged that parents have special duties toward their children. We would note here that people stand in roughly the same relationship toward their companion animals as they do toward their children, both with respect to the animals and children themselves and with respect to third parties. Thus, just as we would not excuse a parent who failed to teach his child that he ought not to throw rocks at other children on the ground that the failure was "only" an omission, so too we would not excuse a dog owner who failed to teach her dogs not to bite the neighbors' children on the ground that the failure was a mere omission.

Similarly, we think that a pet owner bears responsibility for her decision not to neuter her pet, even though failure to do so could be characterized as an omission. She owes the duty to third-party victims of the failure to neuter, certainly including the offspring who will have their lives cut short and probably also the animals currently in shelters.

Having said that, we acknowledge that sterilization of companion animals raises serious moral questions. In a perfect world, human beings would not play any direct role in controlling animal reproduction.

HUMAN ABORTION

The problem of human abortion is similar in an important respect: prior events leave only flawed options.

Pro-life activists sometimes tendentiously describe their political adversaries as "pro-abortion."[4] This way of thinking sometimes even finds its way into legislation. For example, a longstanding provision of a federal grant program forbids the expenditure of funds "in programs where abortion is a method of family planning."[5] Although the provision was intended, and has been construed, to prevent expenditures on abortions generally, if read literally it would have virtually no application. After all, almost no one uses an abortion as a *method of family planning*. On the contrary, women resort to abortion because they failed to engage in family planning, or because their family planning (i.e., contraception) failed, or because the pregnancy, if carried to term, would yield a severely disabled family member, which is not at all what was planned. Put differently, just about nobody goes out and *plans* to have an abortion. Women have abortions when they find themselves in circumstances that they would have preferred to avoid.

Thus, just as humans make decisions about animal reproduction under less-than-ideal circumstances, so too individual women make decisions about whether to have an abortion in suboptimal circumstances. Ideally, women would not have any abortions because they would find themselves pregnant only under circumstances in which they wished to be.

As with animal reproduction, so with human reproduction: the fact that circumstances leave only suboptimal choices does not mean that there are no better or worse choices. Some issues are clear-cut. For example, a woman who decides that she will have an abortion has some moral obligation to abort as soon as possible, both to minimize health risks to herself and to ensure that the abortion occurs before fetal sentience.

Thinking about abortion as a choice made under suboptimal conditions also points the way toward broader policy cooperation. By joining campaigns promoting contraception, pro-life activists could reduce the number of unwanted pregnancies and thus the number of abortions as well. To be sure, many people who are pro-life also oppose contraception, typically on religious grounds. But not everyone who is pro-life is anticontraception. Indeed, most people who oppose abortion support contraception, and even people who oppose certain forms of birth control on the ground that they destroy an embryo or prevent implantation of a fertilized egg are often comfortable with the common forms of contraception that prevent ovulation or conception.[6]

As we have explained throughout this book, we have considerable sympathy for some of the views of the pro-life movement, but we nonetheless regard our position as more closely aligned with its rival, the pro-choice movement. For that reason, we are probably not well positioned to give advice to the pro-life movement. But insofar as pro-life readers are interested, our advice would be to work toward a world in which fewer women feel burdened by an unwanted pregnancy, a burden that foreseeably generates the need or desire for an abortion.

IS ZOOPOLIS ZOOTOPIA?

By contrast to our caveat with respect to the pro-life movement, we do regard ourselves as card-carrying members of the animal rights movement. Thus, we have some insider thoughts about how animal rights activists can change the preconditions for the tragic choices we now face regarding animal reproduction and other questions. Our point of departure is a thoughtful and thought-provoking book by Sue Donaldson and Will Kymlicka, *Zoopolis*.

Donaldson and Kymlicka theorize about the sorts of relationships that humans ought to have with other animals. They contend that animal rights theory's focus on the inherent moral value of animals has led animal rights theorists to focus almost exclusively on "the direct violation of basic rights" at the expense of attending to more complex relationships.[7] They imagine a future in which nonhumans fall into roughly three categories, depending on how they prefer to interact with humans: (1) Sovereigns: Humans would respect the *sovereignty* over substantial undeveloped territory of wild animals who either want nothing to do with humans or cannot interact with humans safely; (2) Citizens: Domesticated animals like dogs, who seem to thrive in relationships with humans, would be given *citizenship* rights and duties in accordance with their capacities and preferences; and (3) Denizens: Liminal animals like pigeons, squirrels, and rats—who live among us but not with us—would be treated as *denizens*, entitled to respect and consideration in roughly the same way that human communities now treat welcome human strangers among us. In this world, humans would not *breed* animals, but neither would they generally interfere with animals' own reproduction.

We applaud the efforts of Donaldson and Kymlicka to consider not only the ways in which humans currently mistreat animals but also to think about how humans might interact with animals to our mutual benefit, both now and in a future world in which people more generally have finally come to reject the current, deeply exploitative relationship that we have with our fellow earthlings. That is not to say that we agree with all of their conclusions. In particular, we question the view that it would be possible for sheep, chickens, and cows to live among humans as citizens and (through a human intermediary) to sell their wool, eggs, and milk.[8] We are highly skeptical of this claim, and we also note that such purpose-bred species almost by definition cannot live fully satisfying lives: pigs, steers, turkeys, and "broiler" chickens bred to reach slaughter weight at a very young age endure pain and disability when permitted to grow beyond that weight; laying hens suffer prolapses, extreme calcium deficiencies, and other maladies from having been bred to produce large numbers of eggs[9]; and domesticated sheep need to be sheared only because of selective breeding for excess wool that many are incapable of shedding.[10] In our view, having created these species in the first place, humans bear responsibility for deciding whether to bring into existence any new members of these species or instead to permit the land that would be liberated by a shift to veganism return to nature and to members of other species who can live on their own. In our judgment, the latter choice would be more responsible.[11]

Dogs and cats are different, and we are at least open to the possibility that, in the zoopolis imagined by Donaldson and Kymlicka, it would be appropriate for humans to both live with dogs and cats and to refrain from interfering with their reproduction. But, to point out the obvious, we do not live in the utopian zoopolis, and the most pressing questions today revolve around what to do now and how to get from here to there. We live in a world in which most animals receive no moral consideration, and in which even those animals whose interests humans purport to value—such as dogs and cats—are often treated as mere things (as when they are used in medical and other experiments, and when they are bred and purchased as pets).

In our world as it actually is, the decision to adopt an animal from a shelter is a noble act but one that necessarily entails difficult choices. Dogs are scavengers by nature, so they can thrive on a vegan diet. Our dogs are involuntary vegans, and they are none the worse for it. Some people with adopted cats feed them a vegan diet, and some such cats suffer no ill effects, but there is evidence that cats may be obligate carnivores, meaning that they might not be able to live healthy lives without consuming some meat.[12]

Should a vegan whose cat appears to need meat feed her meat? Should domestic cats be permitted to roam outdoors, where they appear to lead fulfilling lives? Or should human caretakers keep cats indoors, so as to spare the billions of birds and rodents they would otherwise hunt?[13] Is it a sufficient answer that cats tend to live longer lives if they are confined indoors?[14] If it is not possible to provide a home to a cat without bringing about the deaths of other animals, is it wrong to adopt a cat, even if the alternative for that cat is a premature death at a shelter?

And what about the animal shelters themselves? A great many shelters kill animals who could probably be adopted, as the positive experience of some no-kill shelters illustrates.[15] No-kill shelters are able to adopt out more animals by improving their outreach, but they also rely on vigilant control of animal reproduction. Not only do they insist on spaying or neutering every animal they adopt out; no-kill advocates and animal rights advocates more generally promote sterilization of feral cats as well through "trap, neuter, release" programs.[16] Animal advocates promote similar programs for deer as an alternative to lethal population control methods.[17]

None of these approaches to human control of animal reproduction is ideal because no ideal solution is possible given that humans have almost completely appropriated for ourselves the natural environment, including the resources on which other animals depend as well as those other animals themselves. In these circumstances, even the best-intentioned efforts by humans to take affirmative steps to benefit specific animals can really do little more than mitigate the damage that we humans have already done and continue to do.

Having said that, we do not wish to give the impression that all questions about human–animal relations are difficult. Far from it. As we hope we have conveyed throughout this book, all or nearly all of the horrific use to which humans put animals is utterly unjustifiable, leading to a clear moral imperative: each one of us should stop participating in that use and become vegan. Yes, there are some challenging questions about how to imagine the future, but that fact should not blind us to the clear injustices of the present.

NOTES

INTRODUCTION: TWO MOVEMENTS, ONE SET OF ISSUES

1. *See, e.g.*, Mary Eberstadt, *Pro-Animal, Pro-Life*, FIRST THINGS, Jun.–Jul. 2009, at 15, *available at* http://www.firstthings.com/article/2009/05/pro-animal-pro-life-1243228870; Matthew Scully, *Pro-Life, Pro-Animal*, 65(22) NATIONAL REVIEW 35, Nov. 25, 2013, *available at* https://www.nationalreview.com/nrd/articles/363361/pro-life-pro-animal. Per the custom in legal scholarship, citations in this book appear in the format prescribed in THE BLUEBOOK: A UNIFORM SYSTEM OF CITATION (Columbia Law Review Ass'n et al. eds., 19th ed. 2010), except that for the sake of brevity we use fewer explanatory parentheticals than usually appear in law journals and we do not provide the dates on which websites were last visited. We verified all citations of Internet sources before publication.

2. A popular pro-life bumper sticker depicts endangered animals on one side and a human embryo on the other, with the caption "Guess Which One *Isn't* Protected?" For an example that goes in the other direction, consider a 2009 statement by People for the Ethical Treatment of Animals (PETA) spokesman Bruce Friedrich: "I find it grotesquely hypocritical that people who say they are pro-life will, every time they sit down to eat, make a choice to add to the level of misery and cruelty in the world." Matthew Cullinan Hoffman, *Pro-Lifers "Loathsome" and "Grotesquely Hypocritical" for Not Caring About Chickens: PETA Spokesman*, LIFESITENEWS (Jun. 23,

2009, 11:15 AM), http://www.lifesitenews.com/news/archive//ldn/2009/jun
/09062313.

3. *E.g.*, Alabama Pain-Capable Unborn Child Protection Act, § 26-23
B-1-9 (2013); Unborn Child Pain Awareness and Prevention Act, ARK.
CODE ANN. §§ 20-16-1101–1111 (2012); Pain-Capable Unborn Child
Protection Act, NEB. REV. STAT. § 28-3,102–3,111 (2012). The United
States House of Representatives passed a similar bill, but it died in the Sen-
ate. Pain-Capable Unborn Child Protection Act, H.R. 1797, 113th Cong.
(2013).

4. *See NPLA's Mission*, NAT'L PRO LIFE ALLIANCE, http://www.prolife
alliance.com/mission.html.

5. 410 U.S. 113 (1973).

6. *But see* Emily Greene Owens, *Are Underground Markets Really More
Violent? Evidence from Early 20th Century America*, 13 AM. L. & ECON.
REV. 1 (2011). Regarding abortions, see Linda Greenhouse & Reva Siegel,
BEFORE ROE V. WADE: VOICES THAT SHAPED THE ABORTION DEBATE
BEFORE THE SUPREME COURT'S RULING 7 (2010).

7. For answers to some of these questions on the animal rights side, see
Sherry F. Colb, MIND IF I ORDER THE CHEESEBURGER? AND OTHER
QUESTIONS PEOPLE ASK VEGANS (2013).

8. *Exodus* 21:22.

9. *See* John T. Noonan Jr., *Abortion and the Catholic Church: A Summary History*, 12 Nat. L. F. 85, 95, 101, 105, 111–16 (1967). The contemporary Catholic position that abortion is immoral from conception
onward does not necessarily depend on when ensoulment occurs. *See* (Rev.
Dr.) Tadeusz Pacholczyk, *Letter: Embryonic Ensoulment*, NAT'L CATHO-
LIC REG. (Jun. 1, 2003), *available at* http://www.ncregister.com/site/article
/embryonic_ensoulment.

10. *See* Norm Phelps, THE DOMINION OF LOVE: ANIMAL RIGHTS
ACCORDING TO THE BIBLE (2002); Matthew Scully, DOMINION: THE
POWER OF MAN, THE SUFFERING OF ANIMALS, AND THE CALL TO MERCY
(2002). *See also* Charles Camosy, FOR LOVE OF ANIMALS (2013).

11. John Rawls, POLITICAL LIBERALISM 215 (1993).

12. Jeremy Bentham, AN INTRODUCTION TO THE PRINCIPLES OF MOR-
ALS AND LEGISLATION 310 n.1 (Dover Pub. 2007) (1789).

13. *See* Julian Franklin, ANIMAL RIGHTS AND MORAL PHILOSOPHY 7–9
(2007); Tom Regan, *The Case for Animal Rights, in* ANIMAL RIGHTS AND
HUMAN OBLIGATIONS (Tom Regan & Peter Singer eds., 2d ed. 1989) (part 4).

14. This made-up word simply connotes the notion that under various
circumstances the welfare of some people (or nonhuman beings) receives
higher priority than the welfare of others. *See* Derek Parfit, *Equality and
Priority*, 10 RATIO 202 (1997).

15. *See* Michael Moore, PLACING BLAME: A GENERAL THEORY OF THE
CRIMINAL LAW 723 (1997).

16. David DeGrazia, TAKING ANIMALS SERIOUSLY: MENTAL LIFE AND MORAL STATUS 6 (1996). Not everyone sees Singer as an animal rights activist. *See* Gary L. Francione, INTRODUCTION TO ANIMAL RIGHTS: YOUR CHILD OR THE DOG? 148 (2000) (hereafter "INTRODUCTION TO ANIMAL RIGHTS").

17. *See, e.g.,* John Rawls, *Kantian Constructivism in Moral Theory,* 77 J. PHIL. 515 (1980). *See also* Carla Bagnoli, *Constructivism in Metaethics,* STANFORD ENCYCLOPEDIA PHIL. (Sep. 27, 2011), http://plato.stanford.edu/entries/constructivism-metaethics.

18. *See* Richard A. Posner, *The Problematics of Moral and Legal Theory,* 111 HARV. L. REV. 1637, 1641 (1998).

19. *See* Jonathan Haidt, THE RIGHTEOUS MIND: WHY GOOD PEOPLE ARE DIVIDED BY POLITICS AND RELIGION 39–42, 55–56 (2012). *See also* Joshua Greene & Jonathan Haidt, *How (and Where) Does Moral Judgment Work?,* 6 TRENDS IN COGNITIVE SCI. 517, 517 (2002).

1. SENTIENCE OR SPECIES?

1. 550 U.S. 124 (2007).

2. *Id.* at 138–39 (quoting testimony before the Senate Judiciary Committee).

3. *Cage Free Eggs: Behind the Myth,* HUMANEMYTH.ORG, http://www.humanemyth.org/cagefree.htm.

4. AM. VETERINARY MED. ASS'N, AVMA GUIDELINES FOR THE EUTHANASIA OF ANIMALS (2013), *available at* https://www.avma.org/KB/Policies/Documents/euthanasia.pdf.

5. We say that "most" people think this way in recognition of the "deep ecology" movement, which regards nature itself, or in some articulations, all living beings, including nonsentient organisms like plants, as having interests and value. *See* DEEP ECOLOGY FOR THE 21ST CENTURY (George Sessions ed., 1995). We share much of the aesthetic sensibility of deep ecologists, but we nonetheless regard sentience as marking an important moral boundary. Nonetheless, nothing in our argument turns on rejecting the possibility that we might have moral duties that extend beyond what we owe to sentient beings.

6. Gary Francione argues that animal welfare laws actually cause harm by reassuring the public, thereby inducing complacency. *See* Gary L. Francione & Robert Garner, THE ANIMAL RIGHTS DEBATE: ABOLITION OR REGULATION? 4, 26, 51 (2010). One of us has argued similarly: *see* Sherry F. Colb, *An Empty Gesture to Soothe the Conscience: Why We Pass Laws Protecting Chimpanzees and Other Animals from Cruelty,* FINDLAW (Mar. 4, 2009), http://writ.news.findlaw.com/colb/20090304.html. We return to the possibility that animal welfare laws may be counterproductive to the welfare of animals in chapter 5.

7. 7 U.S.C. §§ 2131–2159 (2012).

8. 7 U.S.C. § 2132(g) (2012).

9. Ronald Dworkin, LIFE'S DOMINION: AN ARGUMENT ABOUT ABORTION, EUTHANASIA, AND INDIVIDUAL FREEDOM 30–67 (1994).

10. *Id.* at 42.

11. Kant's view on lying derived from his philosophy that human beings must be treated as ends in themselves, not as means to an end. To lie to another, even to bring about a positive outcome, is to use that person as a means to bring about that outcome. *See* Immanuel Kant, GROUNDWORK FOR THE METAPHYSICS OF MORALS 47 (Allen W. Wood ed., 2002) (1785).

12. Ronald Dworkin, *What Is A Good Life?*, N.Y. REV. BOOKS, Feb. 10, 2011, at 42 (emphasis original), *available at* http://www.nybooks.com /articles/archives/2011/feb/10/what-good-life.

13. *Id.*

14. *See* Jonathan Haidt, THE RIGHTEOUS MIND: WHY GOOD PEOPLE ARE DIVIDED BY POLITICS AND RELIGION 148–49 (2012).

15. Kant, for example, believed so strongly in the duty to refrain from violence that he held suicide to be just as wrongful as homicide. *See, e.g.,* Kant, *supra* note 11, at 47.

16. *See, e.g.,* Julian Franklin, ANIMAL RIGHTS AND MORAL PHILOSOPHY (2007); Tom Regan, *The Case for Animal Rights, in* ANIMAL RIGHTS AND HUMAN OBLIGATIONS (Tom Regan & Peter Singer eds., 2d ed. 1989). We are aware that Kant himself thought that humans did not owe moral duties to animals, see Immanuel Kant, ANTHROPOLOGY FROM A PRAGMATIC POINT OF VIEW 15 (Robert B. Louden & Manfred Kuehn eds., 2006) (1798), although he nonetheless opposed wanton cruelty to animals on the ground that people who are cruel to animals will tend to act cruelly toward other people. *See* Immanuel Kant, LECTURES ON ETHICS 212 (Peter Heath trans., J. B. Schneewind ed., 1997).

17. Martha C. Nussbaum, FRONTIERS OF JUSTICE: DISABILITY, NATIONALITY, SPECIES MEMBERSHIP 325–407 (2007).

18. We place "moment" in quotation marks because conception, depending on how that term is defined, is a process that typically takes between two days and a week. *See* Elizabeth Spahn & Barbara Andrade, *Mis-Conceptions: The Moment of Conception in Religion, Science, and Law*, 32 U.S.F. L. REV. 261, 265, 293–94 (1998). For our purposes, nothing turns on this distinction. The resulting zygote lacks sentience at both the beginning and the end of the process and for many weeks thereafter. *See* Vivette Glover Reader & Nicholas M. Fisk, *Fetal Pain: Implications for Research and Practice*, 106 BJOG: AN INT'L J. OBSTETRICS & GYNAECOLOGY 881, 885 (2005), *available at* http://onlinelibrary.wiley.com/doi/10.1111/j.1471-0528.1999 .tb08424.x/full; Susan Tawia, *When Is the Capacity for Sentience Acquired During Human Fetal Development?*, 1 J. MATERNAL-FETAL AND NEONATAL MED. 153 (1992), *abstract available at* http://informahealthcare.com

/doi/abs/10.3109/14767059209161911. Thus, for simplicity, we adopt the pro-life convention of assuming a conception moment.

19. 2013 Kan. Sess. Laws 779. *See* Kevin Murphy, *Kansas Set to Enact Life-Starts-"At Fertilization" Abortion Law*, REUTERS (Apr. 6, 2013, 5:13 PM), http://www.reuters.com/article/2013/04/06/us-usa-kansas-abortion -idUSBRE93501220130406.

20. *When Does Life Begin?*, NAT'L RIGHT TO LIFE COMM., http://www .nrlc.org/abortion/wdlb/.

21. *See* Audrey White & Becca Aaronson, *Anti-Abortion Groups Push a New Round of Rules*, N.Y. TIMES, Nov. 23, 2012, at A25A; Sherry F. Colb, *Sending Out Partial Birth Announcements: Symbolism and Deception by Pro-Life Legislators*, FINDLAW (Jun. 18, 2003), http://writ.lp.findlaw .com/colb/20030618.html. Not all pro-life activists agree with this approach. *See* Josh Craddock, *Why Fetal Pain Hurts (the Pro-Life Cause)*, LIFESITE-NEWS.COM (Jun. 24, 2013, 4:01 PM), http://www.lifesitenews.com/news /why-fetal-pain-hurts-the-pro-life-cause.

22. *See* Reader & Fisk, *supra* note 18; Tawia, *supra* note 18.

23. Peter Singer, PRACTICAL ETHICS 159–63 (2d. ed. 1999).

24. John T. Noonan Jr., *An Almost Absolute Value in History*, *in* THE MORALITY OF ABORTION 1, 56 (John T. Noonan Jr. ed. 1970).

25. Patrick Lee & Robert P. George, *The Stubborn Facts of Science: Human Embryos Are Human Beings*, NAT'L REVIEW ONLINE (Jul. 30, 2001), http://web.archive.org/web/20121113235110/http://old.nationalreview .com/comment/comment-george073001.shtml.

26. *See, e.g.*, Eileen L. McDonagh, BREAKING THE ABORTION DEAD-LOCK: FROM CHOICE TO CONSENT 181–86 (1996).

27. *See* Elisabeth Rosenthal, *Excommunication Is Sought for Stem Cell Researchers*, N.Y. TIMES, Jul. 1, 2006, at A3; Sheryl Gay Stolberg, *Bush Vetoes Measure on Stem Cell Research*, N.Y. TIMES, Jun. 21, 2007, at A21.

28. We do not claim, of course, that the pro-life thinkers who oppose ani-mal rights would acknowledge the role that sentience plays in their argument.

29. Noonan, *supra* note 24, at 51.

30. *See id.*

31. Mary Anne Warren, *On the Moral and Legal Status of Abortion*, 57 MONIST 43–61 (1973), reprinted in THE ETHICS OF ABORTION 272, 274 (Robert M. Baird & Stuart E. Rosenbaum eds., 3d ed.2001).

32. *See* Gary Francione, *Abortion and Animal Rights: Are They Compa-rable Issues*, *in* ANIMALS AND WOMEN: FEMINIST THEORETICAL EXPLORA-TIONS (Carol J. Adams & Josephine Donovan eds., 1995).

33. Singer, *supra* note 23, at 150, 151.

34. *Id.* at 151.

35. Peter Singer, ANIMAL LIBERATION 1 (1975).

36. One relatively early champion of extending moral concern to non-humans noted the challenge that animal rights advocates posed to "society's

belief that we can distinguish between human and animal moral interests on the basi[s] of rationality, linguistic ability, the human soul, a God-granted dominion over animals, or the facts that humans are unique in being moral *agents*. . . . " Andrew N. Rowan, OF MICE, MODELS, & MEN 258 (1984) (emphasis in original).

37. *See, e.g.*, Inbal Ben-Ami Bartal *et al.*, *Empathy and Pro-Social Behavior in Rats*, 334 SCIENCE 1427; Donald M. Broom, *Pigs Learn What a Mirror Image Represents and Use it to Retain Information*, 78 ANIMAL BEHAVIOUR 1037 (2009); R. Allen Gardner & Beatrice T. Gardner, *Teaching Sign Language to a Chimpanzee*, 165 SCIENCE 664 (1969); Gavin R. Hunt, *Manufacture and Use of Hook-Tools by New Caledonian Crows*, 379 NATURE 249 (1996); S. Millot *et al.*, *Innovative Behaviour in Fish: Atlantic Cod Can Learn to use an External tag to Manipulate a Self-feeder*, 17(3) ANIM. COGN. 779–85 (May 2014).

38. *See, e.g.*, Norm Phelps, THE DOMINION OF LOVE: ANIMAL RIGHTS ACCORDING TO THE BIBLE (2002); Matthew Scully, DOMINION: THE POWER OF MAN, THE SUFFERING OF ANIMALS, AND THE CALL TO MERCY (2002).

39. *See* Jonathan Balcombe, SECOND NATURE: THE INNER LIVES OF ANIMALS (2011).

40. *See, e.g.*, *Dog Saves Owner by Calling 911*, YOUTUBE (Sep. 15, 2013), https://www.youtube.com/watch?v=dZ5_gJ6b-5Y (originally aired on CNN).

41. We say "presumptively" wrong rather than always wrong because there are circumstances in which pain may be necessary. For example, a doctor might perform a lifesaving but painful emergency procedure without anesthesia because there is no time to obtain or administer anesthesia. One can quibble about whether the pain is inflicted "intentionally" but justifiably in such circumstances or whether we should instead characterize it as an unintended-but-foreseen side effect. We address related questions of necessity in chapter 2.

42. Jeremy Bentham, AN INTRODUCTION TO THE PRINCIPLES OF MORALS AND LEGISLATION 310 n.1 (Dover Pub. 2007) (1789).

43. See Michael J. Murray, NATURE RED IN TOOTH AND CLAW: THEISM AND THE PROBLEM OF ANIMAL SUFFERING 43–66 (2011); William Lane Craig, *Animal Pain and the Ethical Treatment of Animals*, REASONABLE FAITH (Dec. 12, 2011), http://www.reasonablefaith.org/animal-pain-and-the-ethical-treatment-of-animals.

44. Nussbaum, *supra* note 17, at 327.

45. *See* John Rawls, A THEORY OF JUSTICE 75 (1971).

46. *NHE Fact Sheet*, CTRS. FOR MEDICARE & MEDICAID SERVS. (Jan. 9, 2013), http://www.cms.gov/Research-Statistics-Data-and-Systems/Statistics-Trends-and-Reports/NationalHealthExpendData/NHE-Fact-Sheet.html.

47. *See, e.g.*, Melanie Joy, Why We Love Dogs, Eat Pigs and Wear Cows: An Introduction to Carnism (2011).

48. Nicolette Hahn Niman, *Dogs Aren't Dinner: The Flaws in an Argument for Veganism*, Atlantic (Nov. 4, 2010), available at http://www.theatlantic.com/health/archive/2010/11/dogs-arent-dinner -the-flaws-in-an-argument-for-veganism/66095/.

49. *Id.*

50. This concept was first introduced in J. O. Urmson, *Saints and Heroes, in* Essays in Moral Philosophy 198–216 (A. I. Melden ed. 1958). *See* David Heyd, *Superogation*, Stanford Encyclopedia Phil. (Sep. 27, 2011), http://plato.stanford.edu/archives/win2012/entries/superero gation/.

51. We use the phrase "pet owners" because the law currently regards companion animals as the property of the humans who house them. By doing so, however, we certainly do not endorse this classification.

52. For example, Norway and Sweden each spent roughly $5 billion on foreign aid in 2012. *See Top Ten Donors of Foreign Aid*, http://www .mapsofworld.com/world-top-ten/world-top-ten-doners-of-foreigner-aid-map.html. Yet these figures represent only a small fraction of the countries' total spending: according to the CIA World Factbook, Norway's estimated 2012 government expenditures totaled $206.7 billion and Sweden's were $289.3 billion. *The World Factbook: Field Listing: Budget*, Cent. Intelligence Agency, https://www.cia.gov/library/publications/the-world -factbook/fields/2056.html.

53. Many Americans do not object to the killing of foreigners in war, but that is because they regard wartime killing—including wartime killing of innocent civilians as "collateral damage"—as justified. As we have been at pains to note throughout this chapter, for now we are considering only whether moral consideration is owed in the first place, not whether some interest suffices to override that moral consideration.

54. *See, e.g.*, Richard B. Brandt, *Toward a Credible Form of Utilitarianism, in* Morality and the Language of Conduct 107 (Hector-Neri Castañeda & George Nakhnikian eds., 1963).

55. The original formulation of the trolley problem arose in an article about the morality of abortion. Philippa Foot, *The Problem of Abortion and the Doctrine of the Double Effect*, 5 Oxford Rev. 5, 8, available at http:// spot.colorado.edu/~heathwoo/phil3100,SP09/foot.pdf. For one take on the ramifications of various philosophical views on one's approach to the trolley problem, see Judith Jarvis Thomson, *The Trolley Problem*, 94 Yale L. J. 1395, 1404–14 (1985).

2. THE NECESSITY DEFENSE

1. Vegans tend to include in the category of "nonfood" some animals, like bivalves, that might not be sentient. We understand and would accordingly characterize this potential overinclusiveness as an effort on the part of vegans to err on the side of caution, rather than as a reflection of the view that it is immoral to kill or consume a truly nonsentient organism.

2. *See* Nathan J. Winograd, *The Indictment of Wayne Pacelle*, NATHANWINOGRAD.COM (Aug. 9, 2011), http://www.nathanwinograd .com/?p=6510. *See also* Gary L. Francione, Op-Ed., *We're All Michael Vick*, PHILADELPHIA DAILY NEWS, Aug. 22, 2007, at 25; Sherry F. Colb, *The Homage Vice Pays to Virtue: Lessons of the Michael Vick Story*, FINDLAW (Sep. 10, 2007), http://writ.news.findlaw.com/colb/20070910.html.

3. *See* Alexandra Caspero, *Building a Healthy Vegetarian Meal: Myths and Facts*, ACADEMY OF NUTRITION AND DIETETICS (Jan. 28, 2014), http://www.eatright.org/resource/food/nutrition/vegetarian-and-special-diets /building-a-healthy-vegetarian-meal-myths-and-facts.

4. *See, e.g.*, Neal Barnard, THE GET HEALTHY, GO VEGAN COOKBOOK 21–23 (2010); T. Colin Campbell & Thomas M. Campbell II, THE CHINA STUDY: THE MOST COMPREHENSIVE STUDY OF NUTRITION EVER CONDUCTED AND THE STARTLING IMPLICATIONS FOR DIET, WEIGHT LOSS, AND LONG-TERM HEALTH 111–82 (2006); Caldwell B. Esselstyn, PREVENT AND REVERSE HEART DISEASE: THE REVOLUTIONARY, SCIENTIFICALLY PROVEN, NUTRITION-BASED CURE 5–6, 33–34 (2007); Joel Fuhrman, EAT TO LIVE: THE AMAZING NUTRIENT-RICH PROGRAM FOR FAST AND SUSTAINED WEIGHT LOSS 85–87 (2011) [hereinafter Fuhrman, EAT TO LIVE]; Joel Fuhrman, THE END OF DIABETES: THE EAT TO LIVE PLAN TO PREVENT AND REVERSE DIABETES 84–87 (2012) [hereinafter FUHRMAN, THE END OF DIABETES]; Julieanna Hever, THE COMPLETE IDIOT'S GUIDE TO PLANT-BASED NUTRITION 5–7 (2011).

5. Philip J. Tuso *et al.*, *Nutritional Update for Physicians: Plant-Based Diets*, 17 PERMANENTE J. 61, 61 (Spring 2013).

6. *See* Fuhrman, EAT TO LIVE, *supra* note 4, at 101, 197; Fuhrman, THE END OF DIABETES, *supra* note 4, at 81–82; Jean-Philippe Peyrat *et al.*, *Plasma Insulin-Like Growth Factor-1 (IGF-1) Concentrations in Human Breast Cancer*, 29 EUR. J. CANCER 492, 492 (1993). There is some evidence that the adverse effects of IGF-1 occur only in people under the age of sixty-five. *See* Srinivas Teppala and Anoop Shankar, *Association Between Serum IGF-1 and Diabetes Among U.S. Adults*, 33(10) DIABETES CARE 2257 (2010), http://care.diabetesjournals.org/content/33/10/2257.full.pdf.

7. For a more thorough discussion of how plant-based diets contribute to health and well-being while animal-based foods do the opposite, see Sherry F. Colb, MIND IF I ORDER THE CHEESEBURGER? AND OTHER QUESTIONS PEOPLE ASK VEGANS 25–36 (2013).

8. We say "almost" because some ranchers and their allies do claim that grazing animals on pasture is not only sustainable but affirmatively helps the planet through a natural cycling of nutrients from plants to animals and back again through manure. *See* Michael Pollan, THE OMNIVORE'S DILEMMA: A NATURAL HISTORY OF FOUR MEALS (2006); Joel Salatin, FOLKS, THIS AIN'T NORMAL: A FARMER'S ADVICE FOR HAPPIER HENS, HEALTHIER PEOPLE, AND A BETTER WORLD (2011). Yet these claims do not withstand critical scrutiny. Consider that every time a young healthy animal is removed for slaughter, nutrients are removed from the cycle. Or that grass-fed cattle appear to emit *more* planet-warming greenhouse gases than the grain-fed cattle raised on factory farms. *See* James E. McWilliams, *The Myth of Sustainable Meat*, N.Y. TIMES, Apr. 12, 2012, at A31, *available at* http://www.nytimes.com/2012/04/13/opinion/the-myth-of-sustainable-meat.html. Salatin's response to McWilliams appears to assume, mistakenly, that McWilliams was making an affirmative argument for factory farming rather than making the more fundamental point that so-called sustainable animal agriculture is not in fact sustainable. *See* Joel Salatin, *Joel Salatin Responds to New York Times' "Myth of Sustainable Meat"* GRIST, Apr. 17, 2012, http://grist.org/sustainable-farming/farmer-responds-to-the-new-york-times-re-sustainable-meat.

9. *See* Food and Agriculture Organization of the United Nations, *Livestock's Long Shadow: Environmental Issues and Options* 91, 213 (Nov. 29, 2006) (citing Simon D. Donner, *Surf or Turf? Shifting from Feed to Food Cultivation Could Reduce Nutrient Flux to the Gulf of Mexico*, 17 GLOBAL ENVTL. CHANGE 105 [2006]).

10. *See* Robert Goodland and Jeff Anhang, *Livestock and Climate Change*, World Watch 10 (Nov./Dec. 2009), available at http://www.worldwatch.org/files/pdf/Livestock%20and%20Climate%20Change.pdf.

11. For a fascinating treatment of the many ways in which the consumption of animal products, including land and marine animals, has caused global depletion and endangers the future of our planet, see Richard Oppenlander, COMFORTABLY UNAWARE: WHAT WE CHOOSE TO EAT IS KILLING US AND OUR PLANET (2011).

12. *See* Glynnis MacNicol, *WATCH: Maria Bartiromo Gets Booed for Asking Herman Cain About Sexual Harassment Allegations*, BUS. INSIDER (Nov. 9, 2011, 9:08 PM), http://www.businessinsider.com/maria-bartiromo-booed-herman-cain-sexual-harassment-allegations-2011-11.

13. For an analysis of how negative duties (duties of nonharm) consistently trump duties of rescue, see Philippa Foot, *The Problem of Abortion and the Doctrine of Double Effect*, 5 OXFORD REV. 5 (1967).

14. *See Vegans Save 198 Animals a Year*, PETA (Dec. 13, 2010), http://www.peta.org/b/thepetafiles/archive/2010/12/13/vegans-save-185-animals-a-year.aspx.

15. *See* Colb, *supra* note 7, 80–94.

16. Polls from as far back as the mid-1990s have yielded this result. An Associated Press poll from 1996 found that two-thirds of Americans agree with the following statement: "An animal's right to live free of suffering should be just as important as a person's right to live free of suffering." The same poll found that 59 percent of Americans believe killing animals for fur is "always wrong" and that 51 percent believe killing animals for sport is "always wrong." *See* David Foster, *Animal Rights Activists Getting Message Across: New Poll Findings Show Americans More in Tune with 'Radical' Views*, CHI. TRIB., Jan. 25, 1996, at C8.

17. *See* Douglas J. Lisle & Alan Goldhamer, THE PLEASURE TRAP: MASTERING THE HIDDEN FORCE THAT UNDERMINES HEALTH & HAPPINESS 83–84 (2006).

18. For further discussion of how much pleasure can be found in vegan food, see Colb, *supra* note 7, 15–24.

19. In a partially autobiographical book, Twain laments the low quality of food in Europe and sets out a menu of American foods he prefers. The menu includes such items as "[f]ried chicken, Southern style," "[s]oft-shell crabs, Connecticut shad," and "American roast beef." Mark Twain, A TRAMP ABROAD 276–78 (Dover Publications 2003) (1880).

20. *Letter from Mark Twain to London Anti-Vivisection Society* (May 26, 1899) *in* MARK TWAIN'S BOOK OF ANIMALS (JUMPING FROGS: UNDISCOVERED, REDISCOVERED AND CELEBRATED WRITINGS OF MARK TWAIN), at 139 (Shelley Fisher Fishkin ed., 2011).

21. In Ancient Greece, both the philosopher Pythagoras (and many of his followers) and the religious group known as the Orphics are known to have practiced a vegetarian lifestyle since at least the sixth century B.C. *See* Colin Spencer, THE HERETIC'S FEAST: A HISTORY OF VEGETARIANISM 38–55, 61–63 (1993). Pythagoras was once quoted as associating meat eating with the murder of humans, saying: "For as long as men massacre animals, they will kill each other. Indeed, he who sows the seed of murder and pain cannot reap joy and love." Jon Wynne-Tyson, THE EXTENDED CIRCLE: A DICTIONARY OF HUMANE THOUGHT 260 (1985) (quote reported by Ovid). A number of Platonists, including Plutarch and Porphyry, lived at least part of their lives as vegetarians. Porphyry, in fact, wrote an entire book on the subject. Porphyry, ON ABSTINENCE FROM ANIMAL FOOD (Shirley Hibberd trans., London, William Horsell, 1851). More recently, the Jewish American author Isaac Bashevis Singer advocated strongly for vegetarianism, going so far as to compare the exploitation of animals to the Holocaust. Isaac Bashevis Singer, *The Letter Writer, in* THE COLLECTED STORIES 250, 271 (1982): "In relation to [animals], all people are Nazis; for the animals, it is an eternal Treblinka." Many great religious figures have also abstained from eating meat, including Buddha, who believed that "the eating of meat extinguishes the seed of Great Kindness." THE MAHAYANA MAHAPARINIRVANA SUTRA 52 (Kosho Yamomoto trans., 2007), *available at*

http://www.nirvanasutra.net/convenient/Mahaparinirvana_Sutra_Yamamoto _Page_2007.pdf. In addition, some current practitioners of Buddhism and Jainism find inspiration in these faith traditions for veganism. *See* Victoria Moran, *Show Notes: Buddhism, Jainism, Veganism* (Aug. 20, 2015), mainstreetvegan.net/show-notes-buddhism-jainism-veganism. The blind poet and philosopher Al-Ma'arri, who lived from 973 to 1058, not only observed a strict vegan diet but also wrote a poem, entitled "I No Longer Steal from Nature," that championed his vegan lifestyle. *See* Gary L. Francione, *On Veganism from a Medieval Arab Poet*, ANIMAL RIGHTS: THE ABOLITIONIST APPROACH (Nov. 28, 2010), http://www.abolitionistapproach.com /on-veganism-from-a-medieval-arab-poet.

22. *See* Aysha Akhtar, ANIMALS AND PUBLIC HEALTH: WHY TREATING ANIMALS BETTER IS CRITICAL TO HUMAN WELFARE 132–67 (2012); Gary L. Francione, INTRODUCTION TO ANIMAL RIGHTS: YOUR CHILD OR THE DOG? 31–49 (2000).

23. For a comprehensive review of the history and methodology of the Draize eye test, see Kirk R. Wilhemus, *The Draize Eye Test*, 45 SURV. OPHTHALMOLOGY 493 (2001). John Draize's initial paper on the topic was published in 1944. John H. Draize, Geoffrey Woodard, & Herbert O. Calvery, *Methods for the Study of Irritation and Toxicity of Substances Applied Topically to the Skin and Mucous Membranes*, 82 J. PHARMACOLOGY 377 (1944).

24. To purchase household products and cosmetics that have not been tested on animals, one can look for the rabbit sign on the product—so designated because of the Draize test's notoriety. For a periodically updated list of American companies that are licensed with the bunny logo, see *Companies That Don't Test on Animals*, PETA'S BEAUTY WITHOUT BUNNIES PROGRAM, http://www.mediapeta.com/peta/PDF/companiesdonttest.pdf. India, Israel, and the European Union (EU) have all banned animal testing for cosmetics. Monica Engebretson, *India Joins the EU and Israel in Surpassing the US in Cruelty-Free Cosmetics Testing Policy*, WORLD POST (Jul. 23, 2013,12:58 PM), http://www.huffingtonpost.com/monica-engebretson /cruelty-free-cosmetics-testing_b_3605460.html. Norway, which is not an EU member, has also adopted such a ban. *See Norway Ban Animal Testing of Cosmetics*, OSLO TIMES (Mar. 12, 2013), http://www.theoslotimes.com /norway-ban-animal-testing-of-cosmetics/.

25. Argentina, Slovakia, and Israel ban all dissection in primary and secondary schools while India bans dissection of mice, rats, and frogs. Italy allows students to opt out of dissection as conscientious objectors. *See Questions and Answers About Dissection*, HUMANE SOCIETY OF THE UNITED STATES (Nov. 13, 2013), http://www.humanesociety.org/issues/dissection/qa/questions _answers.html. The Cummings School of Veterinary Medicine at Tufts University was the first U.S. veterinary school to eliminate all terminal procedures (and most unnecessary invasive procedures) on healthy animals. *See DVM Animal Use*, CUMMINGS SCHOOL OF VETERINARY MEDICINE (Jul. 18, 2012),

http://vet.tufts.edu/dvm/animal_use.html. For a list of other American veterinary and medical schools that offer alternatives to dissection, see *Schools Offering Dissection Alternatives*, ANIMALEARN, http://www.animalearn .org/vetSchools.php. In addition, Canada's veterinary schools have universally ceased performing terminal surgeries on animals. *Alternatives in Education*, NEW ENGLAND ANTI-VIVISECTION SOCIETY, http://www.neavs.org /alternatives/in-education.

26. *See Dissection: The Problem with Dissection and Vivisection*, AMERICAN ANTI-VIVISECTION SOCIETY, http://www.aavs.org/site/c.bkLTK fOSLhK6E/b.6457887/k.238F/Dissection.htm; *Questions and Answers About Dissection*, Humane Society of the United States (Nov. 13, 2013), http://www.humanesociety.org/issues/dissection/qa/questions_answers .html.

27. *See* 21 C.F.R. § 314.610 (2008). The Food and Drug Administration, the agency tasked with regulating the prescription drug industry, claims that "[t]here are still many areas where animal testing is necessary and non-animal testing is not yet a scientifically valid and available option." *Why Are Animals Used for Testing Medical Products?*, U.S. FOOD & DRUG ADMINISTRATION, http://www.fda.gov/AboutFDA/Transparency/Basics/ucm194932 .htm.

28. *See, e.g.*, Laurie Jackson-Grusby, *Modeling Cancer in Mice*, 21 ONCOGENE 5504 (2002); Uwe Koedel & Hans-Walter Pfister, *Models of Experimental Bacterial Meningitis: Role and Limitations*, 13 INFECTIOUS DISEASE CLINICS N. AM. 549 (1999), *abstract available at* http://www .id.theclinics.com/article/S0891-5520%2805%2970094-5/abstract.

29. *See, e.g.*, Akhtar, *supra* note 22; Junhee Seok *et al.*, *Genomic Responses in Mouse Models Poorly Mimic Human Inflammatory Diseases*, 110 PROC. NAT'L ACAD. SCI. U.S. AM. 3507 (2013); Gina Kolata, *Mice Fall Short as Test Subjects for Deadly Illnesses*, N.Y. TIMES, Feb. 12, 2013, at A19.

30. *See* Vijay V. Moghe, Ujjwala Kulkarni, & Urvashi I. Parmar, *Thalidomide*, 50 BOMBAY HOSP. J. 446; James H. Kim & Anthony R. Scialli, *Thalidomide: The Tragedy of Birth Defects and the Effective Treatment of Disease*, 122 TOXICOLOGICAL SCI. 1 (2011).

31. *See* Robert L. Brent, *Drug Testing in Animals for Teratogenic Effects: Thalidomide in the Pregnant Rat*, 64 J. PEDIATRICS 762 (1964); Bara Fintel *et al.*, *The Thalidomide Tragedy: Lessons for Drug Safety and Regulation*, HELIX MAGAZINE (Jul. 28, 2009), http://helix.northwestern.edu/article /thalidomide-tragedy-lessons-drug-safety-and-regulation.

32. *See* Moghe, Kulkarni & Parmar, *supra* note 30, at 446; Kim & Scialli, *supra* note 30, at 1; Fintel *et al.*, *supra* note 31.

33. *See, e.g.*, Robert L. Brent, *Utilization of Animal Studies to Determine the Effects and Human Risks of Environmental Toxicants (Drugs, Chemicals, and Physical Agents)*, 113 PEDIATRICS 984 (2004); Robert H. Green,

The Association of Viral Activation with Penicillin Toxicity in Guinea Pigs and Hamsters, 47 YALE J. BIOLOGY & MED. 166 (1974).

34. For example, the Susan G. Komen Foundation has been criticized for funding animal testing. *See* Ingrid Newkirk, *Susan G. Komen's Other Gaffe*, HUFF. POST (Feb. 3, 2012), http://www.huffingtonpost.com/ingrid-newkirk /komen-animal-testing_b_1253803.html. As of 2012, the Komen Foundation had funded over $740 million in breast cancer research. *Susan G. Komen for the Cure—Animal Testing*, SUSAN G. KOMEN Houston (Oct. 10, 2012, 11:35 AM), http://www.komen-houston.org/news/susan-g-komen-for-the -cure-animal-testing/. By contrast, the Avon Foundation for Women, which also funds millions of dollars' worth of breast cancer research, makes clear on its website that "Avon Foundation funding may not be used to fund stud- ies involving animals." *Breast Cancer Research 2015 Program Guidelines*, AVON FOUNDATION FOR WOMEN, http://www.avonfoundation.org/grants /breast-cancer/research-grant-guidelines/.

35. *What Are the Key Statistics About Breast Cancer?*, AM. CAN- CER SOC'Y (Jan. 31, 2014), http://www.cancer.org/cancer/breastcancer /detailedguide/breast-cancer-key-statistics. Meanwhile, the incidence rate of breast cancer—defined as the number of new cases per 100,000 American women—is higher now than it was in 1975, although it has consistently dropped since 1999. *SEER Stat Fact Sheets: Breast Cancer*, NAT'L CANCER INST., http://seer.cancer.gov/statfacts/html/breast.html. The mortality rate, as of 2010, was 22 deaths per 100,000 American women; in 1975, that number was 31 per 100,000. *Id.*

36. In 2008 China saw 15,625 new cases of breast cancer and 3,414 deaths from breast cancer, for an incidence rate of about 2.5 per 100,000 women and a mortality rate of about 0.5 per 100,000 women. *See* Wan-qing Chen *et al.*, *Incidence and Mortality of Breast Cancer in China, 2008*, 4 THORACIC CANCER 59 (2013). Similar rates have been reported for Papua New Guinea, although the incidence has risen in recent years, perhaps due to Westernization. *See* Bob Kuska, *Breast Cancer Increases on Papua New Guinea*, 91 J. NAT'L CANCER INST. 994, 995 (1999). "The incidence [of breast cancer in Japan] is approximately one fifth of that in the United States." Robert H. Yonemoto, *Breast Cancer in Japan and the United States: Epidemiology, Hormone Receptors, Pathology, and Survival*, 115 ARCHIVES SURGERY 1056, 1056 (1980). As of 2012 the breast cancer incidence rate across all of East Asia was just 27 new cases per 100,000 women; the mor- tality rate was 6 per 100,000. *Breast Cancer: Estimated Incidence, Mortality and Prevalence Worldwide in 2012*, GLOBOCAN 2012: INT'L AGENCY FOR RES. ON CANCER, http://globocan.iarc.fr/Pages/fact_sheets_cancer.aspx.

37. In his comprehensive study of nutritional patterns and health out- comes in China, T. Colin Campbell found striking variations in the incidence of breast cancer across different regions of China and a strong correlation between these cancer rates and the amount of animal food in regional diets.

See Campbell & Campbell, *supra* note 4, at 85–86 (2006). Further evidence of the diverse health benefits of avoiding eating animal products can be found in Esselstyn, *supra* note 4; Kenneth K. Carroll & Laura M. Braden, *Dietary Fat and Mammary Carcinogenesis*, 6 NUTRITION & CANCER 254 (1984); Michael Greger, *Breast Cancer*, NUTRITIONFACTS. ORG, http://nutritionfacts.org/topics/breast-cancer/; Michael Greger, How Do Plant-Based Diets Fight Cancer?, CARE2 (Oct. 3, 2012, 9:30 AM), http://www.care2.com/greenliving/how-do-plant-based-diets-fight-cancer .html; Michael Greger, *Breast Cancer Survival and Soy*, CARE2 (Apr. 20, 2012, 9:30 AM), http://www.care2.com/greenliving/breast-cancer-survival -and-soy.html.

38. The Cleveland Clinic, ranked by *U.S. News and World Report* as the best hospital in the nation for cardiology and heart surgery, has a McDonald's on site. *Top-Ranked Hospitals for Cardiology and Heart Surgery*, U.S. NEWS & WORLD REPORT, http://health.usnews.com/best-hospitals /rankings/cardiology-and-heart-surgery; *Cleveland Clinic, McDonald's*, McOHIO, http://www.mcohio.com/17243. The clinic has made some effort to close its McDonald's, but the restaurant remains; it is far from alone among hospitals in offering "fast food" to its patrons. *See* Elana Gordon, *Fast Food Chains in Cafeterias Put Hospitals in a Bind*, NPR (Apr. 9, 2012, 1:42 PM), http://www.npr.org/blogs/thesalt/2012/04/05/150091951 /fast-food-chains-in-cafeterias-put-hospitals-in-a-bind.

39. "[S]tudies indicate that chicken is almost as dangerous as red meat for the heart. . . . The best bet for overall health is to significantly limit or eliminate all types of meat—red and white." Fuhrman, EAT TO LIVE, *supra* note 4, 69–70.

40. In other words, if people's consumption of animal products contributes to their contraction of a disease, then the "necessary" research that harms animals in order to find a cure for that disease is made necessary only by a prior act of violence against animals. Similarly, if a person initiates an attack against another, then in the ensuing battle kills his opponent to protect his own life, the killer may lose his claim of self-defense because his need to kill to protect his own life would not have arisen but for his own initial violent action. Many jurisdictions do not allow a self-defense claim at all under these circumstances. See Model Penal Code § 3.04(2) (b)(i).

41. *See* Francione, *supra* note 22, 32.

42. *See* Akhtar, *supra* note 22.

43. *See* Lars Thomsen and Reuben Proctor, VEGANISSIMO A TO Z: A COMPREHENSIVE GUIDE TO IDENTIFYING AND AVOIDING INGREDIENTS OF ANIMAL ORIGIN IN EVERYDAY PRODUCTS (2013); Eliza Barclay, *Is Your Medicine Vegan? Probably Not*, NPR (Mar. 15, 2013, 6:42 PM), http:// www.npr.org/blogs/health/2013/03/13/174205188/is-your-medicine-vegan

-probably-not (citing the Thomsen and Proctor book). For a list of vegan alternatives to pharmaceutical drugs, see Thomsen & Proctor 278.

44. Valves from pigs and cows have been the most commonly used in heart valve replacement surgery. *See, e.g.,* Kok Hooi Yap *et al., Aortic Valve Replacement: Is Porcine or Bovine Valve Better?,* 16 INTERACTIVE CAR-DIOVASCULAR & THORACIC SURGERY 361 (2013). Mechanical heart valves offer a nonanimal alternative, although a patient receiving this type of valve will need to take blood thinning medication daily for the rest of his or her life. See *Aortic Valve Replacement,* UNIV. MARYLAND MED. CENTER (Feb. 4, 2014), http://umm.edu/programs/heart/services/services/cardiac-surgery /valve-surgery/replacement; *Heart Valve Replacement,* ST. JUDE MEDICAL (Jan. 19, 2010). A number of studies have reported no overall difference in quality of life between patients receiving tissue valves and those receiving mechanical valves. *See, e.g.,* Artyom Sedrakyan *et al.,* Quality of Life After Aortic Valve Replacement with Tissue and Mechanical Implants, 128 J. THORACIC & CARDIOVASCULAR SURGERY 266, 266, 271 (2004); Mariano Vicchio *et al., Tissue Versus Mechanical Prostheses: Quality of Life in Octogenarians,* 85 ANNALS THORACIC SURGERY 1290, 1295 (2008). Yet another procedure uses the patient's own pulmonary (lung) valve to replace the diseased heart valve. See *The Ross Procedure,* UNIV. S. CAL., http://www .cts.usc.edu/rossprocedure.html. One study found that patients undergoing this procedure report a better subsequent quality of life than patients receiving a mechanical valve. See Axel Notzöld *et al., Quality of Life in Aortic Valve Replacement: Pulmonary Autografts Versus Mechanical Prostheses,* 37 J. AM. C. CARDIOLOGY 1963, 1965 (2001). Finally, human heart valves provide yet another alternative, but this option requires a willing donor (as human organs, unlike porcine or bovine organs, are not taken against the owner's will).

45. A number of philosophers have criticized utilitarianism for its inability to properly address this kind of an example. *See, e.g.,* Judith Jarvis Thomson, *The Trolley Problem,* 94 YALE L.J. 1395, 1396 (1985).

46. *R v. Dudley & Stephens,* [1884] Q.B. 273 (Eng.).

47. 410 U.S. 113 (1973). Indeed, even the Texas statute that was struck down as unconstitutional in *Roe* allowed abortions to save the life of the mother. *Id.* at 118. The *Roe* Court noted that "[s]imilar statutes [were] in existence in a majority of the States." *Id.* at 118 & n.2 (providing a long list of state statutes).

48. *See id.* at 164–65; *Planned Parenthood of Southeastern Pa. v. Casey,* 505 U.S. 833, 879 (1992) (reaffirming this portion of *Roe*'s holding); *Ayotte v. Planned Parenthood of N. New Eng.,* 546 U.S. 320, 327–28 (2006).

49. *See* Catholic Church, *Catechism of the Catholic Church,* 2271, *available at* http://www.vatican.va/archive/ENG0015/__P7Z.HTM ("Since the first century the Church has affirmed the moral evil of every procured

abortion."); Second Vatican Council, *Gaudium et Spes*, Sec. 51, *available at* http://www.vatican.va/archive/hist_councils/ii_vatican_council/documents /vat-ii_const_19651207_gaudium-et-spes_en.html (1958). A hospital in Phoenix reportedly lost its Catholic affiliation when it permitted an abortion to save a woman's life and did not accede to the Church's demand that it promise never to permit such abortions again. *See* Editorial, *A Matter of Life or Death*, N.Y. TIMES, Dec. 23, 2010, at A32.

50. *See* Foot, *supra* note 13, 5, 6. *See also* Paul VI, *Humanae Vitae* (Jul. 25, 1968), in 13 POPE SPEAKS 329, 337 (1969), available at http://www.vatican .va/holy_father/paul_vi/encyclicals/documents/hf_p-vi_enc_25071968 _humanae-vitae_en.html; U.S. Conference of Catholic Bishops, ETHICAL AND RELIGIOUS DIRECTIVES FOR CATHOLIC HEALTH CARE SERVICES 26 (5th ed. 2009) (Directive 47). *See generally* Edwin F. Healy, S.J., MEDICAL ETHICS (1956).

51. Article 8 of the "Rome Statute," which established the International Criminal Court, criminalizes attacks that unintentionally result in civilian casualties only when they are undertaken with knowledge that "clearly excessive" civilian casualties or injuries will result. *Rome Statute of the International Criminal Court* art. 8, ¶ 2(b)(iv), Jul. 17, 1998, 2187 U.N.T.S. 90, 95. *See also Response to Communications Received Regarding Iraq, Letter from Luis Moreno-Ocampo, Chief Prosecutor of the International Criminal Court* (Feb. 9, 2006), *available at* http://www.icc-cpi.int/NR/rdonlyres /F596D08D-D810-43A2-99BB-B899B9C5BCD2/277422/OTP_letter_to _senders_re_Iraq_9_February_2006.pdf.

52. *See Rome Statute of the International Criminal Court* art. 8, ¶ 2(b)(i), Jul. 17, 1998, 2187 U.N.T.S. 90, 95.

53. *See* Foot, *supra* note 13, at 6, 14. Foot uses the example of a hysterectomy performed to save the life of a pregnant woman but inevitably killing the fetus inside of her.

54. The affirmative defense of "necessity," which might otherwise benefit the man throwing his companion out of a sinking lifeboat, does not typically extend to cases of homicide. *See, e.g., Oswald v. Bertrand*, 374 F.3d 475, 481 (7th Cir. 2004) (citing *R v. Dudley & Stephens*, [1884] Q.B. 273 (Eng.) along with a number of American cases). *Cf.* United States v. Holmes, 26 F. Cas. 360, 367 (C.C.E.D. Pa. 1842) (No. 15,383).

55. The fetus, of course, need not be male for this analysis to make sense. We have chosen to use the male pronoun only for simplicity's sake, since the mother is necessarily female.

56. Conservative pundit Ann Coulter has even written that she has "never heard of anyone who thinks abortion should not be 'available' to save the life of the mother." Ann Coulter, *Where's That Religious Fanatic We Elected?*, ANNCOULTER.COM (Jan. 27, 2005), http://www.anncoulter .com/columns/2005-01-27.html. Indeed, countries such as Brazil prohibit abortion in almost all circumstances but allow abortions that are necessary

to save the life of the mother. *See* Código Penal [C.P.] art. 128 (Braz.) (allowing abortions "se não há outro meio de salvar a vida da gestante" [if there is no other way to save the life of the pregnant woman] and also providing an exception in the case of rape, but in no other cases). However, despite Coulter's contention, there are countries—like Chile, El Salvador, and Nicaragua—that ban all abortions, with no "life of the mother" exception. *See* Constitución Política de la República de Chile [C.P.] art. 19 ("La ley protege la vida del que está por nacer." [The law protects the life of those about to be born]); Cód Pen. de Chile tit. VII, arts. 342–45 (2014); Cód. Sanit. de Chile lib. 5, art. 119 ("No podrá ejecutarse ninguna acción cuyo fin sea provocar un aborto." [No action may be executed that has as its goal the inducement of abortion.]); Ley No. 603, 26 Oct. 2006, Ley de Derogación al art. 165 del Código Penal Vigente [Derogation of art. 165 of the Penal Code], La Gaceta, Diario Oficial [L.G.], 17 Nov. 2006 (Nicar.); Decreto No. 1030, arts. 133–137, 1998 (El Salvador); 1 United Nations, ABORTION LAWS: A GLOBAL REVIEW 58, 83, 120 (2002); 2 United Nations, ABORTION LAWS: A GLOBAL REVIEW 173 (2002).

57. *See* Sherry F. Colb, *To Whom Do We Refer When We Speak of Obligations to "Future Generations"? Reproductive Rights and the Intergenerational Community*, 77 GEO. WASH. L. REV. 1582, 1607 (2009).

58. Indeed, the pro-life movement within this country has emphasized the criminalization and punishment of those who perform abortions while seemingly excusing the pregnant woman in all cases, even though she has ordered the killing that they classify as murder. *See, e.g.*, *New York Congressman Peter King: Criminalize Doctors Who Perform Abortion* (Aug. 30, 2012) [hereinafter Interview with Peter King], *available at* http://www .democracynow.org/2012/8/30/new_york_congressman_peter_king _criminalize; Douglas Burns, *Republican Pawlenty's 1st Take: No 'Criminal Sanction' for Abortion*, DAILY TIMES HERALD (May 31, 2011), http:// carrollspaper.com/main.asp?SectionID=1&SubSectionID=1&Article ID=12186. *See also* Sherry F. Colb, *What Proponents of the "Rape Exception" Teach Us About Abortion*, FINDLAW (Jul. 11, 2007), http://writ.news .findlaw.com/colb/20070711.html.

59. *See* *CNN/ORC Poll*, CNN (Aug. 24, 2012, 4:00 PM), http://i2.cdn .turner.com/cnn/2012/images/08/24/rel8a.pdf; Emily Swanson, *Abortion Poll: Vast Majority Support Legal Abortion for Rape Victims*, HUFFINGTON POST (Oct. 31, 2012, 9:10 AM), http://www.huffingtonpost.com/2012/10/31 /abortion-poll-legal-access-rape-victims_n_2044973.html.

60. *See* Healy, MEDICAL ETHICS, *supra* note 50, at 205–6; *Pro-Life Answer to the Rape Question*, STUDENTS FOR LIFE OF AM., http://studentsfor life.org/prolifefacts/prolife-answer-to-the-rape-question/; *What About Rape?*, FEMINISTS FOR LIFE, http://www.feministsforlife.org/what-about-rape/. Others, like 2012 Senate hopeful Richard Mourdock, focus less on the innocence of the unborn child and more on the possible role played by a higher

power. *See* Jonathan Weisman, *Rape Remark Jolts a Senate Race, and the Presidential One, Too,* N.Y. TIMES, Oct. 25, 2012, at A16.

61. One mother whose child was conceived through rape, while testifying before the Louisiana Senate Committee on Health and Welfare, described her son as "a living, breathing torture mechanism that replayed in my mind over and over the rape." Andrew Solomon, FAR FROM THE TREE: PARENTS, CHILDREN, AND THE SEARCH FOR IDENTITY 491 (2012). Drawing on his interviews with rape victims, Solomon concludes: "Ready access to a safe abortion allows a woman who keeps a child conceived in rape to feel that she is making a decision rather than having the decision forced upon her. . . . Raped women require unfettered independence in this arena: to abort or carry to term; to keep the child or give him up for adoption." *Id.* at 485.

62. *See NBC News/Wall Street Journal Survey,* WALL STREET J. (Apr. 2013), http://online.wsj.com/public/resources/documents/APRILNBCWSJPOLL 04112013.pdf; *CNN/ORC Poll, supra* note 59.

63. *See* Jed Rubenfeld, *The Riddle of Rape-by-Deception and the Myth of Sexual Autonomy,* 122 YALE L.J. 1372, 1430–31 (2013).

64. *See* Colb, *supra* note 57, at 1614.

65. Studies measuring the fetal loss rate associated with amniocentesis report rates ranging from 0.06 percent to 1 percent. See R. Douglas Wilson, Sylvie Langlois, & Jo-Ann Johnson, *Mid-Trimester Amniocentesis Fetal Loss Rate,* 29 J. OBSTETRICS & GYNAECOLOGY CANADA 586, 588 (2007) (summarizing); *Tests and Procedures: Amniocentesis,* MAYO CLINIC (Oct. 10, 2012), http://www.mayoclinic.org/tests-procedures/amniocentesis/basics/risks /prc-20014529; *see also* Anthony O. Odibo *et al., Revisiting the Fetal Loss Rate After Second-Trimester Genetic Amniocentesis: A Single Center's 16-Year Experience,* 111 OBSTETRICS & GYNECOLOGY 589, 593 (2008).

66. Joe Hilley, SARAH PALIN: A NEW KIND OF LEADER 129 (2008). Indeed, Palin herself seemed to indicate as much in a 2009 speech. *See* Mary Ann Akers, *Report: Palin Says She Considered Abortion,* WASH. POST (Apr. 17, 2009, 11:22 AM), http://voices.washingtonpost.com/sleuth/2009/04 /report_palin_says_she_consider.html (citing an AOL News report).

67. For a number of moving stories detailing the highs and lows of parenting a child with Down syndrome, see chapter 4 ("Down Syndrome") in Solomon, *supra* note 61.

68. In the United States, doctors commonly view twenty-four weeks as the limit of viability. *See* Maria A. Morgan, Robert L. Goldenberg, & Jay Schulkin, *Obstetrician-Gynecologists' Practices Regarding Preterm Birth at the Limit of Viability,* 21 J. MATERNAL-FETAL & NEONATAL MED. 115, 117 (2008). However, some literature suggests the theoretical viability limit might arrive as early as twenty-two weeks. *See, e.g.,* Manuel R. G. Carrapato, *Can We Establish a Universal Lower Limit of Viability? What Are the Medical and Ethical Implications?,* in 2 TEXTBOOK OF PERINATAL MEDICINE 61, 61 (Asim Kurjak & Frank A. Chervenak eds., 2006). Fetuses delivered before

the twenty-four-week mark of gestation rarely survive; those born between twenty-four and twenty-six weeks face substantially better—but still far from comfortable—odds of survival. *See* Grzegorz H. Breborowicz, *Limits of Fetal Viability and Its Enhancement*, 5 EARLY PREGNANCY 49, 49 (2001); Sarah J. Kilpatrick *et al.*, *Outcome of Infants Born at 24–26 Weeks' Gestation: I. Survival and Cost*, 90 OBSTETRICS & GYNECOLOGY 803, 803 (1997); Béatrice Larroque, *et al.*, *Survival of Very Preterm Infants: Epipage, a Population Based Cohort Study*, 89 ARCHIVES DISEASE CHILDHOOD: FETAL & NEONATAL EDITION F139, F140 (2004). The amount of care required by these preterm infants can often generate staggering costs. In 1997 one study indicated that the average cost to produce a survivor out of a baby born at twenty-four weeks was $294,749. See Kilpatrick *et al.* at 803.

69. Some state statutes reflect a similar mode of analysis, though with viability in place of sentience as the marker of life and less regard for the bodily integrity of the mother. *See* Sherry F. Colb, *A New York Woman Is Arrested for Self-Induced Abortion: What Does This Tell Us About Abortion Law?*, VERDICT (Dec. 30, 2011), http://verdict.justia.com /2011/12/30/a-new-york-woman-is-arrested-for-self-induced-abortion.

70. *See* James A. Thomson *et al.*, *Embryonic Stem Cell Lines Derived from Human Blastocysts*, 282 SCIENCE 1145 (1998).

71. *See, e.g.*, Scott Klusendorf, *Is Embryonic Stem Cell Research Morally Complex?*, LIFE TRAINING INST., http://prolifetraining.com/resources /five-minute-2/; J. C. Willke, *I'm Pro Life and Oppose Embryonic Stem Cell Research*, LIFE ISSUES INST., http://www.lifeissues.org/2000/11/im-pro -life-oppose-embryonic-stem-cell-research/.

72. *See* Curt R. Freed, *Will Embryonic Stem Cells Be a Useful Source of Dopamine Neurons for Transplant into Patients with Parkinson's Disease?*, 99 PROC. NAT'L ACAD. SCI. U.S. AM. 1755, 1757 (2002); Kristine K. Freude *et al.*, *Soluble Amyloid Precursor Protein Induces Rapid Neural Differentiation of Human Embryonic Stem Cells*, 286 J. BIOLOGICAL CHEMISTRY 24624, 24624, 24274 (2011); Tingyu Qu *et al.*, *Human Neural Stem Cells Improve Cognitive Function of Aged Brain*, 12 NEUROREPORT 1127, 1132 (2001); Thomson *et al.*, *supra* note 70, at 1147.

73. For example, former presidential candidate John McCain has voiced his support for embryonic stem cell research due to "the potential it has for curing some of the most terrible diseases that afflict mankind." Mary Lu Carnevale, *McCain Speaks Out Against Abortions*, WALL ST. J. (Jul. 17, 2008, 3:05 PM), http://blogs.wsj.com/washwire/2008/07/17/mccain-speaks -out-against-abortions/. In addition, Republican representative Charlie Dent was the co-sponsor (with Democrat Diana DeGette) of a bill, introduced in the House in June 2013, which aimed to "provide for human stem cell research, including human embryonic stem cell research." Stem Cell Research Advancement Act of 2013, H.R. 2433, 113th Cong. (2013). *See also* Katharine Q. Seelye, *The President's Decision: The Overview; Bush Gives His*

Backing for Limited Research on Existing Stem Cells, N.Y. TIMES, Aug. 10, 2001, at A1, *available at* http://www.nytimes.com/2001/08/10/us/president-s-decision-overview-bush-gives-his-backing-for-limited-research.html. The full video of Bush's August 2001 speech is available on YouTube. *George W. Bush: On Stem Cell Research*, YOUTUBE (uploaded Apr. 3, 2009), https://www.youtube.com/watch?v=EAiZp5jTo4I.

74. *See* Interview with Peter King, *supra* note 58 (indicating that "the doctor, not the woman" should face "penalties" for performing an abortion).

75. On Dr. Josef Mengele, *see* Helena Kubica, THE CRIMES OF JOSEF MENGELE, IN ANATOMY OF THE AUSCHWITZ DEATH CAMP 317, 323–25 (Yisrael Gutman & Michael Berenbaum eds., 1998). On the Tuskegee syphilis experiments, *see* U.S. *Public Health Service Study at Tuskegee: The Tuskegee Timeline*, CENTERS FOR DISEASE CONTROL & PREVENTION (Sep. 24, 2013), http://www.cdc.gov/tuskegee/timeline.htm. Nineteenth-century doctor James Marion Sims, among other achievements in gynecology, developed the first successful operation to cure a condition known as vesicovaginal fistula. He is lauded by many as the "father of modern gynecology." However, much of his medical research consisted of experimental operations on slave women whose level of consent remains a subject of debate. Thus, he remains a sharply divisive figure among historians and medical scholars alike. For example, Harriet A. Washington, MEDICAL APARTHEID: THE DARK HISTORY OF MEDICAL EXPERIMENTATION ON BLACK AMERICANS FROM COLONIAL TIMES TO THE PRESENT 2 (2008), describes the "gruesome reality" of Sims's operations: "Each naked, unanesthetized slave woman had to be forcibly restrained by the other physicians through her shrieks of agony as Sims determinedly sliced, then sutured her genitalia." Yet L. Lewis Wall, *The Medical Ethics of Dr. J. Marion Sims: A Fresh Look at the Historical Record*, 32 J. MED. ETHICS 346, 349 (Jun. 2006), describes Sims's slave patients as "desperate for help" and Sims as "a dedicated and conscientious physician." For an article that attempts to acknowledge both Sims's achievements and his shortcomings, see Jeffrey S. Martin, *J. Marion Sims, the Father of Gynecology: Hero or Villian?*, 97 S. MED. J. 500 (2004).

3. REPRODUCTIVE SERVITUDE

1. *See* Lucinda Finley, *Contested Ground: The Story of Roe v. Wade and Its Impact on American Society*, *in* 2 CONSTITUTIONAL LAW STORIES 333 (Michael C. Dorf ed., 2009).

2. The majority said that "it seems unexceptionable to conclude some women come to regret their choice to abort the infant life they once created and sustained. Severe depression and loss of esteem can follow." 550 U.S. at 159. The Court cited an amicus brief filed by, among others, "180 women injured by abortion." *See Brief for Sandra Cano et al. as Amici Curiae*

Supporting Petitioner, Gonzales v. Carhart, 510 U.S. 124 (2007) (No. 05-380), at 22–24.

3. Judith Jarvis Thomson, *A Defense of Abortion*, 1 PHIL. & PUB. AFF. 47, 48 (1971).

4. *Id.* at 47.

5. *Id.* at 59.

6. Providing evidence of this consensus, the conservative periodical the *National Review* recently published an article on its website by Reggie Littlejohn, the president of a group called Women's Rights Without Frontiers, in which she wrote: "Pro-choice and pro-life advocates can agree: No one should support forced abortion, because it is not a choice." Reggie Littlejohn, *China Hasn't 'Eased' Its One-Child Policy*, NAT'L REV. ONLINE (Nov. 18, 2013, 9:55 AM), http://www.nationalreview.com/corner/364200/china-hasnt-eased-its-one-child-policy-reggie-littlejohn.

7. The ceremony is known as a "mizuko kuyō." *See* Anne Page Brooks, *Mizuko Kuyō and Japanese Buddhism*, 8 JAPANESE J. RELIGIOUS STUD. 119 (1981); Bardwell Smith, *Buddhism and Abortion in Contemporary Japan: Mizuyuko Kuyō and the Confrontation with Death*, 15 JAPANESE J. RELIGIOUS STUD. 3 (1988).

8. Almost every state has a provision, known as a "conscience clause," that allows doctors who object on moral, ethical, or religious grounds to refuse to provide abortions. *See, e.g.*, ALASKA STAT. § 18.16.010(b) (2012); ARIZ. REV. STAT. ANN. § 36-2154 (2013); ARK. CODE ANN. § 20-16-304(5) (2013); CAL. HEALTH & SAFETY CODE § 123420 (West 2013); COLO. REV. STAT. § 25-6-102(9) (2013); CONN. AGENCIES REGS. § 19-13-D54 (2013); DEL. CODE ANN. tit. 24, § 1791 (2013); FLA. STAT. § 390.0111(8) (2013); IDAHO CODE ANN. § 18-612 (2008); 720 ILL. COMP. STAT. 510/13 (2012); MASS. GEN. LAWS ch.112, § 12I (2012); N.J. STAT. ANN. §§ 2A:65A–1 & 2A:65A–2 (West 2013). For a list of states' "conscience clause" laws, see *State Policies in Brief: Refusing to Provide Health Services*, GUTTMACHER INST. (Apr. 1, 2014), https://www.guttmacher.org/statecenter/spibs/spib_RPHS.pdf. In addition, the federal "Church Amendments" clarify that federal funding of hospitals cannot be conditioned on an agreement to provide abortions. 42 U.S.C. § 300a–7 (2012).

9. The relevant passage is found in the Mishnah, at chapter 7, verse 6 of the Oholot tractate (within the Tehorot order): "If a woman is in hard labor [and her life cannot otherwise be saved], one cuts up the child within her womb and extracts it member by member, because her life comes before that of the child. But if the greater part [or the head] was delivered, one may not touch it, for one may not set aside one person's life for the sake of another." *See* Joseph G. Schenker, *The Beginning of Human Life: Status of Embryo Perspectives in Halakha (Jewish Religious Law)*, 25 J. ASSISTED REPRODUCTION & GENETICS 271, 273.

10. *See* U.S. CONST. amend. XIV ("All persons born or naturalized in the United States . . . and subject to the jurisdiction thereof, are citizens of the United States. . . .").

11. 410 U.S. 113, 157–58 (1973).

12. *See id.* at 163–64. *Planned Parenthood of Southeastern Pa. v. Casey,* 505 U.S. 833 (1992) cut back on *Roe* in some respects but reaffirmed the viability line. *See id.* at 846.

13. *See* Manuel R. G. Carrapato, *Can We Establish a Universal Lower Limit of Viability? What Are the Medical and Ethical Implications?, in* 2 TEXTBOOK OF PERINATAL MEDICINE 61, 61 (Asim Kurjak & Frank A. Chervenak eds., 2006); Maria A. Morgan, Robert L. Goldenberg, & Jay Schulkin, *Obstetrician-Gynecologists' Practices Regarding Preterm Birth at the Limit of Viability,* 21 J. MATERNAL-FETAL & NEONATAL MED. 115, 117 (2008).

14. *E.g.,* Alabama Pain-Capable Unborn Child Protection Act, ALA. CODE §§ 26-23B-1-9 (2013); Unborn Child Pain Awareness and Prevention Act, ARK. CODE ANN. §§ 20-16-1401–1410 (2012); Pain-Capable Unborn Child Protection Act, NEB. REV. STAT. §§ 28-3,102–3, 111 (2012); Preborn Pain Act, TEX. HEALTH & SAFETY CODE ANN. § 171.044. The United States House of Representatives passed a similar bill but it failed in the Senate. Pain-Capable Unborn Child Protection Act, H.R. 1797, 113th Cong. (2013).

15. *See* chapter 7 ("Are You Against Abortion?") in Sherry F. Colb, MIND IF I ORDER THE CHEESEBURGER? AND OTHER QUESTIONS PEOPLE ASK VEGANS (2013); Laurence H. Tribe & Michael C. Dorf, ON READING THE CONSTITUTION 60–61 (1993).

16. *Compare, e.g.,* N.Y. Penal Law §§ 125.05–125.27 (criminalizing various forms of homicide) *with* N.Y. Penal Law § 35.15 (providing a defense for those who have killed or injured another in self-defense). *See also* Model Penal Code §§ 210.1–210.4 (criminalizing homicide); Model Penal Code § 3.04 (self-defense provision).

17. *See* Daniel Schiff, ABORTION IN JUDAISM, 59–61 (2002).

18. The same is true for male victims and female perpetrators, but for simplicity (and because the victimization commonly goes in this direction), we shall refer to the perpetrator of rape as male and to the victim as female.

19. India is a prime example of this phenomenon. Despite laws banning the practice (*see* The Pre-natal Diagnostic Techniques [Regulation and Prevention of Misuse] Amendment Act, 2002, No. 14 of 2003, India Code [2010], *available at* http://indiacode.nic.in/), one study has estimated that half a million females are aborted on the basis of sex every year in India. Prabhat Jha *et al., Low Male-to-Female Sex Ratio of Children Born in India: National Survey of 1.1 million Households,* 367 LANCET 211, 217 (2006). China faces a similar problem. *See* Law on Maternal and Infant Health Care (promulgated by Order No. 33 of the President of the People's Republic of

China, Oct. 27, 1994, effective Jun. 1, 1995), *available at* http://www.npc
.gov.cn/englishnpc/Law/2007-12/12/content_1383796.htm; Population and
Family Planning Law (promulgated by Order No. 63 of the People's Republic of China, Dec. 29, 2001, effective Sept. 1, 2002), *available at* http://www
.gov.cn/english/laws/2005-10/11/content_75954.htm; Jing-Bao Nie, *Non-
Medical Sex-Selective Abortion in China: Ethical and Public Policy Issues
in the Context of 40 Million Missing Females*, 98 BRIT. MED. BULL. 7, 8
(2011). In 2012 the U.S. House of Representatives considered and rejected
a bill that would have banned sex-selective abortions in the United States.
Jennifer Steinhauer, *House Rejects Bill to Ban Sex-Selective Abortions*, N.Y.
TIMES, Jun. 1, 2012, at A20.

20. *See* Jody Raphael, RAPE IS RAPE: HOW DENIAL, DISTORTION, AND
VICTIM BLAMING ARE FUELING A HIDDEN ACQUAINTANCE RAPE CRI-
SIS 48–49 (2013) (discussing the rape allegations against WikiLeaks founder
Julian Assange); Sherry F. Colb, *Rape by Deception, Rape by Impersonation,
and a New California Bill*, VERDICT (May 1, 2013), http://verdict.justia
.com/2013/05/01/rape-by-deception-rape-by-impersonation-and-a-new
-california-bill; Sherry F. Colb, *The Jerusalem "Rape by Deception" Case:
Can a Lie Transform Consensual Sex Into Rape?*, FINDLAW (Aug. 4, 2010),
http://writ.corporate.findlaw.com/colb/20100804.html.

21. These laws vary by state. Some states do not permit birth parents to
officially consent to adoption until a period of days has passed since birth.
E.g., Mass. Gen. Laws ch. 210, § 2 (2012) (four days); W. Va. Code § 48-22-
302(a) (2013) (three days). Other states allow immediate consent upon the
birth of the child but allow consent to be revoked within a period of time
thereafter. *E.g.*, Md. Code Ann., Fam. Law § 5-339 (2012) (thirty days). Still
others allow consent to be given even before birth but allow for revocation
for a period of time after birth. *E.g.*, Ala. Code § 26-10A-13 (2011) (providing that consent may be given at any time, but "may be withdrawn within
five days after birth or within five days after signing of the consent or relin-
quishment, whichever comes last"). For a comprehensive survey of state laws
in this area, see Elizabeth J. Samuels, *Time to Decide? The Laws Governing
Mothers' Consents to the Adoption of Their Newborn Infants*, 72 TENN. L.
REV. 509, 541–48 (2005).

22. *See* Andrea Gavinelli & Miyun Park, *Farm Animal Welfare: In Legislatures, Corporate Boardrooms, and Private Kitchens, in* STATE OF THE
ANIMALS 129, 130, 135–36 (2007).

4. DEATH VERSUS SUFFERING

1. Epicurus, *Letter to Menoeceus, in* GREEK AND ROMAN PHILOSOPHY
AFTER ARISTOTLE: READINGS IN THE HISTORY OF PHILOSOPHY 50 (Jason
L. Saunders ed., 1994).

2. *See* Francis W. Newman, *Epicureanism, Ancient and Modern*, 84 FRASER'S MAG. 606, 611 (1871), *reprinted in* 111 LITTELL'S LIVING AGE 771, 774 (1871).

3. *See, e.g.*, Jaime Solano *et al.*, *A Note on Behavioral Responses to Brief Cow–Calf Separation and Reunion in Cattle (Bos indicus)*, 2 J. VETERINARY BEHAV.: CLINICAL APPLICATIONS & RES. 10, 11 (2007).

4. *See, e.g.*, Timothy Pachirat, EVERY TWELVE SECONDS: INDUSTRIALIZED SLAUGHTER AND THE POLITICS OF SIGHT 144–45 (2011); Gary L. Francione, INTRODUCTION TO ANIMAL RIGHTS: YOUR CHILD OR THE DOG? 12 (2000).

5. *See* Frederike Kaldewaij, *Animals and the Harm of Death, in* 2 THE ANIMAL ETHICS READER 54 (Susan J. Armstrong & Richard G. Botzler eds., 2008).

6. For the most part, Regan defines the category of beings that are "subjects of a life" by identifying the criteria for inclusion as opposed to providing an exhaustive list of the creatures that satisfy those criteria. He explains that "individuals are subjects-of-a-life if they have beliefs and desires; perception, memory, and a sense of the future, including their own future; an emotional life together with feelings of pleasure and pain, preference- and welfare-interests; the ability to initiate action in pursuit of their desires and goals; a psychophysical identity over time; and an individual welfare in the sense that their experiental life fares well or ill for them, logically independently of their utility for others and logically independently of their being the object of anyone else's interests." Tom Regan, THE CASE FOR ANIMAL RIGHTS 243 (2004). One commentator has offered that Regan's criteria are "likely to be satisfied by many species of birds, and quite possibly by reptiles, amphibians and fish," but that "[l]iving human beings in persistent vegetative states might not" and "humans in irreversible coma almost certainly would not" qualify. Mark Rowlands, 2 ANIMAL RIGHTS: MORAL THEORY AND PRACTICE 59–60 (2009).

7. Peter Singer, PRACTICAL ETHICS 133 (1993).

8. Others go much further in pointing out animals' "inabilities." *See* Neel Burton, *The Seven Things Only Human Beings Can Do*, PSYCH. TODAY (Aug. 27, 2012), http://www.psychologytoday.com/blog/hide-and-seek /201208/the-seven-things-only-human-beings-can-do; J. Neil Schuman, *Fifty Things Animals Can't Do*, PULPLESS (Dec. 7, 2000), http://www.pulpless .com/jneil/fifty.html. For further argument against the idea that animal rights should hinge on human characteristics, *see* Gary L. Francione, *Animals— Property or Persons?, in* ANIMAL RIGHTS: CURRENT DEBATES AND NEW DIRECTIONS 129–30 (Cass R. Sunstein & Martha C. Nussbaum eds., 2005). For the argument that characteristics beyond sentience may sometimes be a necessary predicate to legal rights, see Steven M. Wise, DRAWING THE LINE: SCIENCE AND THE CASE FOR ANIMAL RIGHTS 33–34 (2003).

9. *See generally* Aristotle, NICOMACHEAN ETHICS (Christopher Rowe trans., Oxford University Press 2002).

10. *See* Jonathan Balcombe, SECOND NATURE: THE INNER LIVES OF ANIMALS (2011); Marc Bekoff, THE EMOTIONAL LIVES OF ANIMALS: A LEADING SCIENTIST EXPLORES ANIMAL JOY, SORROW, AND EMPATHY—AND WHY THEY MATTER (2008).

11. *See* Thomas Nagel, *What Is It Like to Be a Bat?*, 83 Phil. Rev. 435 (1974).

12. "For as far as any intelligent being can repeat the idea of any past action with the same consciousness it had of it at first, and with the same consciousness it has of any present action; so far it is the same personal self." John Locke, AN ESSAY CONCERNING HUMAN UNDERSTANDING 247 (Prometheus Books 1995).

13. *See* Robert Nozick, PHILOSOPHICAL EXPLANATIONS 29–43 (1983); Derek Parfit, REASONS AND PERSONS (1986); Bernard Williams, *The Self and the Future*, 79 PHIL. REV. 161 (1970).

14. Hume addressed personal identity in book 1, part 4, section 6 of his "Treatise of Human Nature." *See* David Hume, A TREATISE OF HUMAN NATURE 116–21 (CreateSpace Independent Publishing, 2012).

15. *See id.* at 116–17.

16. Like many ancient Greek philosophers, Heraclitus is known to us today primarily through the writings of Plato. *See* Plato, CRATYLUS 68 (Benjamin Jowett trans., 2006). *See also* Leonardo Tarán, *Heraclitus: The River-Fragments and Their Implications*, 20 ELENCHOS 9, 10 (1999).

17. *See* THE CONNECTED DISCOURSES OF THE BUDDHA: A TRANSLATION OF THE SAMYUTTA NIKAYA 551 (Bhikkhu Bodhi trans., 2003); THE THREE BASIC FACTS OF EXISTENCE I: IMPERMANENCE (*Anicca*) (Buddhist Publication Soc'y, 1981), *available at* http://www.bps.lk/olib/wh/wh186.pdf. *See also* James Giles, *The No-Self Theory: Hume, Buddhism and Personal Theory*, 43 PHIL. E. & W. 175, 175 (1993).

18. *See* Thomas Hobbes, 1 THE ENGLISH WORKS OF THOMAS HOBBES OF MALMESBURY 136–37 (William Molesworth ed., 2004). For other treatments of the paradox of the ship of Theseus, both direct and indirect, see Aristotle, PHYSICS 106–7 (David Bostock and Robin Waterfield trans., 2008); Locke, *supra* note 12, at 242–43; Nozick, *supra* note 13, at 33–34; John Bowin, *Aristotle on Identity and Persistence*, 41 APEIRON 63, 63 (2008); Wesley Cooper, *Nozick, Parfit and Platonic Glasses*, 20 SORITES 98 (2008). The puzzle first appears in the writings of Plutarch. Plutarch, *Theseus, in* PLUTARCH LIVES: THESEUS AND ROMULUS, LYCURGUS AND NUMA, SOLON AND PUBLICOLA 49 (Bernadotte Perrin trans., 1914).

19. John Perry, IDENTITY, PERSONAL IDENTITY, AND THE SELF xi (2002).

20. *See* Williams, *supra* note 13.

21. *Compare* Geoffrey Lean, *I Was in a Coma but I Could Hear Every Word*, INDEPENDENT, Sep. 10, 2006, at 40, *and* Adrian M. Owen, *Detecting Awareness in the Vegetative State*, 313 SCIENCE 1402, 1402 (2006), *with* Lionel Naccache, *Is She Conscious?*, 313 SCIENCE 1395 (2006).

22. *See* Mads Gilbert *et al.*, *Resuscitation from Accidental Hypothermia of 13.7°C with Circulatory Arrest*, 355 LANCET 375, 375 (2000); *Frozen Woman: A Walking Miracle*, CBS News (Feb. 3, 2000, 2:06 PM), http://www.cbsnews.com/news/frozen-woman-a-walking-miracle/.

23. *See* Robert Gottlieb, *Back From Heaven—The Science*, NY REV. OF BOOKS 36 (Nov. 6, 2014).

24. *See* Richard Thaler, *Toward a Positive Theory of Consumer Choice*, 1 J. ECON. BEHAV. & ORG. 39, 44 (1980); *It's Mine, I Tell You*, ECONOMIST, Jun. 21, 2008, at 95–96.

25. *See* Jack L. Knetsch, *The Endowment Effect and Evidence of Nonreversible Indifference Curves*, 79 AM. ECON. REV. 1277, 1278 (1989).

26. *See* Gregory Klass & Kathryn Zeiler, *Against Endowment Theory: Experimental Economics and Legal Scholarship*, 61 UCLA L. REV. 2 (2013).

27. *See* Ori J. Herstein, *Why "Nonexistent People" Do Not Have Zero Well-Being but No Well-Being at All*, 30 J. APPLIED PHIL. 136 (2013).

28. *See* Hilary Putnam, THE COLLAPSE OF THE FACT/VALUE DICHOTOMY (2004); Richard Rorty, PHILOSOPHY AND THE MIRROR OF NATURE 178 (1979); Richard Rorty, *Solidarity or Objectivity?*, *in* OBJECTIVITY, RELATIVISM AND TRUTH: PHILOSOPHICAL PAPERS 23–24 (1990). *See* Hume, *supra* note 14, at 208.

29. Oregon Death with Dignity Act, OR. REV. STAT. §§ 127.800–127.995 (2013); Patient Choice and Control at End of Life Act, VT. STAT. ANN. tit. 18, §§ 5281–92 (2012); Washington Death with Dignity Act, WASH. REV. CODE § 70.245.010–70.245.904 (2013); Baxter v. State, 224 P.2d 1211, 1222 (Mont. 2009).

30. *See* Lydia Saad, *Doctor-Assisted Suicide Is Moral Issue Dividing Americans Most*, GALLUP (May 31, 2011), http://www.gallup.com/poll/147842/doctor-assisted-suicide-moral-issue-dividing-americans.aspx (showing that 45 percent of Americans called doctor-assisted suicide "morally acceptable" in a Gallup poll). *Cf.* James A. Colbert, Joann Schulte, & Jonathan N. Adler, *Physician-Assisted Suicide—Polling Results*, 369 N.E. J. MED. e15 (2013) (reporting that 67 percent of American respondents to a poll in a medical journal opposed physician-assisted suicide).

31. *See* M. Scott Peck, DENIAL OF THE SOUL: SPIRITUAL AND MEDICAL PERSPECTIVES ON EUTHANASIA AND MORTALITY 132, 189 (1997).

32. The U.S. Supreme Court credited such fears in its 1997 ruling upholding a state ban on physician-assisted suicide. Washington v. Glucksberg, 521 U.S. 702, 732–34.

33. *E.g.*, Alabama Pain-Capable Unborn Child Protection Act, ALA. CODE §§ 26-23B-1-9 (2013); Unborn Child Pain Awareness and Prevention

Act, ARK. CODE ANN. §§ 20-16-1401–1410 (2012); Pain-Capable Unborn Child Protection Act, NEB. REV. STAT. §§ 28-3,102–3,111 (2012); Preborn Pain Act, TEX. HEALTH & SAFETY CODE ANN. § 171.044.

34. *See* David F. Forte, *Life, Heartbeat, Birth: A Medical Basis for Reform*, 74 OHIO ST. L.J. 121, 134 (2013).

PART II: MOVEMENTS

1. Charles Tilly and Sidney Tarrow, CONTENTIOUS POLITICS 45 (2007).

2. We say "often" rather than "always" or even "usually" because we are mindful of findings that by some measure violence frequently succeeds. *See* William A. Gamson, THE STRATEGY OF SOCIAL PROTEST 72–88 (2d ed. 1990).

5. STRATEGY

1. *See* Gaston V. Rimlinger, WELFARE POLICY AND INDUSTRIALIZATION IN EUROPE, AMERICA, AND RUSSIA 122 (1971).

2. *E.g.*, Seymour Martin Lipset & Gary Marks, *How FDR Saved Capitalism*, HOOVER DIG., no. 1, Jan. 30, 2001, *available at* http://www.hoover.org/research/how-fdr-saved-capitalism.

3. *See* David Whitford, THE CURSE OF HAM IN THE EARLY MODERN ERA: THE BIBLE AND THE JUSTIFICATIONS FOR SLAVERY 2, 105–6 (2009).

4. *See* Eugene D. Genovese, A CONSUMING FIRE: THE FALL OF THE CONFEDERACY IN THE MIND OF THE WHITE CHRISTIAN SOUTH 15, 31, 51–52 (1998).

5. *Quoted in* Carol S. Glasser, *The Radical Debate: A Straw Man in the Movement?*, *in* THE RISE OF CRITICAL ANIMAL STUDIES: FROM THE MARGINS TO THE CENTRE 241, 244 (Nik Taylor and Richard Twine, eds. 2014).

6. Maria do Mar Castro Varela & Nikita Dhawan, *Normative Dilemmas and the Hegemony of Counter-Hegemony*, *in* HEGEMONY AND HETERONORMATIVITY: REVISITING 'THE POLITICAL' IN QUEER POLITICS, 91, 100–101 (Maria do Mar Castro Varela *et al.* eds., 2011).

7. Francione maintains a website, *Animal Rights: The Abolitionist Approach*, at http://www.abolitionistapproach.com/.

8. The litigation and other activities undertaken by the Nonhuman Rights Project are detailed on its website, http://www.nonhumanrightsproject.org.

9. James M. Jasper, *A Strategic Choice to Collective Action: Looking for Agency in Social-Movement Choices*, 9(1) MOBILIZATION 1, 7–9 (Feb. 2004).

10. *HSUS Quotes*, HUMANE WATCH, http://www.humanewatch.org/hsus_quotes/.

11. The major animal welfare organizations are hardly unique in focusing on their own support rather than on real progress. Consider the parallel of "environmental leaders" who "whistle past the graveyard of global warming politics" because "the membership rolls and the income of the big environmental organizations have grown enormously," even as the broad support for effective environmental strategy has become very shallow. Michael Shellenberger and Ted Norhaus, THE DEATH OF ENVIRONMENTALISM: GLOBAL WARMING POLITICS IN A POST-ENVIRONMENTAL WORLD 11 (2004), *available at* http://www.thebreakthrough.org/images/Death_of_Environmentalism.pdf. For a critique of environmentalists for failure to address the impact of animal agriculture, *see* COWSPIRACY: THE SUSTAINABILITY SECRET (A.U.M. Films & First Spark Media 2014).

12. *See Reclaiming Abolitionism: It's Time for Us to Take a Stand for Animals*, VOICES FOR ANIMALS, http://vfaonline.org/index.php/alerts/general-alerts/41-alerts/alertsgeneral/185-reclaiming-abolitionism (noting that a pig farmer sits on the board of HSUS).

13. As of April 2015, video of the debate was available at http://youtu.be/akFdn-sa3EM. Francione also published short written versions of his view and of Friedrich's view on his blog at http://www.abolitionistapproach.com/the-abolitionist-approach-and-farm-sanctuary-discuss-happy-meat-abolition-and-welfare-reform/#.Us2h5NK1xcY.

14. The evidence is at best thin. Friedrich relies on a study by Kansas State economists. Gyln T. Tonsor & Nicole J. Olynk, U.S. MEAT DEMAND: THE INFLUENCE OF ANIMAL WELFARE MEDIA COVERAGE 1 (2010), *available at* http://www.agmanager.info/livestock/marketing/AnimalWelfare/MF2951.pdf. That study looked at media attention to species-specific animal welfare concerns and found that such attention is correlated with reduced demand for poultry and pork (but not beef) for up to six months. The authors concluded that such media attention led to reallocation of consumer purchasing to "nonmeat" food without indicating how much of that displaced demand was for other animal products such as eggs and dairy. Thus, the Tonsor and Olynk analysis barely constitutes any evidence, much less proof, that welfare campaigns lead people to become vegan. Nick Cooney of Mercy for Animals makes similar claims to those made by Friedrich, but these also appear to be mostly speculative. *See* Nick Cooney, *Welfare Reform and Vegan Advocacy: The Facts*, FARM SANCTUARY (Aug. 21, 2012), *available at* http://ccc.farmsanctuary.org/welfare-reform-and-vegan-advocacy-the-facts (listing several studies that indicate that animal welfare reforms drive up the prices of animal products but that also concede that demand for those products remains relatively inelastic as well as listing two studies indicating that, in other contexts, small changes in social attitude can prime individuals for large ones).

15. For example, after KFC adopted controlled-atmosphere killing of chickens, PETA ended its boycott of KFC in Canada nd begin handing out

free samples of a new vegan KFC menu item. *PETA Ends Boycott of KFC*, Canada.com (Jul. 15, 2008), http://www.canada.com/windsorstar/story .html?id=d79e8d75-e2b6-430e-a2da-8bdad12c776c.

16. *See also* Lee Hall, *An Interview with Professor Gary L. Francione on the State of the U.S. Animal Rights Movement*, Friends of Animals (Summer 2002) http://friendsofanimals.org/programs/animal-rights/issues-ideas /gary-l-francione-state-us-animal-rights-movement; Sherry F. Colb, *An Empty Gesture to Soothe the Conscience: Why We Pass Laws Protecting Chimpanzees and Other Animals from Cruelty*, FindLaw (Mar. 4, 2009), http://writ.news.findlaw.com/colb/20090304.html; James LaVeck, *Truthiness Stranger than Fiction: The Hidden Cost of Selling the Public on "Cage-Free" Eggs*, Satya, Feb. 2007, *available at* http://www.satyamag.com/feb07 /laveck.html.

17. Sandra Higgins, *Enriched Cages and Embodied Prisons: A Report on the EU Directive Banning Battery Cages for Egg Laying Hens* 21 (2013), available at http://www.edenfarmanimalsanctuary.com/wp-content /uploads/2013/05/Enriched-Cages-and-Embodied-Prisons.pdf.

18. Carrie P. Freeman, Framing Farming: Communications Strategies for Animal Rights (2014).

19. *See, e.g.*, Nat'l Right to Life Educ. Trust, *Pain of the Unborn* 1–2 (2004), *available at* http://www.nrlc.org/uploads/factsheets/FS20Unborn Pain.pdf; Steven Ertelt, *Late-Term Abortion Practitioner LeRoy Carhart Hampered by New Nebraska Pro-Life Laws*, LifeNews (Apr. 13, 2010), http://archive.lifenews.com/state4993.html; National Right to Life Committee, National Right to Life Applauds U.S. Supreme Court Ruling Upholding Partial-Birth Abortion Ban Act (Apr. 18, 2007), https://www.nrlc.org /communications/releases/2007/release041807/; Drew Zahn, *New Law Bans Picking Baby's Sex by Abortion*, WorldNetDaily (May 23, 2009), http:// www.wnd.com/?pageId=98886.

20. Bruce Friedrich, *Getting from A to Z: Why Animal Activists Should Support Incremental Reforms to Help Animals*, Huffington Post (Feb. 21, 2011, 10:28 AM), http://www.huffingtonpost.com/bruce-friedrich /getting-from-a-to-z-why-p_b_825612.html.

21. 18 U.S.C. § 1531 (2006). *See, e.g.*, Ariz. Rev. Stat. Ann. § 36-449.03(D)(4); Ind. Code Ann. § 16-34-2-1.1(a)(1)(D); Mich. Comp. Laws Ann. § 333.17015; R.I. Gen. Laws § 23-4.7-3; Va. Code Ann. § 18.2–76.

22. *See, e.g.*, Ala. Code §§ 13A-11-240 to -247; Ark. Code Ann. § 5-62-104; Ohio Rev. Code Ann. § 959.131 (prohibiting cruelty to a "companion animal" and specifically excluding livestock from the definition).

23. *See Horse Slaughter—Related Statutes*, Michigan State University Animal Legal & Historical Center, http://www.animallaw.info /statutes/topicstatutes/sttohorsl.htm (listing numerous state statutes banning or regulating horse slaughter).

24. *See, e.g.*, N.M. Stat. Ann. § 30-18-1(I)(4); Texas Penal Code § 42.09(f)(2). These standard practices include extremely painful and frightening procedures. *See Factory Farming, Chickens*, Farm Sanctuary, http://www.farmsanctuary.org/learn/factory-farming/chickens/ (noting that, because of excessive pecking concerns that arise in crowded conditions, laying hens have part of their beaks cut off, and that "a chicken's beak is filled with nerves, and debeaking can result in severe and possibly chronic pain").

25. Elizabeth L. Decoux, *Speaking for the Modern Prometheus: The Significance of Animal Suffering to the Abolition Movement*, 16 Animal L. 9, 31–35 (2009); *PETA's Farmed Animal Campaigns: Some Improvements Made; Many More Still Needed*, People for the Ethical Treatment of Animals, http://www.peta.org/about/learn-about-peta/farmed-animal-campaigns.aspx.

26. *See, e.g.*, *Oppose Regulations Because*, American Right to Life, http://americanrtl.org/regs (urging opposition to every law that regulates killing of the unborn because such regulations, "end with the meaning, 'and then you can kill the baby'"). *Compare* Jill Stanek, *Purely Fanatical*, WorldNetDaily (Jun. 13, 2007), http://www.wnd.com/?pageId=42048 (characterizing those opposed to anything less than a ban as "fanatical" and their stance as "the equivalent of saying one cannot pull any victims from a burning building if all cannot be pulled out"). One indication of the continuing pro-life commitment to the full personhood of even the earliest embryos is evident in the embrace of embryo donation and adoption as comparable to the adoption of born children. *See, e.g. Snowflakes Embryo Adoption Testimonials*, Nightlight Christian Adoptions, http://www.nightlight.org/snowflakes-embryo-adoption-testimonials/.

27. Guttmacher Institute, *Facts on Induced Abortion in the United States* 1 (May 2010), *available at* http://www.guttmacher.org/pubs/fb_induced_abortion.pdf (indicating graphically the number of abortions among women aged fifteen to forty-four, showing an increase from an annual rate of 16.3 per 1,000 in 1973 to a high of 29.3 per 1,000 in 1981 followed by a decreasing trend through 2005, when the number was 19.4 per 1,000).

28. *See* Mark Bittman, *We're Eating Less Meat. Why?*, N.Y. Times (Jan. 10, 2012), http://opinionator.blogs.nytimes.com/2012/01/10/were-eating-less-meat-why.

29. *See* Rosanna Mentzer Morrison, *Major Trends in U.S. Food Supply, 1909–99*, 23 Food Rev. 8, 11 (2000); Vaclav Smil, *Eating Meat: Evolution, Patterns, and Consequences*, 28 Population and Dev. Rev. 599, 609–14 (2002). *See also Farm Animal Statistics: Slaughter Totals*, Humane Society of the United States (Apr. 17, 2014), http://www.humanesociety.org/news/resources/research/stats_slaughter_totals.html.

30. *See* Bonnie Liebman, *The Changing American Diet: A Report Card*, Nutrition Action Newsletter (Ctr. for Science in the Pub. Interest),

Sep. 2013, at 10, *available at* http://cspinet.org/new/pdf/changing_american
_diet_13.pdf.

31. *See* John J. McGlone & Janeen Salak-Johnson, *Changing from Sow Gestation Crates to Pens: Problem or Opportunity?*, Manitoba Swine Seminar (2008), http://www.thepigsite.com/articles/2672/changing-from-sow-gestation-crates-to-pens-problem-or-opportunity; Jim Mason & Peter Singer, Animal Factories 3 (1990) ("In 1967, 44 percent of commercial layers were in cages; by 1978, 90 percent were in cages").

32. Ctrs. for Disease Control, U.S. Dep't of Health and Human Servs., Assisted Reproductive Technology Success Rates: National Summary and Fertility Clinic Reports 68 (2007); Nicholas Wade, *Pioneer of in Vitro Fertilization Wins Nobel Prize*, N.Y. Times, Oct. 4, 2010, http://www.nytimes.com/2010/10/05/health/research/05nobel.html.

33. *See* Father Tadeusz Pacholcyzk, *What Should We Do with the Frozen Embryos?*, Nat'l Catholic Bioethics Ctr. (Jun. 2009), http://www.ncbcenter.org/page.aspx?pid=478 (noting that even frozen embryos eventually die from "decay or 'freezer burn'").

34. Amanda Gardner, *Most Americans Back Embryonic Stem Cell Research: Poll*, U.S. News & World Report (Oct. 7, 2010), http://health.usnews.com/health-news/managing-your-healthcare/research/articles/2010/10/07/most-americans-back-embryonic-stem-cell-research-poll.html.

35. Genetics & Pub. Pol'y Ctr., *Public Awareness and Attitudes About Reproductive Genetic Technology* 5 (2004), *available at* http://web.archive.org/web/20120105075941/http://www.dnapolicy.org/images/reportpdfs/PublicAwarenessAndAttitudes.pdf.

36. Guttmacher Institute, *supra* note 27, at 1.

37. *Id.*

38. *Id.*

39. *See* Food and Agriculture Organization, The State of Food and Agriculture 136 (2009), *available at* http://www.fao.org/docrep/012/i0680e/i0680e.pdf.

40. *See* Sharon S. Brehm & Jack W. Brehm, Psychological Reactance: A Theory of Freedom and Control 4 (1981) ("In general, [reactance] theory holds that a threat to or loss of a freedom motivates the individual to restore that freedom"). The magnitude of reactance will vary based upon the importance of the freedom and perceived gravity of the threat. *Id.* at 37–98. *See also* Sharon Begley, *Lies of Mass Destruction*, Newsweek, Aug. 25, 2009, *available at* http://www.newsweek.com/why-we-believe-lies-even-when-we-learn-truth-78775 (citing Steven Hoffman explaining the phenomenon of "motivated reasoning," in which "'[r]ather than search rationally for information that either confirms or disconfirms a particular belief . . . people actually seek out information that confirms what they already believe'").

41. Jo-Ann Tsang, *Moral Rationalization and the Integration of Situational Factors and Psychological Processes in Immoral Behavior*, 6(1) Rev. Gen. Psychol. 25, 25–26 (2002).

42. *See* Daryl J. Bem, *Self-Perception: An Alternative Interpretation of Cognitive Dissonance Phenomena*, 73 Psychol. Rev. 183, 183 (1967).

43. *See* Barbara S. Kisilevsky *et al.*, *Effects of Experience on Fetal Voice Recognition*, 14 J. Psychol. Sci. 220, 222 (2003); Janet L. Hopson, *Fetal Psychology*, 31(5) Psychol. Today 44 (1998), *available at* http://www.leaderu.com/orgs/tul/psychtoday9809.html.

44. In response to questions that readers have raised about the intense and highly emotional politics of abortion in the United States (which may seem to belie our suggestion that most pro-choice Americans have a shallow commitment to their position on abortion), we want to clarify that we are making a relative rather than an absolute point. People may indeed be very passionate about their pro-choice views—and may even choose political candidates accordingly, a luxury completely unavailable to advocates of animal rights—but for most people, given their daily practices, the desire to believe that abortion is morally acceptable is likely to be less intense than the desire to believe that consuming animal products is morally acceptable.

45. Jonathan Safran Foer, *Eating Animals* 6 (2009).

46. *See* Planned Parenthood of Southeastern Pa. v. Casey, 505 U.S. 833, 899–900 (1992); Hodgson v. Minnesota, 497 U.S. 417, 497–501 (1990); Ohio v. Akron Ctr. for Reproductive Health, 497 U.S. 502, 510–15 (1990); Planned Parenthood v. Danforth, 428 U.S. 52 (1976).

47. *See* Michael C. Dorf and Sidney Tarrow, *Strange Bedfellows: How an Anticipatory Countermovement Brought Same-Sex Marriage into the Public Arena*, 39(2) L. & Soc. Inquiry 449 (2014).

48. *See, e.g.*, Laurence H. Tribe, Abortion: The Clash of Absolutes 135 (1990).

49. *See* Gonzales v. Carhart, 550 U.S. 124, 138 (2007).

50. In describing the pro-life position as the "movement" and the pro-choice position as the "countermovement," we do not mean to be taking a position on which came first. We use "counter" here simply to mean something like "opposite." For a discussion of the complex interaction between movements and countermovements, see Dorf and Tarrow, *supra* note 47.

51. *See, e.g.*, Ark. Code Ann. § 20-16-903(b); Ind. Code Ann. § 16-34-2-1.1(a).

52. We put to one side state laws that are upsetting in other ways, like the North Carolina law that required a doctor to show and describe a fetal ultrasound to any woman seeking an abortion while the doctor is performing the abortion. That law was held invalid as an impermissible interference with a doctor's right to free speech in Stuart v. Camnitz, 774 F.3d 238 (4th Cir. 2014).

53. Jeff Jacoby, *Choosing to Eliminate Unwanted Daughters*, Boston Globe, Apr. 6, 2006, http://www.boston.com/bostonglobe/editorial _opinion/oped/articles/2008/04/06/choosing_to_eliminate_unwanted _daughters/ ("[I]n a 2006 Zogby poll, an overwhelming 86% of Americans agreed that [sex-selection abortion] should be illegal.").

54. Brief for Respondents, Planned Parenthood of Southeastern Pa. v. Casey, 505 U.S. 833 (1992) (Nos. 91-744, 91-902), 1992 WL 12006423 at *4 ("The one provision of the act which does contain an outright prohibition, § 3204(c) (no abortion to be performed solely because of the sex of the unborn child), was not challenged."); Sherry F. Colb, *China Announces That It Will Criminalize Sex-Selection Abortions: What, if Anything, Should the U.S. Do About the Practice in This Country?*, Findlaw (Jan. 26, 2005), http://writ.news.findlaw.com/colb/20050126.html.

55. *See CNN Poll: Wide Divide over Abortion*, CNN (Mar. 6, 2014), http://politicalticker.blogs.cnn.com/2014/03/06/cnn-poll-wide-divide-over -abortion/; *Abortion*, Gallup (2013), http://www.gallup.com/poll/1576 /abortion.aspx.

56. *See* Catherine Donaldson-Evans, *Yale Student Insists Abortion Art Project Is Real, Despite University's Claims of "Creative Fiction,"* Fox News (Apr. 18, 2008), http://www.foxnews.com/story/0,2933,351730,00 .html (describing a woman who claimed to have repeatedly impregnated herself and then had abortions to create an art installation).

57. *Cf.* Roger Scruton, *Animal Rights*, City J., Summer 2000, *available at* http://www.city-journal.org/html/10_3_urbanities-animal.html.

58. *See* Stephen Budiansky, The Covenant of the Wild: Why Animals Chose Domestication 59–62 (1992); Angelique Chao, *Why Animal Lovers Should Eat Meat*, Simple Good and Tasty, http://simple goodandtasty.com/2010/04/23/why-animal-lovers-should-eat-meat (Apr. 23, 2010, 11:01 PM). For a thorough response, see Sherry F. Colb, Mind if I Order the Cheeseburger? And Other Questions People Ask Vegans 156–72 (2013).

59. *See, e.g.*, *Review of the Welfare of Animals in Agriculture: Hearing Before the Subcomm. on Livestock, Dairy, and Poultry of the H. Comm. of Agriculture*, 110th Cong. 22–23 (2007) (statement of Barbara Determan, National Pork Producers Council); Animal Agric. Alliance, *Agriculture's Commitment to Animal Well-Being* 2 (2008), available at http://thehill.com /sites/default/files/aniag2_agriculturescommitmenttoanimalwellbeing_0.pdf; Merritt W. Harper, Animal Husbandry for Schools 81–100, 157–71 (1915); John L. Tormey & Rolla C. Lawry, Animal Husbandry 246 (1920).

60. *See* Darian B. Ibrahim, *A Return to Descartes: Property, Profit, and the Corporate Ownership of Animals*, 70 Law & Contemp. Probs. 89, 91–97 (2007); Peter Singer, Animal Liberation 96–97 (1990).

61. *See, e.g.,* Terry McSweeney, *Prop. 2 Opponents Say Measure Is Harmful,* ABC News (Oct. 21, 2008), http://abclocal.go.com/kgo /story?section=news/state&id=6462628; Margot Roosevelt, *Campaign '06: Treating Pigs Better in Arizona,* Time, Nov. 06, 2006, *available at* http:// www.time.com/time/nation/article/0,8599,1555372,00.html.

62. For criticism of the agreement as doing very little for laying hens, see Voices for Animals, *Reclaiming Absolutism: It's Time for Us to Take a Stand for Animals,* http://vfaonline.org/index.php/alerts/general-alerts/41-alerts /alertsgeneral/185-reclaiming-abolitionism; Urgent Action Alert, *Stop the Rotten Egg Bill,* http://stoptherotteneggbill.org/site/c.8qKNJWMwFbLUG /b.7865469/k.3BC1/Humane_Farming_Association_enriched_cages _battery_cages_United_Egg_Producers.htm.

63. Sherry F. Colb, *A Prisoner Seeks Vegan Food in Prison: Why Refusing Him Is Both Illegal and Foolish,* Findlaw (Mar. 31, 2010), http://writ.news .findlaw.com/colb/20100331.html. *See also* Jova v. Smith, 582 F.3d 410, 417 (2d Cir. 2009). *But see* Spies v. Voinovich, 173 F.3d 398. For examples of proposed legislation to protect those who want to opt out of participating in animal harm, see H.R. 4870 § 2(b), 111th Cong. (2010); Assem. B. A07804 § 6, 2009–10 Reg. Sess. (N.Y. 2009).

64. Bryan Walsh, *Getting Real About the Price of Cheap Food,* Time, Aug. 21, 2009, *available at* http://content.time.com/time/magazine /article/0,9171,1917726,00.html (noting that because of corn subsidies "[t]he U.S. agricultural industry can now produce unlimited quantities of meat and grains at remarkably cheap prices" but that "fruits and vegetables do not receive the same price supports as grains").

65. As Professor Freeman puts it, vegan advocacy should problematize commodification of animals, not merely cruel treatment of animals. *See* Freeman, *supra* note 18, at 125.

66. *See, e.g.,* Ariz. Rev. Stat. Ann. § 36-2154; N.Y. Civ. Rights § 79-i.

67. *See* Rust v. Sullivan, 500 U.S. 173, 192–203 (1991). *See also* Nina J. Crimm, *The Global Gag Rule: Undermining National Interests by Doing to Foreign Women and NGOs What Cannot Be Done at Home,* 40 Cornell Int'l L.J. 587, 590 (2007).

68. Olivia Gans & Mary Spaulding Balch, *When They Say . . . , You Say . . .,* National Right to Life Committee 10 (2013), available at http://www.nrlc.org/uploads/WhenTheySayPacket.pdf; *Where We Stand,* Pro-life Action League, http://www.prolifeaction.org/faq/stand.php.

69. *See Urgent Congressional Alert: Urge Congress to Reject Embryo-Killing Research,* National Right to Life Committee (May 4, 2005), http://www.nrlc.org/archive/news/2005/NRL05/Alert050405.html. *See also Embryo Donation and Adoption 101,* Embryo Adoption Awareness Center, http://www.embryoadoption.org/donors/embryo_adoption_101.cfm.

70. For the downside of such an approach, if one views embryos as qualitatively distinct from persons, see Sherry F. Colb, *The Costs of the Bush Administration's Promoting "Embryo Adoption"*, FINDLAW (Aug. 28, 2002), http://writ.lp.findlaw.com/colb/20020828.html.

71. *See* Mary Esch, *Cow Torture Video: Willet Dairy Caught Burning off Cows' Horns, Chopping Calf's Tail in Mercy for Animals Exposé*, HUFFINGTON POST (Jan. 27, 2010, 4:20 PM), http://www.huffington post.com/2010/01/27/cow-torture-video-willet-_n_438403.html. *See also* Anna Schecter & Brian Ross, *Got Milk? Got Ethics? Animal Rights v. U.S. Dairy Industry*, ABC NEWS (Jan. 26, 2010), http://abcnews.go.com/Blotter /animal-rights-us-dairy-industry/story?id=9658866&page=1.

72. *See* Michael C. Dorf, *The Supreme Court's Responsibility for Recent Death Penalty Mishaps*, VERDICT (Jan. 29, 2014), http://verdict .justia.com/2014/01/29/supreme-courts-responsibility-recent-death-penalty-mishaps.

73. Neither PETA nor Mercy for Animals possesses data on the veganism rates of their respective memberships. It should be noted, however, that PETA even employs some nonvegans. *Frequently Asked Questions about Working for PETA/FSAP*, PEOPLE FOR THE ETHICAL TREATMENT OF ANIMALS, http://www.peta.org/about-peta/work-at-peta/jobs-faq/.

74. Eddie Lama, *Sadly, Happy Meat*, SATYA, Sept. 2006, available at http:// www.satyamag.com/sept06/lama.html; Gary L. Francione, *"Happy Meat:" Making Humans Feel Better About Eating Animals*, ANIMAL RIGHTS: THE ABOLITIONIST APPROACH (Jun. 25, 2009, 3:20 AM), http://www.abolitionist approach.com/happy-meat-making-humans-feel-better-about-eating -animals/.

75. *Chickens*, ANIMALS AUSTRALIA UNLEASHED, http://www.unleashed .org.au/animals/chickens.php. *See also* C. M. Sherwin *et al.*, *Comparison of the Welfare of Layer Hens in 4 Housing Systems in the UK*, 51 BRITISH POULTRY SCIENCE 488, 488–89 (2010).

76. *See, e.g.*, Megan Lane, *Some Sausages Are More Equal than Others*, BBC (Feb. 1, 2007), http://news.bbc.co.uk/2/hi/6295747.stm.

6. GRAPHIC IMAGES

1. Michael J. New, *The Pro-Life Legacy of Dr. Bernard Nathanson*, NATIONAL REVIEW ONLINE (Feb. 22, 2011, 11:51 AM), http://www .nationalreview.com/corner/260358/pro-life-legacy-dr-bernard-nathanson -michael-j-new. The video is available at http://www.silentscream.org/.

2. Reedu Taha, *Barbi Twins Milk 'Earthlings' Spotlight in Australia*, HUFFINGTON POST (May 26, 2010, 10:05 AM), http://www.huffington post.com/reedu-taha/barbi-twins-milk-earthlin_b_586632.html. The video is available at http://earthlings.com/.

3. One example is portrayed in *The Witness*, a documentary film available at http://www.witnessfilm.org/.

4. Gonzales v. Carhart, 550 U.S. 124, 159–60 (2007) (emphasis added).

5. *See, e.g., Meet Your Meat*, PETA, http://www.peta.org/videos/meet-your-meat/; PETA, *Official "Glass Walls" Video by Paul McCartney*, You-Tube (Apr. 12, 2013), https://www.youtube.com/watch?v=ql8xkSYvwJs; HumaneMYTH, *Silencing the Lambs*, Vimeo (2011), http://vimeo.com/13613159; Nation Earth, *Earthlings*, Vimeo (2014), http://vimeo.com/95571304.

6. *See* Department of Animal Science, *Dairy Teaching & Research Center*, Michigan State University, http://www.ans.msu.edu/facilities/dairy_teaching_research_center; Daniel M. Weary, Jennifer Jasper, & Maria J. Hotzel, *Understanding Weaning Distress*, 110 App. Animal Behaviour Sci. 24 (2008); Richard L. Wallace, *Market Cows: A Potential Profit Center*, Univ. Ill. Urbana-Champaign (Mar. 13, 2002), http://www.livestocktrail.illinois.edu/dairynet/paperDisplay.cfm?ContentID=354; Tanya Dewey & Jessica Ng, *Bos Taurus*, Animal Diversity Web (2001), http://animaldiversity.ummz.umich.edu/accounts/Bos_taurus/.

7. *House of Cards: Chapter 14* (Netflix online release Feb. 14, 2014).

8. The scene begins at approximately twenty-eight minutes.

9. *E.g.* Jason Babcock, *Approval Sought for Slaughterhouse*, S. Md. Newspapers Online (July 23, 2010), http://ww2.somdnews.com/stories/07232010/entetop161611_32331.shtml; Amy J. Fitzgerald, *A Social History of the Slaughterhouse: From Inception to Contemporary Implications*, 17 Human Ecology Review 58, 58–59 (2010); Tove Skaarup, Slaughterhouse Cleaning and Sanitation 2.1.1 (1985), *available at* http://www.fao.org/docrep/003/x6557e/X6557E00.htm#TOC.

10. For example, a campaign by Farm Animal Rights Movement (FARM) pays passersby one dollar each to watch a graphic four-minute video of factory farm conditions and slaughter. According to FARM, this campaign decreases animal consumption by roughly ten animals per year per viewer. Jasmine Elist, *FARM Campaign Pays Viewers $1 to Watch Graphic Anti-Meat Video*, Los Angeles Times (May 25, 2012), http://articles.latimes.com/2012/may/25/local/la-me-gs-campaign-pays-viewers-1-to-watch-graphic-antimeat-video-20120525.

11. PETA, *Official "Glass Walls" Video*.

12. *E.g.*, Paula Moore, *Shocker: Mom Finds Parts of Dead Chickens in Chicken Soup*, PETA (Mar. 20, 2014), http://www.peta.org/blog/mom-finds-dead-chickens-soup/.

13. Sherry F. Colb, *Probabilities in Probable Cause and Beyond: Statistical Versus Concrete Harms*, 73 Law & Contemp. Probs. 69, 70–71 (2010); Sherry F. Colb, Mind if I Order the Cheeseburger? And Others Questions People Ask Vegans 65–79 (2013).

14. Carol Sanger, *Seeing and Believing: Mandatory Ultrasound and the Path to a Protected Choice*, 56 UCLA L. REV. 351 (2008), *available at* http://uclalawreview.org/pdf/56-2-2.pdf.

15. Planned Parenthood v. Casey, 505 U.S. 833, 872 (1992) (quoting Webster v. Reprod. Health Servs., 492 U.S. 490, 511 [1989], stating that "[t]he Constitution does not forbid a State or city, pursuant to democratic processes, from expressing a preference for normal childbirth," so long as it does not impose an "undue burden" on a woman's ability to choose abortion); Rust v. Sullivan, 400 U.S. 173, 201 (1990).

16. Farming in the Fertile Crescent may have begun up to twelve thousand years ago. Melinda A. Zeder, *Domestication and Early Agriculture in the Mediterranean Basin: Origins, Diffusion, and Impact*, 10 PROCEEDINGS OF THE NATIONAL ACADEMY OF SCIENCES 11597 (2008). Modern *Homo sapiens*, in contrast, have existed for around two hundred thousand years. John L. Bradshaw, HUMAN EVOLUTION: A NEUROPSYCHOLOGICAL PERSPECTIVE 185 (2003).

17. Jim Mason, AN UNNATURAL ORDER: THE ROOTS OF OUR DESTRUCTION OF NATURE 52 (2004); Eugene S. Hunn, *On the Relative Contribution of Men and Women to Subsistence among Hunter-Gatherers of the Columbia Plateau: A Comparison with Ethnographic Atlas Summaries*, 1 J. ETHNOBIOLOGY 124 (1981). The percentage of animal food in the diets of pre-agricultural societies varied based on climate. *See* Loren Cordain *et al.*, *Plant-Animal Subsistence Ratios and Macronutrient Energy Estimations in Worldwide Hunter-Gatherer Diets*, 71 AM. J. CLIN. NUTR. 682 (2000).

18. Paul Halstead, *Farming and Feasting in the Neolithic of Greece: The Ecological Context of Fighting with Food*, 31 DOCUMENTA PRAEHISTORICA 151, 156–57 (2004).

19. Malcom Potts & Martha Campbell, *History of Contraception*, 6 OBSTETRICS AND GYNECOLOGY 2 (2002). The original physician's oath prescribed by Hippocrates recognized the possibility of abortion, even while forbidding it. The oath read in part, "I will neither give a deadly drug to anybody who asked for it, nor will I make a suggestion to this effect. Similarly I will not give to a woman an abortive remedy." Peter Tyson, *The Hippocratic Oath Today*, NOVA (March 27, 2001), http://www.pbs.org/wgbh/nova/body/hippocratic-oath-today.html.

20. Joyce E. Salisbury, ENCYCLOPEDIA OF WOMEN IN THE ANCIENT WORLD 1 (2001).

21. Dave Grossman, ON KILLING: THE PSYCHOLOGICAL COST OF LEARNING TO KILL IN WAR AND SOCIETY 27 (1996).

22. *E.g.*, Free Animal Video, *Mother Cows Upset When Calf Taken Away Undercover Video*, YOUTUBE, https://www.youtube.com/watch?v=BWM5jYORSDg; Michael Lanfield, *The Price of Milk, Cheese (Dairy) and Veal—the Separation of a Cow and Her Calf*, YOUTUBE, https://

www.youtube.com/watch?v=SYJPbrxdn8w; Humane Society of the United States, *Slaughterhouse Investigation: Cruel and Unhealthy Practices*, You-Tube, https://www.youtube.com/watch?v=zhlhSQ5z4V4.

23. Cherilyn van Berkel, *Abortion Work: Health Care's Best Kept Secret*, 21 Canadian Association for Social work Review 5 (2004) (indicating abortion providers feel some tension but also gratification).

24. Stephen Vincent, *Bernard Nathanson Dead at 84*, National Catholic Register (Feb. 21, 2011), http://www.ncregister.com/daily-news /bernard-nathanson-dead-at-84/.

25. Gail A. Eisnitz, Slaughterhouse: The Shocking Story of Greed, Neglect and Inhumane Treatment Inside the U.S. Meat Industry (1997).

26. *E.g., id.* at 120–21.

27. *Id.* at 91.

28. Amy J. Fitzgerald *et al.*, *Slaughterhouses and Increased Crime Rates: An Empirical Analysis of Spillover from "The Jungle" into the Surrounding Community*, 22 Organization and Environment 158 (2009).

29. Peaceable Kingdom: The Journey Home (Tribe of Heart 2009).

30. Timothy Pachirat, Every Twelve Seconds: Industrialized Slaughter and the Politics of Sight (2011).

31. *Id.* at 138.

32. So-called ag-gag laws reflect such efforts. *See, e.g.*, Utah Code Ann. § 76-6-112 (LexisNexis 2012).

33. *See* Alison B. Linas, *Virginia's War on Women: How Forcing Women to Have an Ultrasound Before Abortion Is Unconstitutional*, 16 Rich. J.L. & Pub. Int. 47, 53 (2012).

34. *See* Stuart v. Camnitz, 774 F.3d 238 (4th Cir. 2014).

35. Eisnitz, *supra* note 25, at 93.

36. "In some American slaughterhouses, more than three-quarters of the workers are not native English speakers; many can't read any language, and many are illegal immigrants. . . . A wage of $9.50 an hour seems incredible to men and women who come from rural areas in Mexico where the wages are $7 a day. . . . They tend to be poor, vulnerable, and fearful. From the industry's point of view, they are ideal workers: cheap, largely interchangeable, and disposable." Eric Schlosser, *The Chain Never Stops*, Mother Jones (July/Aug. 2001), *available at* http://www.motherjones.com/politics/2001/07 /dangerous-meatpacking-jobs-eric-schlosser.

37. Melanie Joy, Why We Love Dogs, Eat Pigs, and Wear Cows: An Introduction to Carnism 96 (2010).

38. Michael Pollan, The Omnivore's Dilemma: A Natural History of Four Meals 349 (2006).

39. *Id.* at 361.

40. *See* Food and Agriculture Organization, The State of Food and

AGRICULTURE 136 (2009), *available at* http://www.fao.org/docrep/012/io680e/io680e.pdf.

41. *Fact Sheet: Induced Abortion in the United States*, GUTTMACHER INSTITUTE (July 2014), http://www.guttmacher.org/pubs/fb_induced_abortion.html.

7. VIOLENCE

1. *See* Stephen Singular, THE WICHITA DIVIDE 201–14 (2011).

2. Henry Schuster, *Domestic Terror: Who's Most Dangerous?* CNN (Aug. 24, 2005, 2:14 PM), http://www.cnn.com/2005/US/08/24/schuster.column/index.html.

3. The possible exception is Dutch right-wing politician Pim Fortuyn, who was killed in 2002 by Dutch animal rights activist Volkert van der Graaf. However, "what prompted Van der Graaf's action was never clear." Ian Buruma, MURDER IN AMSTERDAM 38 (2006). Although Van der Graaf opposed factory farming and fur, and Fortuyn wore fur, "Van der Graaf appears to have been bothered by other aspects of Fortuyn, to do more with personality than any specific environmental policies." *Id.*

4. Joseph M. Gitlin, *US Animal-Rights Extremists Firebomb Scientists' Home, Car*, ARS TECHNIA (Aug. 9, 2008, 6:10 AM), http://arstechnica.com/uncategorized/2008/08/us-animal-rights-extremists-firebomb-scientists-home-car/.

5. *See Pro-Abortion Violence: Setting the Record Straight*, HUMAN LIFE INTERNATIONAL, http://www.hli.org/resources/pro-abortion-violence-setting-the-record-straight/; *see also* Animal Rights Extremism, SPEAKING OF RESEARCH, http://speakingofresearch.com/extremism-undone/ar-extremism/.

6. For a month-by-month catalogue of anti-abortion violence between 1973 and 2001, ranging from the petty to the murderous, see Patricia Baird-Windle & Eleanor J. Bader, THE TARGETS OF HATRED 39–322 (2001).

7. NARAL Pro-Choice America, *Anti-Choice Violence and Intimidation*, http://www.prochoiceamerica.org/media/fact-sheets/abortion-anti-choice-violence.pdf, at 12.

8. *See* Daniel Cressey, *Animal Research: Battle Scars*, NATURE, Feb. 23, 2011, at 453, http://www.nature.com/news/2011/110223/full/470452a.html.

9. The Freedom of Access to Clinic Entrances Act is codified at 18 U.S.C. § 248 (1994). State buffer zone laws include COLO. REV. STAT. § 18-9-122 (1993). The Animal Enterprise Terrorism Act is codified at 18 U.S.C. § 43 (2006). State ag-gag laws include UTAH CODE ANN. § 76-6-112 (LexisNexis 2012).

10. *See* Dara Lovitz, MUZZLING A MOVEMENT (2010).

11. William A. Gamson, THE STRATEGY OF SOCIAL PROTEST 79 (2d ed. 1990).

12. *See McCullen v. Coakley*, 134 S. Ct. 2518 (2014); *Animal Legal Defense Fund v. Otter*, 2015 WL 4623943 (D. ID. 2015) (holding Idaho ag-gag law unconstitutional).

13. We say "generally" in acknowledgment of case law that permits punishment of persons who violate judicial injunctions based on laws later found to be unconstitutional. *See* Walker v. City of Birmingham, 388 U.S. 307 (1967).

14. *'The Jews' by Gandhi—From Harijan, November 26, 1938* (Nov. 26, 1938), *in* THE JEWS AND PALESTINE, 1921–1948 (E. S. Reddy eds.), *available at* http://www.gandhiserve.org/information/writings_online/articles /gandhi_jews_palestine.html#'The Jews'.

15. *Gandhi, the Jews & Zionism: Martin Buber's Open Letter to Gandhi Regarding Palestine*, JEWISH VIRTUAL LIBRARY (Fed. 24, 1939), *available at* http://www.jewishvirtuallibrary.org/jsource/History/BuberGandhi.html.

16. *See* Michael Walzer, *Political Action: The Problem of Dirty Hands*, 2(2) PHIL. & PUB. AFF. 160, 167–68 (Winter 1973). For a less nuanced view, see Charles Krauthammer, *The Truth About Torture: It's Time To Be Honest About Doing Terrible Things*, 11(12) THE WEEKLY STANDARD 21 (Dec. 5, 2005).

17. This was the position taken by the corporate plaintiffs before the Supreme Court in *Hobby Lobby* [Hobby Lobby Stores, Inc. v. Sebelius, 870 F.Supp.2d 1278 (W.D. Okla. 2010), *rev'd*, 723 F.3d 1114 (10th Cir. 2013), *aff'd in part & rev'd in part*, Burwell v. Hobby Lobby Stores, Inc., 134 S.Ct. 2751 (2014).

18. *See, e.g.*, Mary Ziegler, *Sexing Harris: The Law and Politics of the Movement to Defund Planned Parenthood*, 60 BUFF. L. REV. 701, 701–6 (2012).

19. The Guttmacher Institute estimated that there were 43.8 million abortions worldwide in 2008, with a rate that year of 28 per 1,000 women ages fifteen to forty-four. *See In Brief: Fact Sheet* (Jan. 2012), *available at* http://www.guttmacher.org/pubs/fb_IAW.html. It estimated that there were roughly one million abortions in the United States in 2011. *See Fact Sheet: Induced Abortion in the United States* (Jul. 2014), http://www.guttmacher .org/pubs/fb_induced_abortion.html. Collecting official data from various sources, A. Mood and P. Brooke, *Estimating The Number of Farmed Fish Killed in Global Aquaculture Each Year* 19 (July 2012) (table), *available at* http://fishcount.org.uk/published/std/fishcountstudy2.pdf, provides the following estimates of the number of animals of the following types killed in 2010 for direct or indirect human consumption: 4 billion mammals; 60 billion birds; and 1 trillion to 3 trillion fish.

20. *See, e.g.*, CNN Wire Staff, *Italian Region to Pay Women Not to Have Abortions*, CNN WORLD (Jun. 3, 2010, 9:40 AM), http://www.cnn .com/2010/WORLD/europe/06/03/italy.abortions/.

21. Numerous books by medical professionals point to the health advantages of a diet free of animal products (especially if one also reduces or eliminates highly processed foods). *See, e.g.*, Neal Barnard, DR. NEAL BARNARD'S PROGRAM FOR REVERSING DIABETES (2008); T. Colin Campbell and Thomas Campbell II, THE CHINA STUDY (2006); Caldwell B. Esselstyn, PREVENT AND REVERSE HEART DISEASE (2008). Michael Greger, MD, maintains a website, NutritionFacts.org, that synthesizes peer-reviewed scientific studies of nutrition, which overwhelmingly support a diet free of animal foods.

22. Anisa Mullins, *Vegans Save 185 Animals a Year*, PETA BLOG (Dec. 13, 2010), http://www.peta.org/blog/vegans-save-185-animals-year/.

23. *Pet Statistics*, ASPCA, http://www.aspca.org/about-us/faq/pet-statistics.

24. *See Unwanted Males Killed at Birth*, PETA BLOG (Sept. 1, 2009), http://www.peta.org/blog/unwanted-males-killed-birth/; *see also Farm Animal Statistics: Slaughter Totals*, HUMANE SOCIETY OF THE UNITED STATES, http://www.humanesociety.org/news/resources/research/stats_slaughter _totals.html.

25. *See, e.g.*, Julie Zauzmer, *Families Claim Beagles Released from Virginia Research Lab*, WASH. POST, Jul. 15, 2013, at 1.

26. Slaughterhouse workers exhibit among the highest rates of illness and injury of any industry, and annual turnover rates of 200 percent are "not uncommon." Amy J. Fitzgerald, *A Social History of the Slaughterhouse: From Inception to Contemporary Implications*, 17(1) HUMAN ECOLOGY REV. 58, 64 (2010), *available at* http://www.humanecologyreview.org /pastissues/her171/Fitzgerald.pdf.

27. *See* Gary L. Francione, INTRODUCTION TO ANIMAL RIGHTS: YOUR CHILD OR THE DOG xxii–xxiii (2000).

28. *See generally* Sherry F. Colb, *The Impact of Reproductive Rights Today on the Composition of Future Generations: To Whom Do We Refer When We Speak of Obligations to "Future Generations"? Reproductive Rights and the Intergenerational Community*, 77 GEO. WASH. L. REV. 1582 (2009).

29. *See* Coker v. Georgia, 433 U.S. 584 (1977); Kennedy v. Louisiana, 554 U.S. 407 (2008).

CONCLUSION

1. Phil Brooke, COMPASSION IN WORLD FARMING, PIG WELFARE: TOWARDS SHARED PRIORITIES FOR THE FUTURE 15–16 (2008), *available at* http://www.ciwf.org.uk/media/3818874/pig-welfare-position-paper.pdf.

2. Miho Nagasawa *et al.*, *Oxytocin and Mutual Communication in Mother-Infant Bonding*, 6 FRONT. HUM. NEUROSCI. art. 31, 1 (2012); Allison M. J. Anacker and Annaliese K. Beery, *Life in Groups: The Roles of Oxytocin in Mammalian Sociality*, 7 FRONT. BEHAV. NEUROSCI. art.185, 4 (2013).

3. Glenda Taylor, *How Do Mother Dogs Show Affection to Puppies?*, THE NEST, http://pets.thenest.com/mother-dogs-show-affection-puppies-9451 .html; *see also* Robyn L. Ritchey and Michael B. Hennessy, *Cortisol and Behavioral Responses to Separation in Mother and Infant Guinea Pigs*, 48 BEHAVIORAL AND NEURAL BIOLOGY 1, 1 (Jul. 1, 1987).

4. *See, e.g.*, Chris Rostenberg, *Pro-Abortion or Pro-Life, Which Side Is Really Extreme?*, LIFE NEWS (May 27, 2014), http://www.lifenews.com/2014/05/27 /pro-abortion-or-pro-life-which-side-is-really-extreme/; Peter Jesserer Smith, *Democratic Lawmakers Push "Pro-Abortion Agenda on Steroids"*, NAT'L CATHOLIC REGISTER (Jun. 26, 2014), http://www.ncregister.com/daily-news /democratic-lawmakers-push-pro-abortion-agenda-on-steroids/.

5. 42 U.S.C.A. § 300a-6.

6. William Saletan, *Do Pro-Lifers Oppose Birth Control?*, SLATE (Jan. 14, 2014), http://www.slate.com/blogs/saletan/2014/01/15/do_pro_lifers _oppose_birth_control_polls_say_no.html ("At a minimum, 78 percent of all respondents who said abortion was morally wrong also said that birth control was morally acceptable."). On support for contraception that prevents ovulation or conception, note, for example, that the plaintiffs in a prominent 2014 Supreme Court case sought a religious exception to regulations under the Affordable Care Act requiring that their corporate employees receive employer-based health insurance covering contraception, but they only objected to those forms of contraception that they regarded as abortifacients. *See* Brief for Respondents, *Sebelius v. Hobby Lobby Stores* 3, *available at* http://sblog.s3.amazonaws.com/wp-content/uploads/2013/10 /No-13-354-Brief-for-Respondents.pdf. Moreover, even former Republican vice presidential candidate and social conservative darling Sarah Palin supports educating students on condom use. *See* Seema Mehta, *GOP Ticket Split Over Condom Use*, L.A. TIMES (Sept. 6, 2008), http://articles.latimes .com/2008/sep/06/nation/na-sexed6.

7. Sue Donaldson & Will Kymlicka, ZOOPOLIS 157 (2011).

8. *See id.* at 135–39. The authors might have reconsidered their endorsement of using animals for their secretions since authoring the book because they spoke of *Zoopolis* at a conference in April 2014 as an approach to life with animals the day after abolition, when everyone has become vegan. *See* Sue Donaldson & Will Kymlicka, *Talk at Rutgers-Newark Law Conference on Animal Ethics: Abolition, Regulation or Citizenship* (Apr. 11, 2014).

9. *See* Toby G. Knowles *et al.*, *Leg Disorders in Broiler Chickens: Prevalence, Risk Factors and Prevention*, 2 PLoS ONE e1545, 1 (Feb. 6, 2008); V. Bruggeman *et al.*, *Physiology, Endocrinology, and Reproduction: Feed Allowance—Genotype Interactions in Broiler Breeder Hens*, 84 POULTRY SCI. 298, 298 (2005); *The Chicken Industry*, PETA, http://www.peta.org /issues/animals-used-for-food/factory-farming/chickens/chicken-industry/; *What's Wrong With Backyard Eggs?*, peacefulprairie.org/backyard-eggs .htm.#4.

10. Jesse Hirsch, *Will a Sheep's Wool Grow Forever?*, MODERN FARMER (Jul. 24, 2013), http://modernfarmer.com/2013/07/will-sheep/.

11. For more on the subject of why extinction is just in the case of domesticated farmed animals, see Sherry F. Colb, MIND IF I ORDER THE CHEESEBURGER? AND OTHER QUESTIONS PEOPLE ASK VEGANS 156–72 (2013).

12. *Compare Vegetarian Cats and Dogs*, PETA, http://www.peta.org/living/companion-animals/vegetarian-cats-dogs/ *with* Christina M. Gray *et al.*, *Nutritional Adequacy of Two Vegan Diets for Cats*, 225 J. AM. VET. MED. ASS'N 1670, 1675 (2004).

13. Natalie Angier, *That Cuddly Kitty Is Deadlier than You Think*, N.Y. TIMES (Jan. 29, 2013), http://www.nytimes.com/2013/01/30/science/that-cuddly-kitty-of-yours-is-a-killer.html.

14. Stephanie Watson, *Should You Have an Indoor Cat or an Outdoor Cat?*, WEBMD, http://pets.webmd.com/cats/features/should-you-have-an-indoor-cat-or-an-outdoor-cat.

15. Nathan Winograd & Jennifer Winograd, *The Lie at the Heart of the Killing: The Myth of Pet Overpopulation*, NATHAN J. WINOGRAD (Mar. 12, 2013), http://www.nathanwinograd.com/?p=12245; Nathan J. Winograd, REDEMPTION: THE MYTH OF PET OVERPOPULATION AND THE NO KILL REVOLUTION IN AMERICA (2009).

16. *See A Model Feral Cat Policy*, NO KILL ADVOCACY CENTER (Nov./Dec. 2006), http://www.nokilladvocacycenter.org/wp-content/uploads/2011/10/FeralPolicy.pdf.

17. *See, e.g.*, Lisa Foderaro, *A Kinder, Gentler Way to Thin the Deer Herd*, N.Y. TIMES A14 (Jul. 6, 2013).

INDEX